FOOD INSPIRED BY NATURE
PETER GILMORE

QUAY

MURDOCH BOOKS

nature-based cuisine

I am inspired by nature and have coined the term 'nature-based cuisine' to describe my food. Nature offers us so much diversity — a natural elegance and beauty — and it is the organic nature of food, its textures and flavours that is at the heart of my cooking.

I have been growing vegetables in my home garden for the past seven years and it has changed the way I cook. Reconnecting with nature in this way has given me a better understanding of the life cycle of plants and an awareness of each stage of growth — from the first tiny seedlings and shoots, to the flowers, leaves, fruit and seed pods — all of which I incorporate in my cooking. The seasons, too, present an astonishing array of fruit and vegetables, and my passion for rare or unusual heirloom vegetables has given me access to a wonderful variety of boutique food crops. Nature has provided me with a large palette to work from and, in turn, my presentation has become far more organic in an attempt to represent the natural world.

There are pioneers of this style of cooking, and one of the chefs I most respect is Frenchman Michel Bras, who really developed a close bond with his environment and the natural world, and celebrates the diversity of the vegetable garden in his food. Other contemporaries of this style are people such as Andoni Luis Aduriz, from Mugaritz in Spain, and René Redzepi, from Noma in Denmark.

Another major influence on my style is Japanese cuisine, with its deep connection to nature, respect for the seasons, traditions and overall search for perfection through its presentation, harmony and sense of balance.

What I aim to achieve with my food is a balance that takes into consideration a number of things: the texture of ingredients, mouthfeel, harmony of flavours, and the overall elegance of the visual presentation and proportions. All of these elements need to fit together for the dish to work; this is my creative process.

Texture for me is just as important as flavour, and is such an exciting element in cuisine. When you think about the food that you eat, it is often the texture of the food that you crave — the crispness of an apple, the silkiness of custard or the slipperiness of noodles. What has the most impact, the flavour of ice cream or its texture? It is often the texture of a dessert that really makes an impact — not to say that flavour isn't important. The textural component is a natural part of all ingredients but can be enhanced or altered by different cooking methods. Slicing abalone paper-thin, then briefly sautéing it will give you a totally different texture than braising it whole for six hours, then slicing it thickly. The addition of butter and cream to puréed vegetables drastically changes the texture and mouthfeel.

When considering harmony of flavour, a good place to start is to look at classic flavour matches, such as tomato and basil; lamb, garlic and rosemary; mussels and saffron; and strawberries and cream. These combinations, and hundreds more, work for varying reasons. Sometimes it's juxtaposition, sometimes it's a similarity of flavour nuances building on each other, and sometimes it's purely mysterious as to why some ingredients seem to work so well together.

my journey

It was my mother's passion for cooking that inspired me to be a chef. She was taught how to cook Italian food by Mrs Timeus, the mother of her best girlfriend Luisa, in the early 1960s. Mum also attended Margaret Fulton's cooking classes in the city during the early 1970s, and I would often accompany her as a toddler.

My career as a chef started at age 15 when I did work experience at a restaurant called the Manor House in Balmain. The chef was Jeffrey Almore. He recognised my passion for cooking and, in 1984, when I was 16, offered me the opportunity to start my apprenticeship. I didn't hesitate; I left school and worked for the first three years at the Manor House, starting on bread and salads and washing up. At that time the Manor House was Sydney's big night out dining experience. It opened the door for me to the restaurant industry and it has a special place in my heart as it was where I met my future wife, Kath.

At 19 I left Sydney for Europe. I worked at numerous places in London and in the West Country of England in a country house called Bishopstrow. It was there that I was exposed to some incredible ingredients — wild mushrooms and foie gras from France, Scottish partridge, wild salmon, venison, hare and numerous wonderful vegetables and cheeses. It was the late 1980s, early 1990s, and the kitchen was creative and dynamic and full of enthusiasm for good food.

The three years travelling through Europe and working in the United Kingdom really opened my mind to the possibilities of cuisine. I returned to

Australia and worked in a small guesthouse in the Blue Mountains. It was my first head chef position, and there was just myself and an apprentice in the kitchen, with a dining room that served up to 40 people. I stayed there for three years to concentrate on developing my own style of cooking. This was an invaluable period of my early cooking career. I followed this with a couple of years cooking around Sydney and started my own dessert business with Kath but I missed the buzz of the kitchen and needed to be cooking and creating in a restaurant environment.

At the beginning of 1999 I took on the head chef's role at De Beers restaurant at Whale Beach on Sydney's northern beaches. The brief was to turn it into a standard-setting fine dining restaurant. Within the first year I received a positive review by *The Sydney Morning Herald*'s food critic, Terry Durack, who wrote, 'De Beers houses a young chef with a real talent for sending out beautifully structured food with innate simplicity'. This was my first major review and it was followed by a chef's hat in the 2001 edition of *The Sydney Morning Herald Good Food Guide*. The following year I achieved two chef's hats for my work at De Beers. By this stage, however, De Beers had been put on the market and I decided it was time to look for a new position.

a meeting of great minds

I approached Leon Fink, the owner of Quay restaurant. Leon had developed the restaurant back in 1988 with Tony Bilson, and it wasn't long before it became known as not only a restaurant in a stunning position — right on Sydney harbour — but also as one of Australia's best restaurants, receiving many accolades. This is due in no small part to Leon, who has great passion and an unwavering commitment to the restaurant and the restaurant industry at large. Quay was the restaurant and Leon the restaurateur I really wanted to work with. I expressed this to Leon and a fruitful collaboration was born.

Leon works on instinct and had a gut feeling that I might be right for the position. He had secretly sent trusted friends and family to De Beers to sample my food and asked them to report back on their experience. When these reports came back very positively, he called me for a series of interviews and then decided to take a chance on me. I was young and relatively unknown in the Sydney dining scene. Within 12 months, Leon was rewarded with three chef's hats by *The Sydney Morning Herald Good Food Guide* and, for the first time in its history, Quay was awarded Restaurant of the Year in 2003. The chance Leon gave me to take on this role is something I will always be grateful for. I have been at Quay for nine years now and during this time we have maintained our three-hat status. We have also received a total of four *Sydney Morning Herald Good Food Guide* Restaurant of the Year awards.

In 2009 and 2010 we also received the *Australian Gourmet Traveller* Restaurant of the Year award and have retained our three-star rating in their guide book since 2003. In 2010 Quay was awarded 27th place in the S.Pellegrino World's 50 Best Restaurants, and was named the best restaurant in Australasia.

freedom in cooking

One of the greatest challenges for a cook is to experiment with new combinations to see what works, to develop a good palate, and to coax out and preserve the natural flavour of ingredients. Then there is the balancing act; sometimes you want to intensify the flavour through the cooking process and sometimes you want to minimise the strength of an ingredient through blending it, for the purpose of subtlety.

The freedom of cooking in Australia is that we are not bound by tradition or a set of fixed ideas of how an ingredient should be cooked, what it goes with and how it should be served. This is a double-edged sword of course, as there are many chefs who combine ingredients that should never go together, or try to force cultures and traditions together, or just throw an exotic ingredient into a classical dish to see what happens. This gave rise to the saying 'fusion confusion', but in the right hands this freedom is very powerful and exciting. We have to remember that when new ingredients are introduced into an established cuisine there is, of course, a lot of trial and error — who could imagine Italian cuisine without tomatoes, or Thai cuisine without the chilli, yet 500 years ago these ingredients didn't exist in these countries.

Today, when we have an almost unlimited range of ingredients and are open to so many culinary influences, it is essential that a modern chef works with a real sense of balance and harmony and an understanding and respect for cultural traditions, but with an open mind, imagination, inquisitiveness and intuition. Classic recipes and techniques are essential to modern cuisine — without these marvellous traditions we would have no platform to work from. In Australia we are lucky to have had pioneering chefs with multicultural backgrounds who have pushed the boundaries and educated a dining public.

pleasures of the table

I think a great dining experience is finding a perfect balance of excitement, refinement, professionalism and warmth. Experiencing an original cuisine that reflects the passions of the chef is truly inspiring. The idea of coming to a great restaurant and sitting at a table with beautifully starched white linen and the anticipation of the experience that is to come is one of life's great pleasures. It is about nourishing yourself and delighting your palate and evoking all your senses. I believe fine dining is really an art form and, like all art, you bring your own experiences, prejudices, beliefs and culture to the table. How you interpret what you experience is very individual. My wish is that people bring an open mind and heart to the table.

Dining is about indulgence and being pampered. Good service should be professional, knowledgeable, attentive and intuitive but above all should be welcoming, honest and caring. Of course, your own frame of mind and openness will have an influence on your restaurant experience — you should go to a great restaurant to enjoy the art of what that restaurant has to offer. One of the things you should remember and expect is that the waiters and particularly the sommeliers will have an intimate knowledge of the food and wine that is being served. Communication with the sommelier about the dishes you have selected and compatible wine matches is a service of any good restaurant that should be utilised and should greatly enhance your overall dining experience.

In 2008 I changed the structure of the Quay menu from a traditional three-course à la carte menu to a four-course menu containing three savoury courses and one dessert course, with a choice of four to five dishes in each course. I did this for a variety of reasons. Firstly I found that the main course was too protein dominant. I wanted to include a greater proportion of vegetables in my dishes. Also, to give diners an extra course gave them more variety. We also offer a set eight-course tasting menu.

I think part of a great dining experience is remembering the detail of the dishes you have eaten... a taste memory. An incredible meal can stay in one's memory for a lifetime. The greatest compliment for any chef is when a diner says 'that dish is the best thing I have ever eaten'.

the book

Many of the recipes in this book are quite complex and are comprised of many stages or are made up of smaller recipes, which are then assembled to make the whole. It is important to read the entire recipe through before beginning, as some recipes require marinating overnight or freezing for a few hours, and some require specialised equipment. Some recipes can be broken down into easily achievable components that can be prepared in advance so the final assembly stage isn't overwhelming, or you can take individual components from my dishes and utilise them however you like.

I hope this book gives you inspiration and some insight into my philosophy and shares with you my joy and passion for nature.

Peter Gilmore

foreword

thomas keller, the french laundry

In September 2006, I went on my first trip to Australia. I took several chefs from my team with me to Sydney, including Corey Lee, then the chef de cuisine at The French Laundry, and Mark Hopper, our executive chef at Bouchon, for the Starlight Children's Foundation hosted by my colleague and friend, Neil Perry. During my visit, we all went to Quay restaurant, along with another good friend, Heston Blumenthal. It was the perfect time to relax and unwind after a whirlwind of events. We came for a late lunch and were immediately struck by the views of Sydney harbour surrounding the restaurant. But the bigger surprise came later at the table.

Everything was amazing. The flavour profiles chef Peter Gilmore presented were exquisite and incredibly focussed. I distinctly remember tasting his version of congee, the classic Chinese rice porridge dish. His vision, coupled with his precise techniques and impeccable ingredients, elevated this humble and simple fare to new heights. As the courses continued to arrive, we were impressed by what was in front of us, and even more intrigued by what was to come. It was a profound dining experience made even more memorable by the company of fellow chefs whom I respect and have worked alongside for many years. It was a meal that all of us fondly remember and one that I will always associate with my first trip to Australia.

Peter is one of the next generation of chefs who has made such an impact on our industry and will continue to do so long into the future. His dishes are carefully and thoughtfully composed, and his flavour profiles are a reflection of the produce that abounds in the area. Tremendously dedicated to his craft, he has great command of the fundamentals and is also able to successfully blend the diverse cultures that have influenced the region with integrity and understanding. His cuisine is a brilliant representation of Australian culture today — global, while maintaining its indigenous spirit.

Australia has been a place that I have always had a desire to explore. It is vast with a richness of history that is unique and compelling. Since my first trip, I have been back once more in 2009. Each visit has left me feeling like I had barely scratched its surface. The land produces raw ingredients — be it fruits, vegetables, seafood or meats — that are of the highest quality and diverse in scope. I have started my list of to-dos and to-sees in preparation of my next trip. And one thing I am certain of: I am already anticipating my return visit to Quay, and experiencing Peter's remarkable cuisine once more.

Thomas Keller

the garden

I have become obsessed with the diversity of nature and nowhere is this more greatly emphasised than within the vegetable world, from the rare and almost forgotten vegetables to the heirloom varieties that have been passed on from generation to generation, as well as the endless array of culinary herbs, flowers, buds, stems, leaves, seed pods, nuts, berries and fruits.

SERVES 8

violet potatoes with truffle cream and violets

This is a simple dish of potatoes, truffles and violets. The violet potatoes have a beautiful flavour, especially when freshly dug from the earth. Simply roasting them in the oven to preserve their flavour and serving them with truffles celebrates the best of both worlds — the humble and the rare. The addition of silver leaf is symbolic of the preciousness of the truffles. In some cultures silver is believed to have important health benefits.

ingredients

64 SMALL VIOLET POTATOES
FINE SEA SALT
30 ML (1 FL OZ) OLIVE OIL
ROCK SALT
50 G (1¾ OZ) UNSALTED BUTTER
40 G (1½ OZ) BLACK WINTER TRUFFLE
16 WHITE SWEET VIOLETS
16 PINK SWEET VIOLETS
16 PURPLE SWEET VIOLETS
8 NATIVE VIOLETS
2 X 10 CM (4 INCH) SQUARE SHEETS PURE
    SILVER LEAF

TRUFFLE CREAM
250 ML (9 FL OZ/1 CUP) MILK
10 G (¼ OZ) BLACK WINTER TRUFFLE
FINE SEA SALT
3 G (¹⁄₁₀ OZ) AGAR AGAR POWDER

method

To prepare the truffle cream, heat the milk in a saucepan to simmering point. Using a microplane, grate the truffle and add to the milk. Season with sea salt and allow to infuse off the heat for 15 minutes. Bring the milk back to simmering point and add the agar agar. Whisk in well, then remove the pan from the heat and refrigerate until set. Once the milk is set, place the contents back into a small saucepan and reheat while mixing with a hand-held blender until you have a smooth cream. Put the truffle cream aside until required.

Preheat the oven to 180°C (350°F/Gas 4). Wash the dirt from the potatoes and dry them thoroughly. Place the potatoes on a sheet of foil. Season the potatoes with sea salt and drizzle with the olive oil, then seal the foil to form a package. Prepare a bed of rock salt on a baking tray and place the foil package on the salt. Cook the potatoes in the oven for about 30 minutes, or until they are tender.

Remove the potatoes from the oven and test them with the point of a sharp knife. Peel them while they are hot using a small sharp knife; you can virtually rub away the skin. Cut some of the potatoes in half and leave the smallest ones whole. Melt the butter and brush it liberally over the potatoes, then season with sea salt.

to finish and plate

Arrange the potatoes in small attractive serving bowls. Thinly slice half the truffle and finely julienne the other half. Reheat the truffle cream and place a couple of spoonfuls randomly in between the potatoes. Garnish with sliced and julienned truffle and arrange the violets on top. As a final touch, place a small amount of silver on the dish. Serve immediately.

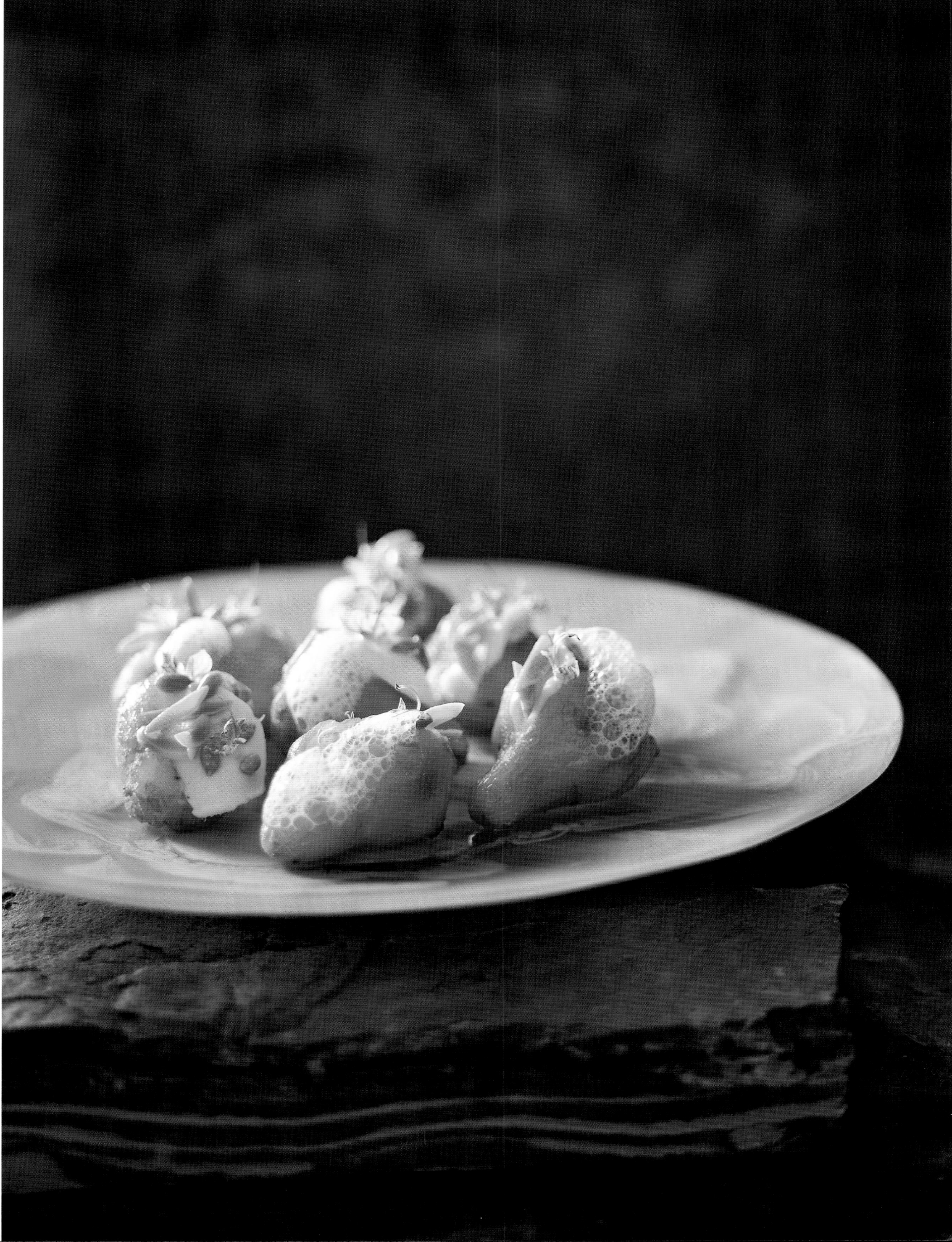

SERVES 8

jerusalem artichokes with toma della rocca and rosemary flowers

This robust vegetarian starter combines the nutty flavour of Jerusalem artichokes with toma della rocca cheese, a soft, creamy Italian cheese made from a blend of sheep's, goat's and cow's milks. The dish is finished with almonds, pine nuts, sunflower seeds, rosemary flowers and a rosemary-scented froth.

ingredients

30 G (1 OZ) BLANCHED WHOLE ALMONDS

30 G (1 OZ) PINE NUTS

30 G (1 OZ) SUNFLOWER SEEDS

30 ML (1 FL OZ) CLARIFIED BUTTER (BASIC RECIPES, PAGE 264)

2 BUNCHES FLOWERING ROSEMARY

400 ML (14 FL OZ) VEGETABLE STOCK (BASIC RECIPES, PAGE 262)

2 G (1/16 OZ) LECITE POWDER

40 MEDIUM-SIZED JERUSALEM ARTICHOKES

250 ML (9 FL OZ/1 CUP) OLIVE OIL

250 G (9 OZ) TOMA DELLA ROCCA CHEESE, RIND REMOVED (OR FRESH GOAT'S CURD)

method

Slice each almond into four slivers lengthways. Put the almonds, pine nuts and sunflower seeds in a frying pan with the clarified butter and fry until golden brown. Drain the nuts and seeds and place on kitchen paper. Remove the rosemary flowers from the rosemary sprigs and place in a covered container in the refrigerator until required.

Heat the vegetable stock in a small saucepan with five sprigs of rosemary. Infuse for 15 minutes over low heat. Remove the rosemary and add the lecite powder to the stock, mix with a hand-held blender for 1 minute and keep warm until required. Steam the Jerusalem artichokes for 10–15 minutes

until they become tender but are still holding their shape. Peel away the skins with a sharp knife, then shallow-fry them in the olive oil in small batches until golden brown. Keep warm in a low–medium oven.

to finish and plate

Make a slit in the golden Jerusalem artichokes and place a teaspoon of toma della rocca cheese inside. Top with the almonds, pine nuts and sunflower seeds. Insert two or three rosemary flowers into the cheese in each Jerusalem artichoke and then arrange the artichokes on serving plates. Froth up the rosemary stock with a hand-held blender and put a little of the froth on top of each Jerusalem artichoke. Serve immediately.

heirloom vegetables

Heirloom vegetables and rare tomato breeds have enjoyed a real renaissance over the past few years and are now available at growers' markets and in seed catalogues. Heirloom vegetables are those varieties that have been in cultivation for at least 50 years, but were eventually relegated to obscurity by the mass-produced commercial varieties. Now, more and more people are demanding fruit and vegetables, such as tomatoes, that taste as they should rather than the insipid ones widely available. People want flavour and diversity not a homogenised product with a good shelf life.

Richard and Nina Kalina, who run Berridale vegetable farm in the Blue Mountains in New South Wales, supply Quay with their gorgeous heirloom cucumbers, tomatoes and eggplants during summer.

The varieties of flavours, colours and shapes of heirloom vegetables are endless. Some varieties of heirloom tomatoes and carrots, such as the Belgium white and Japanese red carrots, are hundreds of years old and in some cases some varieties have only been kept alive through one community or even one family's year on year planting — thus the name heirloom. The original carrot is thought to have been domesticated in Pakistan about 5000 years ago. It was multicoloured with shades of purple, orange, yellow and white.

SERVES 8

heirloom tomato salad

For this salad I use four different varieties, but really you can use any combination of tomatoes you have available. I've combined this salad with goat's and sheep's milk curd and wild and cultivated buds, shoots and flowers.

ingredients

32 LIGURIAN OLIVES
400 G (14 OZ) FRESH GOAT'S CURD
400 G (14 OZ) SHEEP'S MILK YOGHURT
6 PINK BRANDY WINE TOMATOES
4 BLACK OX HEART TOMATOES
24 LOVE BITE TOMATOES
54 MEXICAN MIDGET TOMATOES
8 ORANGE-RED CALENDULA FLOWERS, DRIED
8 SPRIGS PARSLEY FLOWERS
8 WILD ROCKET (ARUGULA) FLOWERS
8 SPRIGS WILD SORREL
8 SPRIGS WILD ELDERFLOWER BUDS
8 WHITE BORAGE BUDS
8 SPRIGS BRONZE FENNEL
1 PUNNET BABY WATERCRESS, TRIMMED
8 CHIVE FLOWER BUDS
8 FLOWERING PEA SHOOTS
4 PRESERVED WILD ITALIAN MOUNTAIN RADICCHIO
10 ML (¼ FL OZ) GRAPESEED OIL
160 ML (5¼ FL OZ) EXTRA VIRGIN OLIVE OIL
FINE SEA SALT

method

Pit the Ligurian olives and chop finely. Put the olives on a sheet of silicone paper and dehydrate them in a low oven, about 60°C (140°F/Gas ¼), for 3–4 hours. (In the restaurant, we place the olives under heat lamps for 3–4 hours.) This will intensify the flavour of the olives. Allow to cool and then store in an airtight container.

Combine the goat's curd and sheep's milk yoghurt together and hang in a muslin cloth over a bowl in the refrigerator for 1–2 hours to remove the excess water, giving you a curd with the consistency of double cream. Keep in an airtight container in the refrigerator until required.

You can use any combination of tomatoes you have available. For the pink brandy wine tomatoes, cut the top and bottom off the tomato to expose the flesh. The pink brandy wine tomato has a very dense flesh with not too many seeds. You will need this type of tomato to be able to cut the cylinders. Using a 2 cm (¾ inch) diameter tube cutter, cut a tube of 3 cm (1¼ inches) in depth from the centre of the tomato. You should be able to get at least four cylinders out of each tomato. For the black ox heart tomatoes, cut them into 2 cm (¾ inch) thick slices, then cut each slice in half. With a paring knife, carefully remove the outside skin and flesh, exposing the seed jelly. Cut the love bite tomatoes in half and leave the Mexican midget tomatoes whole. Pick and sort through all the wild flowers, shoots and buds.

Soak the Italian mountain radicchio in water (four changes), then lightly fry in the grapeseed oil in a non-stick frying pan until crisp.

to finish and plate

Arrange the tomatoes in a half-moon shape on each serving plate. Place one-eighth of the sheep and goat's milk curd in the centre of each semicircle and sprinkle one side of the curd with the dehydrated olives. Arrange a couple of crisp radicchio leaves, as well as all the herbs, buds and flowers attractively on and around the goat's curd. Drizzle the tomatoes with extra virgin olive oil and season with sea salt.

SERVES 8

salad of spring vegetables, herbs and flowers with goat's curd cigars and lemon confit

This salad is inspired by Michel Bras' Gargouillou (salad of vegetables, wild herbs and flowers), my love of gardening and nature's diversity. For this salad use as many seasonal young vegetables, herbs and flowers as you can source. There's nothing quite like growing some of these vegetables yourself and serving them to friends and family. The addition of the goat's curd cigars and lemon confit enhances and complements the natural flavours and textures of the vegetables. This dish is a celebration of the beauty of natural ingredients.

ingredients

8 BABY FENNEL BULBS
8 BABY RED CORE RADISHES
8 RADISH SEED PODS
16 SMALL FRENCH BREAKFAST RADISHES
16 CHERRY BELLE RADISHES
16 BABY KABU (WHITE) TURNIPS
8 BABY PURPLE GARLIC
8 RED MARBLE ONIONS
8 PURPLETTE ONIONS
8 BABY LEEKS
8 BABY PERENNIAL LEEKS
16 SMALL BULB SPRING ONIONS (SCALLIONS)
8 WHITE ASPARAGUS SPEARS
8 GREEN ASPARAGUS SPEARS
8 FRESH PEA PODS
8 BROAD (FAVA) BEANS
8 TINY VIOLET POTATOES
8 BABY RED CARROTS
1 CENTRAL CORE OF PALM HEART
2 GARLIC CHIVE BUDS

8 WHITE BORAGE BUDS
1 NASTURTIUM BUD
8 NASTURTIUM LEAVES
8 FLOWERING PEA SHOOTS
32 SOCIETY GARLIC FLOWERS
8 WASABI FLOWER HEADS
8 RADISH FLOWERS
8 ONION CHIVE FLOWERS
8 ROCKET (ARUGULA) FLOWERS
8 PURPLE SWEET VIOLETS
16 NATIVE VIOLETS
8 PINK SWEET VIOLETS
8 WHITE SWEET VIOLETS
8 SPRIGS BRONZE FENNEL
1 BUNCH LEMON BLOSSOMS
1 PUNNET RED GARNET
8 PARSLEY FLOWERS
GOOD QUALITY EXTRA VIRGIN OLIVE OIL
FINE SEA SALT
LEMON CONFIT (BASIC RECIPES, PAGE 269)

goat's curd cigars

3 SHEETS TUNISIAN BRIK PASTRY
100 ML (3½ FL OZ) MELTED CLARIFIED BUTTER
    (BASIC RECIPES, PAGE 264)
200 G (7 OZ) FRESH GOAT'S CURD

Preheat the oven to 180°C (350°F/Gas 4). Spread the pastry out on the work surface and liberally brush with melted butter. Cut the pastry into 4 x 20 cm (1½ x 8 inch) strips; you will need 16 strips. You will also need 16 stainless-steel rods, 2 cm (¾ inch) in diameter and 6 cm (2½ inches) long. Wrap one strip of pastry around each rod, creating at least a three-layer thickness. Bake the pastry on the rods, join side down, on a baking tray lined with silicone paper for 8 minutes, or until the pastry is golden. Remove from the oven, allow to cool slightly, then remove the pastry cylinders from the rods by sliding them off carefully. Cool completely and store in an airtight container. Put the goat's curd in a small bowl, mix well to soften and transfer into a piping bag.

to finish and plate

Peel and trim the vegetables as necessary. Trim and prepare the herbs and flowers. Blanch each vegetable in boiling salted water separately until just tender, making sure to refresh all of them in iced water to set the colour. Dress all of the vegetables with extra virgin olive oil and season with sea salt. Arrange the vegetables attractively on each serving plate. Fill the cigars with the goat's curd and place two on each plate. Top one with a bunch of red garnet and top the other with a parsley flower. Dab some lemon confit in two or three locations around the plate. Scatter the herbs and flowers around the plates and serve immediately.

SERVES 8

garden peas, truffle custard with truffle and chestnut mushroom consommé

This dish can only be made in early spring with the last of the winter truffles and the first sign of baby spring peas. The combination of the rich truffle custard and the fresh popping flavour of spring peas is a revelation. The truffle and chestnut mushroom consommé has a wonderful intense flavour.

garlic and shallot juices

1 GARLIC CLOVE
3 FRENCH SHALLOTS
10 ML (¼ FL OZ) OLIVE OIL
500 ML (17 FL OZ/2 CUPS) CHICKEN STOCK
    (BASIC RECIPES, PAGE 262)
1 G (1/32 OZ) XANTANA (FERMENTED CORN STARCH)
FINE SEA SALT

To make the garlic and shallot juices, peel the garlic and shallots and finely dice. Sweat the garlic and shallots in a saucepan with the olive oil, without colouring. Add the chicken stock and slowly simmer for 15 minutes, or until the stock has reduced by half. Strain the stock through a fine sieve and discard the diced garlic and shallot. Add the xantana to the liquid and bring back to the boil while whisking. Season with sea salt. This light juice will be used to coat the peas, spring onions and radishes, to add additional flavour to the dish.

truffle and chestnut mushroom consommé

1 KG (2 LB 4 OZ) FRESH CHESTNUT MUSHROOMS
1 LITRE (35 FL OZ/4 CUPS) CHICKEN STOCK
    (BASIC RECIPES, PAGE 262)
30 G (1 OZ) BLACK WINTER TRUFFLE PEELINGS
1 WHITE CELERY STALK (INNER STALK), DICED
1 CARROT, DICED
½ BROWN ONION, DICED
250 G (9 OZ) BUTTON MUSHROOMS
4 EGG WHITES

Preheat the oven to 70°C (155°F/Gas ¼). Line two baking trays with silicone paper, spread the chestnut mushrooms in a single layer on the trays and place in the oven for 4 hours until completely dry. This will intensify the flavour of the stock. Put the chicken stock and 1 litre (35 fl oz/4 cups) of water in a pot. Add the dried mushrooms, truffle peelings, celery, carrot and onion and simmer for 2 hours, or until reduced by half. Skim the surface to remove any fat.

Strain through a sieve lined with muslin cloth into a pot and allow to cool. Meanwhile, to make a raft for the consommé, finely chop the button mushrooms in a food processor. Lightly whisk the egg whites until they form soft peaks, then fold through the mushrooms. Place the cooled stock over medium heat. Vigorously whisk the raft into the stock until well incorporated, stirring occasionally to make sure the raft is not sticking to the bottom. Allow the stock to come close to boiling point, then reduce the heat to the lowest possible setting; you want the stock to be barely simmering. Do not stir the raft again at this point. Cook on very low heat for 30 minutes. Make a hole in the raft to check that it is cooked and that the stock is clear, then cook for 10 minutes. Remove from the heat and set aside for 20 minutes. Ladle the consommé into a sieve lined with a double layer of muslin cloth, making sure you don't break up the raft too much. Taste and season with sea salt if necessary.

to finish and plate

TRUFFLE CUSTARDS (BASIC RECIPES, PAGE 268)
400 G (14 OZ) FRESH SHELLED PEAS
16 BULB SPRING ONIONS (SCALLIONS), TRIMMED
FINE SEA SALT
16 BABY RADISHES
50 G (1¾ OZ) BLACK WINTER TRUFFLE
16 PEA FLOWERS

Place the truffle custards in a steamer and steam for 8–10 minutes until just set. Reheat the garlic and shallot juices. Bring a pan of water to the boil and blanch the peas and spring onions for 1 minute, then drain and add to the garlic and shallot juices. Season the juices with additional sea salt if necessary, then add the baby radishes.

Using a round soup spoon, remove each truffle custard from its mould and place in the centre of a warmed serving bowl. Top the custards with the peas, spring onions and baby radishes, using a slotted spoon to remove any excess juices. Meanwhile, reheat the truffle and chestnut mushroom consommé and pour into a serving jug. Top each custard with some shaved truffle and arrange a few fine slices of truffle around the bowl. Garnish each with two pea flowers. Serve the dish to your guests and pour the consommé at the table.

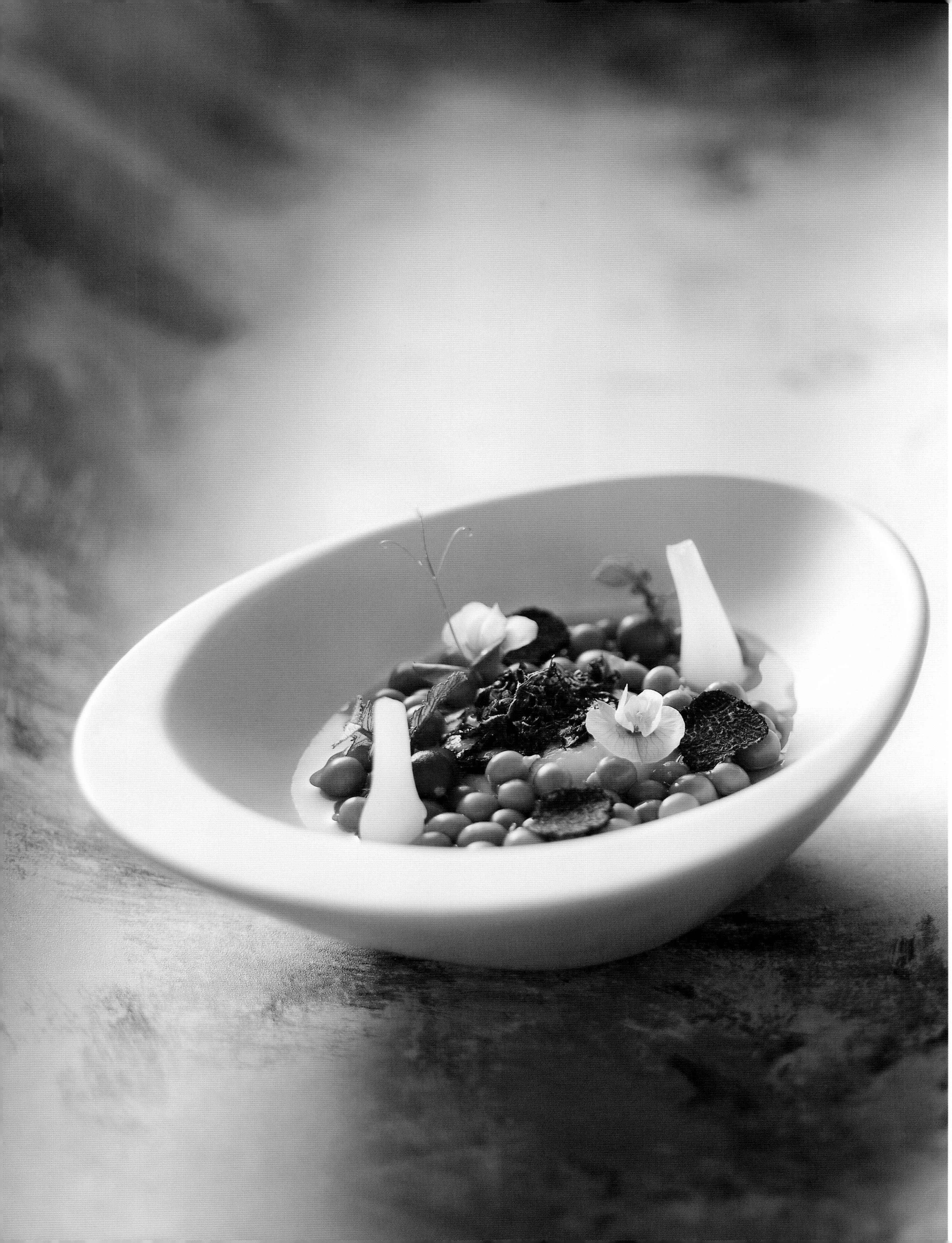

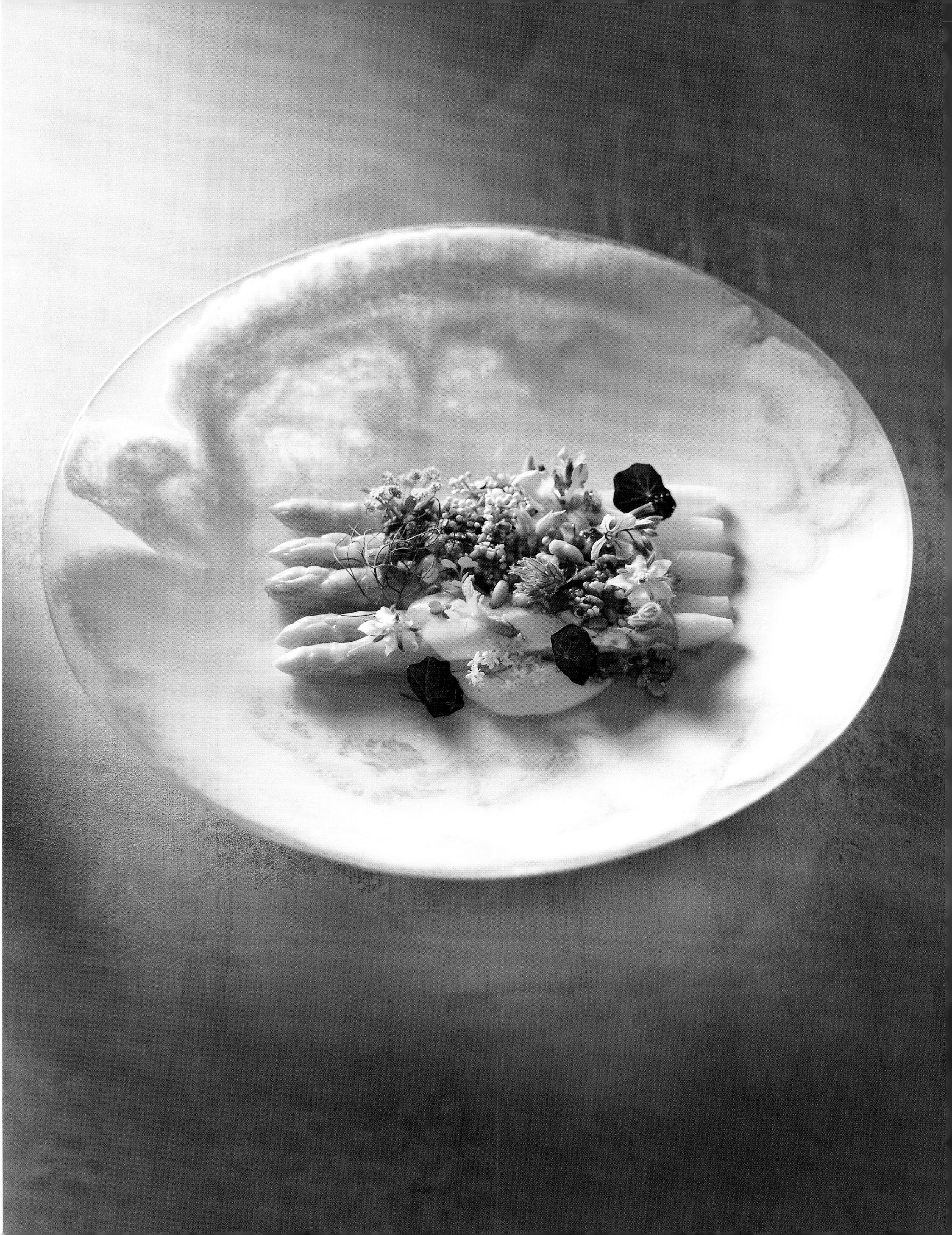

SERVES 8

white asparagus with comte-infused milk curd, roasted nuts and herb flowers

The idea of being able to eat fresh milk curd from the cheese-making process is attractive. Here I have infused grated aged comte in Jersey milk, which has a higher fat content than regular milk, and lightly set it with rennet. It's served immediately while still warm; the curd is delicate yet its flavour echoes the more matured comte. I always look forward to white asparagus in spring.

ingredients

- 1 LITRE (35 FL OZ/4 CUPS) HOMOGENISED JERSEY MILK
- 100 G (3½ OZ) FINELY GRATED AGED COMTE CHEESE
- 100 G (3½ OZ) PINE NUTS
- 100 G (3½ OZ) SUNFLOWER SEEDS
- 10 G (¼ OZ) PUFFED QUINOA
- 200 G (7 OZ) SHELLED AND HALVED HAZELNUTS
- 40 WHITE ASPARAGUS SPEARS
- FINE SEA SALT
- 10 ML (¼ FL OZ) STILL MINERAL WATER
- 3 ML (¹⁄₁₀ FL OZ) VEGETARIAN RENNET
- 100 ML (3½ FL OZ) CLARIFIED BROWN BUTTER (BASIC RECIPES, PAGE 264)
- 100 G (3½ OZ) UNSALTED BUTTER
- 24 NASTURTIUM LEAVES
- 16 ROCKET (ARUGULA) FLOWERS
- 16 CUCUMBER FLOWERS
- 16 WHITE BORAGE FLOWERS
- 16 ELDERFLOWER SPRIGS
- 8 SPRIGS BRONZE FENNEL
- 16 ONION CHIVE FLOWER BUDS
- 8 SPRIGS PARSLEY FLOWERS

method

Preheat the oven to 180°C (350°F/Gas 4). Place the Jersey milk into a saucepan and heat to 90°C (195°F). Add the comte cheese and mix in well. Remove the pan from the heat and allow the cheese and milk to infuse for 15 minutes. Strain the milk through a sieve lined with muslin cloth, and discard any solids. Refrigerate the milk until required.

Roast the pine nuts, sunflower seeds, puffed quinoa and hazelnuts separately in the oven until they are golden brown.

Peel the white asparagus and discard the bottom 5 cm (2 inches) of the spear. Check and trim the lengths so they are uniform. Bring a large pan of salted water to the boil and blanch the asparagus for 4–5 minutes.

Meanwhile, reheat the comte-infused milk until it reaches 40°C (105°F). Check the seasoning and add a little sea salt if necessary. Have eight small Chinese rice bowls ready. Mix the mineral water and rennet together. Stir the milk with a spoon to create a whirlpool effect and add the rennet and water mixture while the milk is swirling. This will ensure an even distribution of rennet. Immediately ladle an equal amount of milk into each rice bowl and allow the curds to set in a warm place. This should only take a couple of minutes.

In a small saucepan, add the brown butter and pine nuts, sunflower seeds, quinoa and hazelnuts. Heat gently to warm the nuts and seeds.

Melt the butter and drain the asparagus. Brush the melted butter over the asparagus and season with sea salt.

to finish and plate

Place five asparagus spears in the centre of each warmed serving plate. Using a small palette knife, release the curds from the edge of the rice bowls, making sure they are completely free. Tip the curd onto the asparagus, then spoon over an equal quantity of the warmed nut, seed and brown butter mixture on to the curds. Attractively arrange all the herbs and flowers on top, and serve immediately.

SERVES 8

roasted globe artichoke, goat's curd and walnut salad

This is a simple salad of roasted globe artichokes, goat's milk curd, rare herbs and a dressing of brown butter, truffle and honey. Walnuts and sliced truffle give it added texture.

ingredients

24 GLOBE ARTICHOKES
JUICE OF 1 LEMON
550 ML (19 FL OZ) EXTRA VIRGIN OLIVE OIL
1 GARLIC CLOVE, FINELY SLICED
1 SPRIG ROSEMARY
1 SPRIG THYME
80 ML (2½ FL OZ) CLARIFIED BROWN BUTTER
 (BASIC RECIPES, PAGE 264)
1 TEASPOON HONEY
40 G (1½ OZ) BLACK WINTER TRUFFLE
FINE SEA SALT
50 ML (1¾ FL OZ) GRAPESEED OIL
32 WALNUT HALVES
250 G (9 OZ) FRESH GOAT'S CURD
64 SPRIGS SALAD BURNET
16 PEA SHOOTS
16 NASTURTIUM LEAVES
64 SPRIGS RED ELK LEAF
32 SPRIGS RED DANDELION
32 RED SHISO LEAVES
1 PUNNET BABY RED GARNET, TRIMMED

method

Peel the artichokes, leaving a small stem. Remove the leaves and choke to expose the bases, then submerge each into a mixture of the lemon juice and 500 ml (17 fl oz/2 cups) of extra virgin olive oil, to prevent them from discolouring while you prepare the remaining artichokes. Place the artichokes in a vacuum bag, add the garlic, rosemary and thyme, as well as 200 ml (7 fl oz) of the olive oil and lemon juice mixture. Seal the bag in a vacuum sealer and steam the artichokes in a temperature-controlled combi oven at 90°C (195°F) for about 15 minutes, or until tender. Alternatively use a zip-lock bag and steam in a steamer. When the artichokes are cooked, remove them from the marinade. Leave half of the artichokes whole and cut the rest in half vertically through the stem.

Take 40 ml (1½ fl oz) of the brown butter and mix it with 50 ml (1¾ fl oz) of extra virgin olive oil and the honey. Finely grate half the truffle into this dressing and add a pinch of sea salt. Whisk the dressing together and reserve until needed.

Put the grapeseed oil and 40 ml (1½ fl oz) of brown butter in a frying pan. Heat the pan and fry the artichokes until they are golden brown. Drain the artichokes on kitchen paper and lightly season with sea salt.

Preheat the oven to 180°C (350°F/Gas 4). Place the walnut halves on a baking tray and roast in the oven for 5–6 minutes or until lightly browned. Remove from the oven and rub in a tea towel to remove as much of the skin as possible, then use the point of a sharp knife to scrape away all the skin, as the skin can be a little bitter. Break the walnuts into pieces and put aside.

to finish and plate

Finely slice the remaining truffle. Divide the artichokes among the serving plates, then spoon 4 teaspoons of goat's curd onto each plate. Lightly dress all the salad leaves and herbs in the truffle and honey dressing. Arrange the leaves and herbs on the plate, sprinkle the sliced truffle and walnut pieces over the salad and drizzle any remaining dressing over the artichokes. Serve immediately.

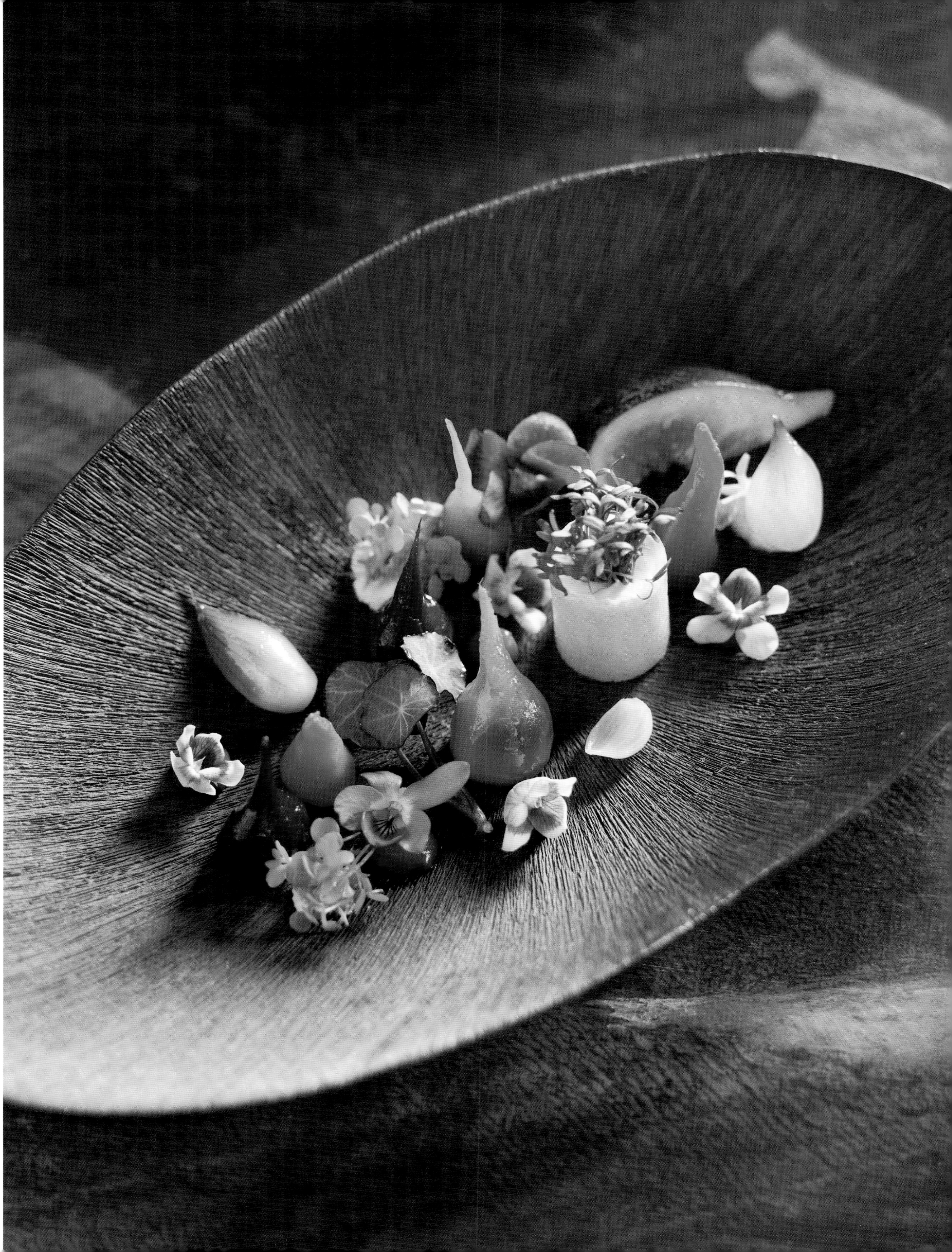

SERVES 8

salad of pink, red and golden beetroot with fig, goat's curd cylinder and truffle honey

This is a wonderful salad to make in autumn, when figs are just coming to the end of their season and baby beetroots are just beginning. I use a combination of red, golden and pink beetroots. The earthy flavour of the beetroot is complemented by an aromatic dressing of truffle-infused honey. The violets also add a subtle perfume and visually lift the dish.

ingredients

16 BABY PINK TARGET BEETROOTS
16 BABY RED BEETROOTS
16 BABY GOLDEN BEETROOTS
FINE SEA SALT
150 ML (5 FL OZ) EXTRA VIRGIN OLIVE OIL
ROCK SALT
50 ML (1¾ FL OZ) ITALIAN WHITE TRUFFLE HONEY
50 ML (1¾ FL OZ) BANYULS VINEGAR
24 SMALL RED ASIAN SHALLOTS
50 ML (1¾ FL OZ) CLARIFIED BUTTER (BASIC RECIPES, PAGE 264)
1 X 20 CM (8 INCH) SQUARE SHEET TUNISIAN BRIK PASTRY
2 FRESH BLACK GENOA FIGS
200 G (7 OZ) FRESH GOAT'S CURD
1 PUNNET BABY RED GARNET, TRIMMED
32 NATIVE VIOLETS
16 PURPLE SWEET VIOLETS
24 SMALL NASTURTIUM LEAVES
2 PUNNETS BABY WATERCRESS, TRIMMED
8 ROSEMARY FLOWERS

method

Preheat the oven to 150°C (300°F/Gas 2). To prepare the beetroots, trim the leaves, leaving 1 cm (½ inch) of stalk. Wash the beetroots well, then dry. Cut a square of foil large enough to hold all the beetroots. Place the beetroots in the middle of the foil, season with sea salt and dress with 50 ml (1¾ fl oz) of olive oil. Wrap the beetroots in the foil to form an airtight parcel. Place the parcel on a baking tray lined with rock salt. The rock salt will stop the beetroots burning on the metal tray. Place the tray in the oven and cook for 15–20 minutes. Open the parcel and test the beetroot with a small knife. When tender, allow the beetroots to cool slightly, then, wearing gloves, rub the skins off with your fingers. Put aside.

To make the dressing, whisk together the white truffle honey and vinegar with a pinch of sea salt. Slowly whisk in the remaining 100 ml (3½ fl oz) of extra virgin olive oil.

Peel the shallots and place them on a sheet of silicone paper. Dress them with a tablespoon of the truffle honey dressing, season with sea salt and

wrap in the paper to form an airtight parcel. Place the shallots on a baking tray lined with rock salt and bake in a 150°C (300°F/Gas 2) oven for 10 minutes, or until the shallots are tender.

To make the brik pastry cylinders, you will need two 1.5 cm (⅝ inch) diameter stainless-steel pipes of about 12 cm (4½ inches) in length. Melt the clarified butter and brush the sheet of pastry. Cut the pastry into 2 cm (¾ inch) thick strips about 10 cm (4 inches) in length and wrap the strips around the stainless-steel rods: you should get four strips on each rod. Bake the pastry on the rods, join side down, on a baking tray lined with silicone paper in a 150°C (300°F/Gas 2) oven for about 5 minutes, or until the pastry is golden. Remove the pastry cylinders from the oven, allow to cool slightly, then remove the pastry cylinders from the rods by sliding them off carefully. Allow to cool completely and store in an airtight container.

to finish and plate

Remove the shallots from the parcel. Place the shallots and remaining juices with the peeled beetroots into a stainless-steel bowl. Dress liberally with the remaining truffle honey dressing and season with sea salt. Arrange the beetroots and shallots onto each serving plate. Cut the figs into quarters and place on the plates. Spoon the goat's curd into a piping bag and fill the pastry cylinders with the curd. Top with some red garnet and arrange on the plates with the violets, nasturtium leaves, watercress and rosemary flowers. Serve immediately.

SERVES 8

steamed and roasted kamo eggplant with fried bamboo fungi and enoki mushrooms

This is a fun and very textural vegetarian dish. Bamboo fungus is a type of mushroom that is grown in the bamboo forests of China. It is sold dried and is available at good Chinese grocery stores. The mushroom is hollow and a perfect vehicle for stuffing — I fill the mushroom with tofu and black sesame seeds but you could use different combinations. This dish is served with wonderful small kamo eggplants, which have very few seeds and a lovely flavour. I like to steam the eggplants before roasting them, which helps maintain a white soft flesh. The dish is accompanied by sesame-coated enoki mushrooms, palm heart, radish pods, garlic cream and seaweed floss.

ingredients

4 JAPANESE KAMO EGGPLANTS (AUBERGINES)
14 G (½ OZ) DRIED WAKAME SEAWEED
20 ML (½ FL OZ) VIRGIN SESAME OIL
8 DRIED BAMBOO FUNGI
100 G (3½ OZ) SILKEN TOFU
FINE SEA SALT
50 G (1¾ OZ) BLACK SESAME SEEDS, GROUND
100 ML (3½ FL OZ) GARLIC CREAM (BASIC RECIPES,
    PAGE 265)
430 ML (15 FL OZ) GRAPESEED OIL
50 G (1¾ OZ) PREPARED JAPANESE SEAWEED
    (JYUNTORO)
200 G (7 OZ) TRIMMED FRESH PALM HEART
200 G (7 OZ) WHITE SESAME SEEDS, ROASTED
200 G (7 OZ) ENOKI MUSHROOMS
100 G (3½ OZ) RICE FLOUR
32 ASIAN RADISH PODS
2 BUNCHES GARLIC CHIVE FLOWERS

method

Put the eggplants into a vacuum bag with the wakame seaweed and sesame oil. Seal the bag in a vacuum sealer and steam in a temperature-conrolled combi oven at 90°C (195°F) for 20 minutes. Alternatively, use a zip-lock bag and steam in a steamer. Allow the eggplant to cool in the bag.

Soak the dried bamboo fungi in cold water for 5 minutes, changing the water three times. Remove the fungi and squeeze out the excess water with your hands, then dry well. Chop the silken tofu into 1 cm (½ inch) dice, put into a bowl and season with a little sea salt. Add the ground black sesame seeds and mix lightly. Spoon the mixture into a piping bag and fill the hollow of each bamboo fungus with the tofu mixture. Refrigerate the stuffed bamboo fungi until required. Make the garlic cream.

To make the seaweed floss, heat 350 ml (12 fl oz) of grapeseed oil in a small saucepan to 180°C (350°F). Add the Japanese seaweed and deep-fry in batches for 30 seconds until the seaweed is light golden in colour. Remove with a slotted spoon and drain on a kitchen cloth. Reserve the oil.

Slice the palm heart on an angle into thin slices and put aside. Finely chop the white sesame seeds and put aside. Trim the enoki mushrooms, leaving 5 cm (2 inches) of stem. Put the rice flour into a bowl and wet with just enough water to make a light, thin batter. Place the bamboo fungi in the batter to lightly coat, then roll it in the chopped sesame seeds, and put aside. Do the same with the enoki mushrooms.

white tea and seaweed broth

½ GARLIC CLOVE, FINELY CHOPPED
½ BUNCH GREEN SPRING ONIONS (SCALLIONS),
    WHITE PART ONLY, FINELY CHOPPED
20 ML (½ FL OZ) GRAPESEED OIL
5 G (⅛ OZ) WHITE TEA LEAVES
10 G (¼ OZ) DRIED WAKAME SEAWEED
WHITE SOY SAUCE, TO TASTE
2 G (1⁄16 OZ) XANTANA (FERMENTED CORN STARCH)

To make a light white tea and seaweed broth, sauté
the garlic and spring onions together in a pan with
the grapeseed oil. Add 400 ml (14 fl oz) of water and
simmer for 10 minutes, then remove from the heat.
Add the white tea and dried wakame and infuse for
4 minutes. Strain the broth and discard the solids.
Taste the broth and season with white soy sauce.
Bring back to simmering point, add the xantana and
whisk well; you should have a very lightly thickened
broth. Put aside.

to finish and plate

Place a small pan of water on to boil and blanch the radish pods for 30 seconds, then drain. Cut the eggplant
into quarters and pan-fry, in batches, in a large non-stick frying pan in 80 ml (2½ fl oz/⅓ cup) of grapeseed
oil until golden brown. Strain the oil used to deep-fry the seaweed and place in a clean saucepan, then bring
back up to deep-frying temperature. Deep-fry the stuffed bamboo fungi until golden brown. Remove from
the oil and drain on a kitchen cloth. Deep-fry the enoki mushrooms until golden brown, then remove and
drain. Reheat the seaweed broth, add the palm heart and simmer for 1 minute.

   On each serving plate, place two quarters of the eggplant. Slice each bamboo fungus in half with a bread
knife to expose the tofu, and place on the plate. Add a spoonful of garlic cream, place the sesame-coated
enoki mushrooms on top and add the palm heart. Garnish with the fried seaweed floss, garlic chive flowers
and radish pods. Add a couple of spoonfuls of the white tea and seaweed broth and serve immediately.

SERVES 8

radishes and turnips with green almonds and almond cream

This simple vegetable dish is a celebration of the diversity that nature produces in just two ingredients: radishes and turnips. There are about 20 varieties available between them, but here I have used only nine. This dish should be served as an accompaniment to a main course or as a vegetable course as part of a degustation menu.

ingredients

40 GREEN ALMONDS (LATE NEW SEASON ALMONDS)
500 ML (17 FL OZ/2 CUPS) MILK
4 WATERMELON RADISHES
12 CHERRY BELLE RADISHES
8 FRENCH BREAKFAST RADISHES
8 PURPLE FRENCH BREAKFAST RADISHES
8 HAILSTONE (WHITE) RADISHES
8 MANTANGHONG RADISHES
16 SMALL PINK TURNIPS
8 HINONA KABU (LONG JAPANESE) TURNIPS
8 LARGE KABU (WHITE) TURNIPS
16 BABY KABU (WHITE) TURNIPS
24 RED MARBLE ONIONS
ALMOND CREAM (BASIC RECIPES, PAGE 265)
150 G (5½ OZ) UNSALTED BUTTER
FINE SEA SALT
24 SOCIETY GARLIC FLOWERS
16 RADISH FLOWERS
24 ONION CHIVE FLOWERS

method

Shell the green almonds. Place the kernels in the milk (this will help to keep them white). Cover and refrigerate until required.

Prepare the radishes and turnips. Peel the watermelon radishes and cut into 5 mm (¼ inch) thick slices, then use a 5 cm (2 inch) round pastry cutter to cut the slices into discs. You will need two discs per portion. Cut four of the cherry belle radishes in half and with a sharp turning knife scrape away the skin of the other eight, leaving a slight bleeding of the red behind on the radish. Leave the French breakfast radishes whole. Leave the purple breakfast radishes whole. Peel the hailstone radishes and leave them whole. Peel the mantanghong radishes with a turning knife and shape into a 3 cm (1¼ inch) barrel.

Pick eight small pink turnips and leave them whole (you only need to gently scrape the outside skin away). Peel the other eight pink turnips and cut them in half lengthways. Slice a 2 cm (¾ inch) disc from the dark purple part of the hinona kabu turnips.

Peel the rest of the turnip very lightly and cut it in half. Peel the large kabu turnips and use a 4 cm (1½ inch) round pastry cutter to cut through the centre of the turnip. Finely slice the core you have cut on a mandolin into 1 mm (¹⁄₁₆ inch) thin slices. You will need about ten slices per portion. Trim the green leaves from the baby kabu turnips, leaving behind 5 mm (¼ inch) of stem. Carefully peel the turnips by rubbing off the skin with a sharp paring knife. Top and tail the red marble onions and peel one layer of the outside skin away. Put aside the prepared radishes, turnips and onions. Leave them soaking in cold water in the refrigerator for no more than 1 hour before cooking.

to finish and plate

Bring a large saucepan of salted water to the boil. You will need to cook all the radishes, turnips and onions at once, starting with the thickest radishes and turnips. The thickest vegetables will need no longer than 3 minutes while the small marble onions will need 1½ minutes. The smallest radishes and turnips will need 1 minute. The fine radish slices will only need 30 seconds.

Meanwhile, reheat the almond cream in a small pan. Drain the green almonds from the milk. Once all the radishes, turnips and onions are cooked, drain them. Melt the butter and generously brush it over the vegetables and season with sea salt. Arrange the radishes, turnips, onions, almond cream, almonds and flowers on each serving plate. Serve while piping hot.

SERVES 8

palm heart and truffle risotto with white corn cream

Australia has a flourishing truffle industry. For the past five years at least, I have been able to buy beautiful Australian black winter truffles that rival the French-imported Perigord truffles. Our truffles are grown on truffle farms in Tasmania, Victoria, New South Wales and Western Australia during the southern hemisphere's winter. It occurred to me that for the first time I could have fresh winter truffles from Australia and fresh summer truffles (imported from Italy) together in the one dish. The risotto is made using aged acquerello rice and fresh palm hearts. Fresh palm hearts have an amazingly crisp texture and a flavour reminiscent of corn, hence the reason for serving it with a white corn cream. This is a wonderful vegetarian dish.

ingredients

2 FRESH PALM HEARTS
2 X 50 G (1¾ OZ) BLACK WINTER TRUFFLES
1 X 50 G (1¾ OZ) ITALIAN SUMMER TRUFFLE
2 FRENCH SHALLOTS
1 SMALL GARLIC CLOVE
100 G (3½ OZ) PARMIGIANO REGGIANO
130 G (6¼ OZ) UNSALTED BUTTER
2–2.5 LITRES (70–87 FL OZ/8–10 CUPS) CHICKEN
    OR VEGETABLE STOCK (BASIC RECIPES, PAGE 262)
500 G (1 LB 2 OZ) ACQUERELLO RICE
FINE SEA SALT

method

Make the purée for the white corn cream (see right). Trim the central top section of the palm heart cores and slice into 40 x 5 mm (¼ inch) thick rounds. Scrub the winter and summer truffles with a brush and wipe with a cloth to remove any traces of dirt.

Peel and finely dice the shallots and garlic, grate the parmesan and dice the butter. Bring 2 litres (72 fl oz/8 cups) of stock to the boil in a saucepan, then remove from the heat. In a separate saucepan, melt 50 g (1¾ oz) of butter and sweat the shallots and garlic, being careful not to add any colour. Add the rice and stir with a wooden spoon so the rice is well coated in the butter and shallots. Slowly add the stock, a small ladle at a time, and cook, stirring, for 15 minutes, or until the rice is al dente. (You may not need to use all of the stock.) Add another 50 g (1¾ oz) of butter and the grated parmesan and mix in well. Take one of the winter truffles and, using a microplane, finely grate the truffle into the rice. Stir well and allow the risotto to sit with a lid on for about 2 minutes.

white corn cream

2 FRENCH SHALLOTS, FINELY DICED
1 SMALL GARLIC CLOVE, FINELY DICED
100 G (3½ OZ) UNSALTED BUTTER
8 COBS FRESH WHITE CORN
1 LITRE (35 FL OZ/4 CUPS) CHICKEN OR VEGETABLE
    STOCK (BASIC RECIPES, PAGE 262)
50 ML (1¾ FL OZ) CREAM (35% FAT)

Sweat the shallots and garlic in a saucepan with 50 g (1¾ oz) of butter, without colouring.

Remove the corn kernels from the cob with a knife. Add the kernels to the shallots and garlic along with the stock. Bring to the boil and cook the corn until all the stock has evaporated. Place the contents of the pan into a blender with the remaining 50 g (1¾ oz) of butter and blend until smooth. Pass the mixture through a drum sieve and hang the corn purée in muslin cloth for a couple of hours to remove the excess moisture. Scoop the purée into a small saucepan and season to taste.

to finish and plate

Heat 500 ml (17 fl oz/2 cups) of stock in a small saucepan, add the palm heart slices and blanch for 1 minute, then strain. Melt the remaining 30 g (1 oz) of butter and brush it over the palm hearts. Season with sea salt. Reheat the white corn purée, whip the cream and fold through the purée. Check and adjust the seasoning if necessary. Remove the lid from the risotto and season with sea salt to taste. Finely slice the remaining winter truffle and summer truffle on a truffle slicer and put aside.

Place a generous spoonful of the risotto in the centre of each plate. Top with small spoonfuls of white corn cream and place the palm heart and truffle slices over the risotto. Serve immediately.

the sea

Seafoods offer the most potential for creative cookery. The sea provides a vast array of textures and flavours, which lend themselves to multiple cooking techniques; from pan-roasting to gentle poaching in butter or stock, baking in salt and seaweed, steaming and searing. And combinations of accompanying flavours offer almost endless possibilities too. However, it is the subtlety and gentle nature of the flavour and texture of seafood that speaks to me as a chef.

sea pearls

Sea Pearls is one of my most original and beautiful seafood dishes; it is a complex dish using many different techniques. This dish is comprised of various seafood delicacies shaped into iridescent pearls. The dish is a culmination of several ideas, inspired from my Sea Treasures dish, which I had been wanting to expand upon. The catalyst for developing the idea of 'edible pearls' came after seeing a photograph of an exhibition of real pearls, featured at the museum. I hadn't realised that pearls came in so many shapes, sizes and colours, and somehow this thought remained in the back of my mind when the idea finally came together.

After the idea's conception came the considerations of flavour and texture and the practicalities of actually producing the dish. When considering flavour compatibility, I assembled an array of ingredients that I felt worked harmoniously together — the saltiness of caviar, the light smokiness of dashi and smoked eel, the aromatic heat of the wasabi and the citrus burst from the yuzu. The textural components are the soft fleshy mouthfeel of the sashimi tuna, the chewy texture of the poached octopus, the jellied dashi and slippery tapioca, the lushness of the sea scallops and crème fraîche and the poppiness of the egg white pearls and caviar.

SERVES 8

dashi jelly and abalone pearl

ingredients

1 X 250 G (9 OZ) LIVE GREEN LIPPED ABALONE
COARSE SEA SALT
750 ML (26 FL OZ/3 CUPS) STILL MINERAL WATER
18 G (¾ OZ) SHAVED DRIED BONITO
18 G (¾ OZ) DRIED KONBU SEAWEED
75 ML (2½ FL OZ) LIGHT SOY SAUCE
30 ML (1 FL OZ) MIRIN
2 SHEETS TITANIUM GELATINE

method

Place the live abalone into an iced water bath for 20 minutes, then remove. Shuck the abalone using a large kitchen spoon. Remove all the organs and guts and, with a sharp pair of scissors, trim off the hard external lip. Lightly scrub the abalone meat with coarse sea salt under running water for 1 minute.

To make the dashi stock, put the mineral water in a small saucepan and bring to the boil. Remove the pan from the heat and add the bonito, konbu seaweed, light soy sauce and mirin and infuse for 20 minutes, then strain through a sieve lined with muslin cloth. Measure 250 ml (9 fl oz/1 cup) of dashi and set aside. Place the remaining dashi in a small saucepan and heat to 90°C (195°F), add the abalone and gently simmer for 15 minutes. Remove the abalone and allow it to cool. Using a very sharp knife or a gear-driven slicing machine, slice the abalone into tissue-paper-thin slices and put aside.

Heat the reserved dashi in a small saucepan to 70°C (155°F). Meanwhile, soak the gelatine sheets in cold water until softened. Squeeze the excess water from the gelatine and add to the dashi. Stir to dissolve the gelatine, then remove the pan from the heat. Allow to cool completely to room temperature. Be careful not to let the dashi set.

Take eight 20 cm (8 inch) squares of plastic wrap and place them over eight coffee cups, leaving a dip in the middle of the plastic. Place 15 ml (½ fl oz) of the dashi stock and three thin slices of abalone into the dip in the plastic. Carefully lift up the four corners of the plastic wrap and twist them together to form a liquid ball a little larger than a cherry tomato. Tie a knot in the plastic so the liquid jelly is completely sealed. Repeat this process until you have eight balls. Place in the refrigerator to set for 2–3 hours before serving.

to finish and plate

Use a small pair of scissors to cut the knot from the dashi pearls and carefully peel away the plastic wrap. Serve on a plate with one of each of the other pearls.

SERVES 8

tapioca, mud crab and yuzu pearl with rosemary flowers and edible silver leaf

ingredients

1 X 800 G (1 LB 12 OZ) LIVE MUD CRAB
1 YUZU OR LEMON
50 G (1¾ OZ) CRÈME FRAÎCHE
FINE SEA SALT
95 G (3¼ OZ/½ CUP) PEARL TAPIOCA
32 ROSEMARY FLOWERS
**2 X 10 CM (4 INCH) SQUARE SHEETS PURE
  SILVER LEAF**

method

Place the live mud crab into a bucket filled with water and plenty of ice for 15 minutes. This will send the crab into a coma, which is a more humane way of treating it. Meanwhile, place a large pot of salted water on the stovetop and bring to the boil. Remove the crab from the iced water, plunge into the boiling water and cook for 10 minutes. Remove the crab and cool for 10 minutes at room temperature, then refrigerate for at least 1 hour to cool completely. Once the crab has cooled, crack the body, legs and claws. Remove the meat and finely shred it; you will need 160 g (5¾ oz) of crabmeat.

Finely zest the yuzu using a microplane. You will need 1 teaspoon of zest. Wrap the zest in a small purse of muslin cloth and tie the neck of the purse tightly with kitchen string. Blanch the zest in boiling water for 30 seconds, then refresh in iced water. Gently squeeze the muslin to remove excess water, then remove the zest from the muslin. Add the zest to the crème fraîche, then thoroughly mix through

the crabmeat. Season with sea salt if necessary, then refrigerate for 15 minutes. This small amount of crème fraîche will help bind the crab. Using your hands, roll the crabmeat into eight small balls, then return the crab balls to the refrigerator for 30 minutes.

Cook the tapioca in boiling water for 10 minutes, or until the tapioca become opaque and the smallest pinprick of white is visible in the centre. Drain the tapioca and allow to cool.

Take eight 20 cm (8 inch) squares of plastic wrap and place them over eight coffee cups. Using 3 teaspoons of tapioca for each pearl, spread the tapioca out in a thin layer on the plastic until you have a circumference of about 5 cm (2 inches). Place one crabmeat ball in the centre of the tapioca. Carefully lift up the four corners of the plastic wrap and twist them together to form a ball of tapioca-lined crab, then tie a knot in the plastic. Repeat this process until you have eight balls. Place in the refrigerator to set for 1 hour before serving.

to finish and plate

Use a small pair of scissors to cut the knot from the tapioca pearls and carefully peel away the plastic wrap. Use a pair of tweezers to insert four rosemary flowers into each pearl. The flowers will be held in place by the sticky tapioca. Cut each sheet of silver leaf into four. Use a pair of tweezers to crinkle the silver leaf and then place it on top of the pearl. Repeat for all eight pearls. Serve on a plate with one of each of the other pearls.

SERVES 8

marinated scallop and lime crème fraîche pearl with wasabi flowers

ingredients

1 TAHITIAN LIME
100 G (3½ OZ) CRÈME FRAÎCHE
FINE SEA SALT
8 LARGE SEA SCALLOPS, WITHOUT ROE
50 ML (1¾ FL OZ) WHITE SOY SAUCE
4 WASABI FLOWER STEMS
8 SMALL NASTURTIUM LEAVES

method

To make the lime crème fraîche, finely zest the lime using a microplane. Wrap the zest in a small purse of muslin cloth and tie the neck of the purse tightly with kitchen string. Blanch the zest in boiling water for 30 seconds, then refresh in iced water. Gently squeeze the muslin to remove excess water. Remove the zest from the muslin. Place the crème fraîche in a bowl and add the blanched zest, 1 teaspoon lime juice and a pinch of sea salt. Whisk together until soft peaks form.

Slice each scallop into six thin discs, about 2 mm (¹⁄₁₆ inch) thick. Briefly marinate the scallop discs in the white soy sauce for 5 seconds. Remove and drain on a clean kitchen cloth.

Take eight 20 cm (8 inch) squares of plastic wrap and place them over eight coffee cups. Place five slightly overlapping slices of scallop on the plastic and 1 teaspoon of lime crème fraîche in the centre. Place one slice of scallop over the crème fraîche. Carefully lift up the four corners of the plastic wrap and twist them together to form a ball of scallop, with the lime crème fraîche contained in the centre. Tie a knot in the plastic. Repeat this process until you have eight balls. Place in the refrigerator to set for 30 minutes before serving.

to finish and plate

Use a small pair of scissors to cut the knot from the scallop pearls and carefully peel away the plastic wrap. Remove the individual wasabi flowers from their stems; you will need 48 flowers. Using a sharp knife, make six small indentations into the scallop flesh. Place a wasabi flower in each slit, then place a small nasturtium leaf in the centre. Serve on a plate with one of each of the other pearls.

SERVES 8

sashimi tuna, horseradish cream and aquaculture caviar pearl

ingredients

10 G (¼ OZ) FINELY GRATED FRESH HORSERADISH

100 G (3½ OZ) CRÈME FRAÎCHE

FINE SEA SALT

250 G (9 OZ) CENTRE-CUT SASHIMI-GRADE TUNA, CUT INTO A 15 CM (6 INCH) LONG, 5 CM (2 INCH) ROUND CYLINDER (ASK YOUR FISHMONGER TO DO THIS FOR YOU)

50 ML (1¾ FL OZ) WHITE SOY SAUCE

10 ML (¼ FL OZ) GRAPESEED OIL

20 G (¾ OZ) AQUACULTURE STURGEON CAVIAR

method

Mix the grated horseradish, crème fraîche and a pinch of sea salt together and lightly whisk until soft peaks form.

Slice the tuna into 3 mm (⅛ inch) thick slices; you will need 24 thin round slices. Briefly marinate each piece of tuna in the white soy sauce for about 5 seconds. Remove and drain on a clean kitchen cloth.

Take eight 20 cm (8 inch) squares of plastic wrap and place them over eight coffee cups. Place three slightly overlapping slices of tuna on the plastic and 1 teaspoon of the horseradish crème fraîche in the centre. Carefully lift up the four corners of the plastic wrap and twist them together to form a ball of tuna, with the horseradish crème fraîche contained in the centre. Tie a knot in the plastic. Repeat this process until you have eight balls. Place in the refrigerator to set for 30 minutes before serving.

to finish and plate

Use a small pair of scissors to cut the knot from the tuna pearls and carefully peel away the plastic wrap. Brush them with a little grapeseed oil, then place a small amount of caviar on the top of each pearl. Serve on a plate with one of each of the other pearls.

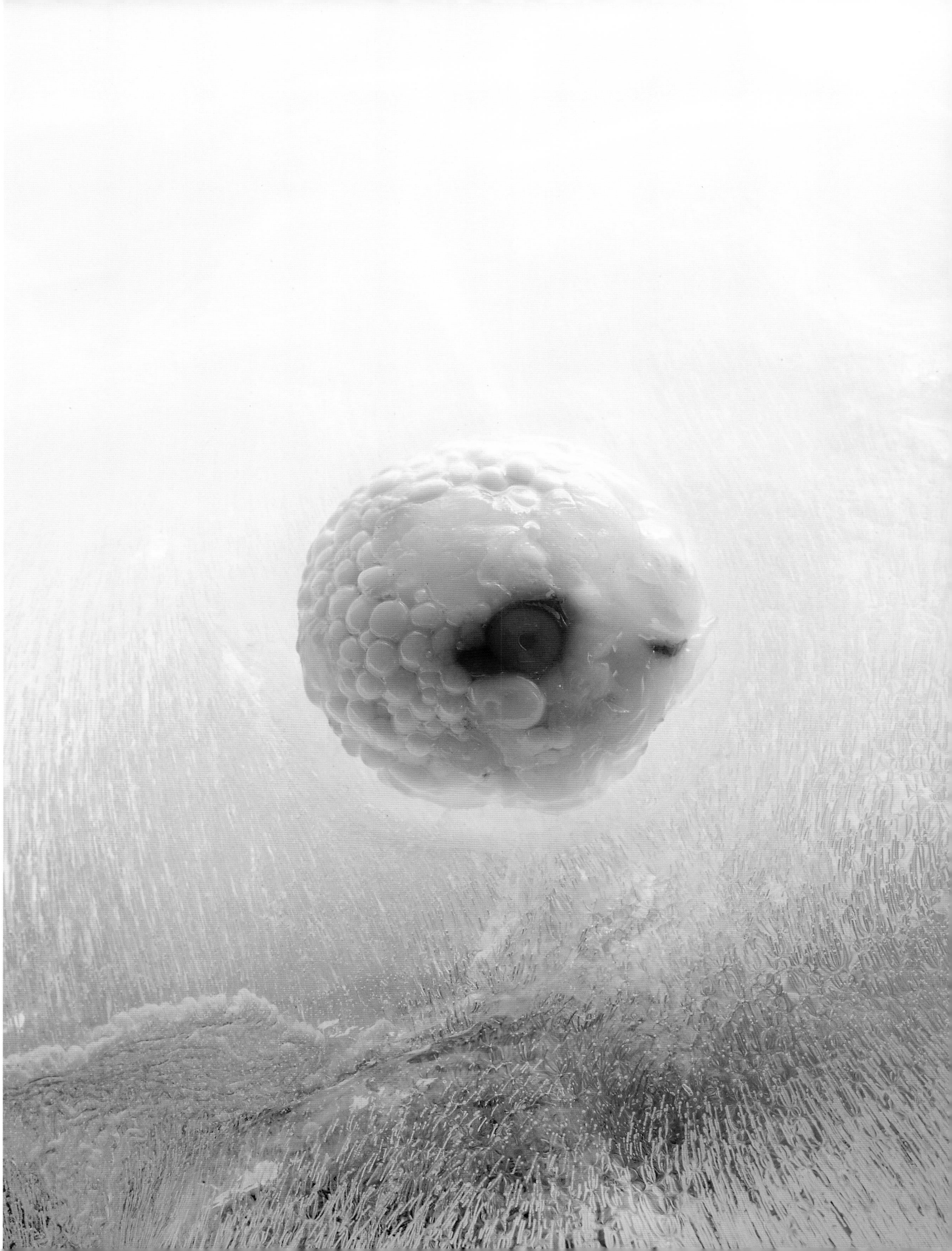

SERVES 8

smoked eel, octopus and egg white pearl

ingredients

70 G (2½ OZ) SMOKED EEL MEAT

200 ML (7 FL OZ) MILK

70 G (2½ OZ) WHITE FLESHED FISH, SUCH AS BLUE
    EYE, SNAPPER OR COD

60 G (2¼ OZ) UNSALTED BUTTER, SOFTENED

40 ML (1¼ FL OZ) EXTRA VIRGIN OLIVE OIL

JUICE OF ½ LEMON

60 G (2¼ OZ) MASHED POTATO

FINE SEA SALT

30 G (1 OZ) CRÈME FRAÎCHE

500 ML (17 FL OZ/2 CUPS) GRAPESEED OIL

100 ML (3½ FL OZ) STRAINED EGG WHITE

1 X 500 G (1 LB 2 OZ) OCTOPUS

COARSE SEA SALT

300 ML (10½ FL OZ) OLIVE OIL

method

To make the smoked eel brandade, first make sure the smoked eel flesh is boneless and skinless. Put the milk in a pan and bring to the boil, then remove the pan from the heat and add the smoked eel. Leave the eel to marinate in the warm milk for 10 minutes, then strain the eel and discard the milk. Steam the white fish until it flakes.

Put the eel and fish in a small bowl. Using a fork, mash them together with 30 g (1 oz) of softened butter. Drizzle over 20 ml (½ fl oz) of extra virgin olive oil and the lemon juice, mixing with the fork as you go. Add the mashed potato and mix well. Add the remaining 30 g (1 oz) of butter and 20 ml (½ fl oz) of extra virgin olive oil and mix well. Season to taste with sea salt. Allow the mixture to cool, then fold in the crème fraîche. Place the mixture in the refrigerator for at least 1 hour.

Take some of the mixture in the palm of your hand and roll into balls the size of a cherry tomato. You will need eight balls. You will have some mixture leftover, which you can use elsewhere.

To make the egg white pearls, put the grapeseed oil in a small saucepan and heat to 70°C (155°F). Using an eye dropper, drop the strained egg white into the oil, drop by drop, in rapid succession. When you have about 30 egg white droplets, stop and gently stir them around. They need about 1 minute in the oil to fully set. Carefully sieve out the egg white pearls

using a fine strainer and place the pearls on a metal tray. Repeat this process several times, maintaining the oil temperature at about 70°C (155°F), until you have a sufficient amount of egg white pearls to coat the eight balls of brandade mixture.

To prepare the octopus, remove the tentacles from the body. You will only need the tentacles for this recipe. With some coarse sea salt, scrub the tentacles under running water. Once fully rinsed, finely slice the tentacles through the suckers into very thin discs. Heat the olive oil to 70°C (155°F) and poach the sliced octopus in batches for about 1 minute, or until opaque. Move the octopus in the oil while poaching to ensure even cooking. Drain and allow to cool.

Take eight 20 cm (8 inch) squares of plastic wrap and place them over eight coffee cups. Place 1 teaspoon of egg white pearls and 10 thin slices of cooked octopus tentacles in the middle of the plastic and spread them out in a thin layer over the plastic. Place one ball of brandade in the centre. Carefully lift up the four corners of the plastic wrap and twist them together to form a ball, then tie a knot in the plastic. The aim is to coat the brandade balls in the egg white pearls and octopus. Repeat this process until you have eight balls. Place in the refrigerator to set for 30 minutes before serving.

to finish and plate

Use a small pair of scissors to cut the knot from the pearls and carefully peel away the plastic wrap. Carefully unwrap the pearls and allow them to come back to room temperature for about 15 minutes before serving. Serve on a plate with one of each of the other pearls.

SERVES 8

poached rock oysters with winter melon, oyster broth and pea flowers

Most oyster aficionados in Australia prefer the Sydney rock oysters over other varieties. I also think they are superior in flavour. If you can't find Sydney rocks you could substitute with flat angasi oysters. In this recipe I have gently poached the oysters in a broth made from oyster juices, shaved bonito and seaweed. The dish is served with Chinese winter melon, oyster cream, radish pods and flowering pea shoots.

ingredients

1 YOUNG WINTER MELON OR HAIRY MELON,
    WITH SMALL SEEDS
OYSTER CREAM (BASIC RECIPES, PAGE 265)
24 UNSHUCKED SYDNEY ROCK OYSTERS
24 RADISH SEED PODS
16 FLOWERING PEA SHOOTS
8 OKRA SPROUTS

OYSTER JUS

12 UNSHUCKED SYDNEY ROCK OYSTERS
4 FRENCH SHALLOTS, FINELY DICED
½ GARLIC CLOVE, FINELY DICED
10 ML (¼ FL OZ) GRAPESEED OIL
1 LITRE (35 FL OZ/4 CUPS) CHICKEN STOCK
    (BASIC RECIPES, PAGE 262)
5 G (⅛ OZ) SHAVED DRIED BONITO
1 TEASPOON DRIED WAKAME SEAWEED
4 G (⅛ OZ) XANTANA (FERMENTED CORN STARCH)

method

Peel the winter melon and cut into 4 cm (1½ inch) thick slices. Using a 3 cm (1¼ inch) round pastry cutter, cut out as many cylinders as you can from the flesh; you will need 16 cylinders. Store the winter melon in cold water in the refrigerator until required. Make the oyster cream.

To make the oyster jus, shuck the 12 oysters, reserving the meat and juice separately. In a small saucepan, gently sauté the shallots and garlic in the grapeseed oil until they are translucent. Add the chicken stock and bring to the boil. Turn the heat down to a very low simmer, then add the oysters, bonito and wakame seaweed. Infuse over low heat for 15 minutes, then remove the pan from the heat and infuse for a further 15 minutes. Add the oyster juice to the pan and then strain the stock through a fine sieve lined with muslin cloth, discarding the oysters. Return the stock to a clean saucepan and reheat to simmering point. Sprinkle in the xantana while whisking. Allow the stock to gently simmer for 10 minutes; it should thicken slightly. Strain the stock through a fine sieve and put aside until required.

Shuck the 24 oysters, reserving all the juice, then pass the juice through a sieve lined with muslin cloth and put aside.

Divide the thickened oyster jus between two saucepans (you should have about 400 ml/14 fl oz in each pan). Bring both pans to boiling point, then turn them both down to a low simmer. In one pan, add the winter melon cylinders and gently poach for 2 minutes, then add the radish pods for the last 30 seconds. Remove the winter melon and radish pods from the oyster jus and keep warm. Add the shucked oysters to the oyster jus and poach the oysters for 1 minute over low heat. Be careful not to overcook the oysters; you just want to get the oysters warm.

Add the reserved oyster juice to the second pan of thickened oyster jus. Stir well and bring the jus up to the boil.

to finish and plate

Gently reheat the oyster cream. Place two cylinders of winter melon and two poached oysters in each serving bowl. Top the oysters with a couple of spoonfuls of oyster cream and then place one oyster on top. Garnish with the radish pods, flowering pea shoots and okra sprouts. Carefully spoon in 2–3 tablespoons of oyster jus and serve immediately.

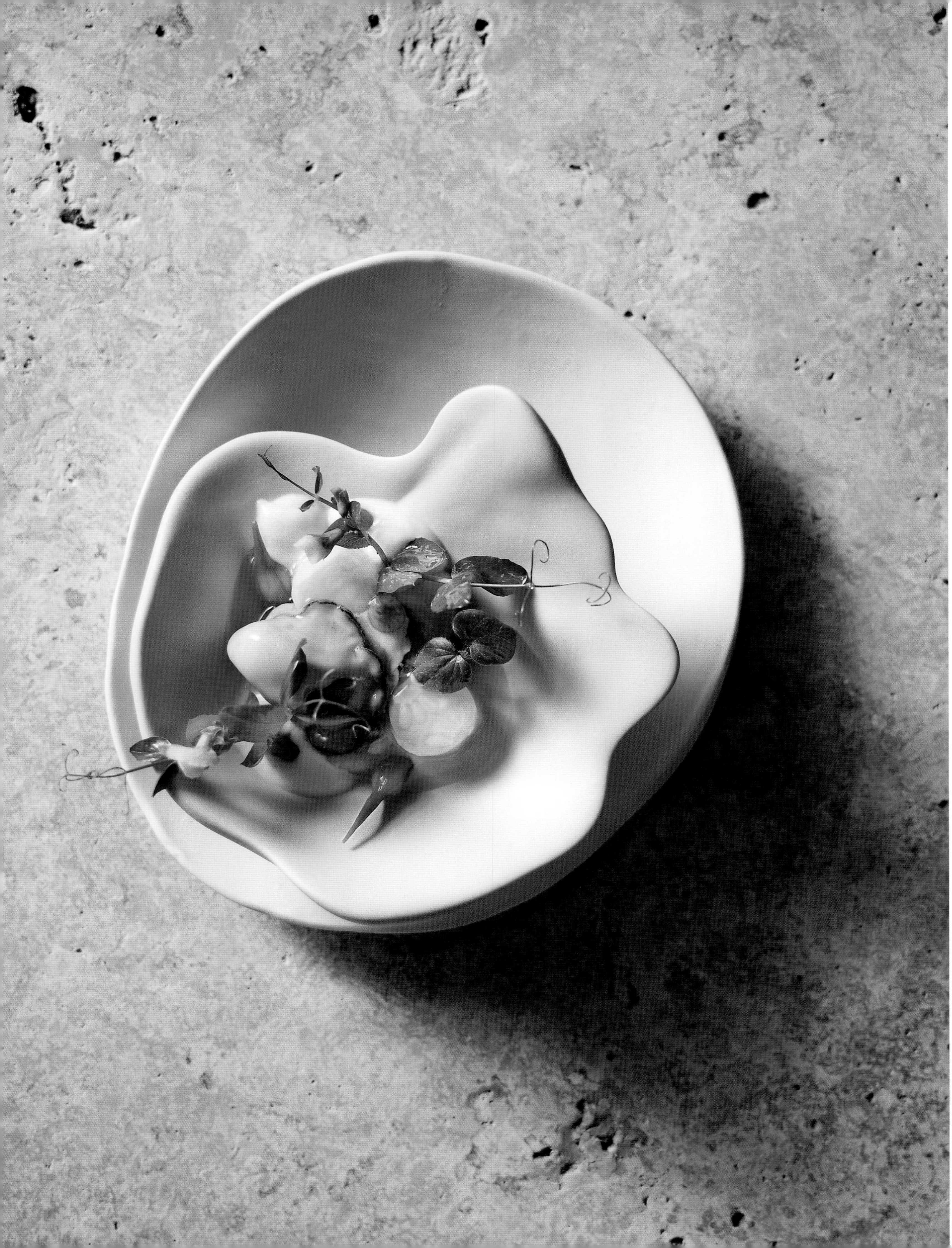

SERVES 8

whole snapper baked in a rock salt and seaweed crust

This is a beautiful way to cook whole fish and is one of my favourite fish dishes. Cooking the fish whole in rock salt and seaweed gives the fish a delicate seaweed perfume and perfectly seasons the flesh. It also seals in all of the natural fish juices, making the flesh incredibly moist and succulent — basically, the fish is steaming in its own juices. The snapper is accompanied by what I like to call stone pot rice. This was inspired by an incredible rice dish that I ate in Japan. The rice was cooked in a heavy stone pot in the oven, which produced rice that was very crisp on the outside and soft on the inside. The pot was then taken to the table, where the waiter added fresh sea urchin roe and then stirred some soft rice through the crispy rice, giving the rice a wonderful nutty, crispy flavour. I have adapted the idea for this recipe, which uses a different method to produce a similar result.

baked snapper

12 G (½ OZ) DRIED WAKAME SEAWEED
4 KG (8 LB) ROCK SALT
1 X 4 KG (8 LB) SNAPPER, GUTTED AND SCALED

Rehydrate the dried wakame seaweed in 3 litres (105 fl oz/12 cups) of cold water for 1 hour. Remove the seaweed from the water (you should now have about 500 g/1 lb 2 oz of seaweed) and tear it into small pieces.

Preheat the oven to 200°C (400°F/Gas 6). Wet the salt with 1 litre (35 fl oz/4 cups) of cold water. You want the salt to be wet but do not add too much water or the salt will dissolve.

Cover the snapper completely in the wakame seaweed. Place half the rock salt on a flat baking tray and form a mound roughly the same size as the fish. Place the seaweed-covered snapper on the salt and cover the fish with the other half of salt. Press the salt around the fish so that the fish is completely encased in the salt. Place the fish into the oven and bake for 35 minutes.

fish head and seaweed glaze

3 SNAPPER HEADS, SPLIT IN HALF (ASK YOUR FISHMONGER TO DO THIS FOR YOU)
100 ML (3½ FL OZ) GRAPESEED OIL
1 SMALL KNOB YOUNG GINGER, FINELY SLICED
½ BUNCH GREEN SPRING ONIONS (SCALLIONS), WHITE PART ONLY, FINELY SLICED
300 ML (10½ FL OZ) DRY SAKE
2 LITRES (70 FL OZ/8 CUPS) CHICKEN STOCK (BASIC RECIPES, PAGE 262)
1 TEASPOON DRIED WAKAME SEAWEED
40 G (1½ OZ) JAPANESE GLUTINOUS RICE
WHITE SOY SAUCE

Remove and discard the eyes and gills from the halved snapper heads, then wash thoroughly under cold running water to remove the excess blood.

In a large pot, lightly brown the snapper heads in the grapeseed oil. Add the ginger and spring onions and sauté for 1 minute. Deglaze with the sake and continue to cook until almost all the sake has evaporated. Add the chicken stock and wakame seaweed and simmer for 30 minutes over low heat. Add the rice and continue to simmer for a further 1 hour, or until the liquid has reduced by half and is lightly thickened from the rice.

Strain the stock through a fine sieve and discard the solids. Return the liquid to a clean saucepan and continue to reduce until you have 400–500 ml (14 fl oz–17 fl oz) of liquid remaining. By now the liquid should be reasonably thick. Season to taste with white soy sauce. Refrigerate until required.

accompaniments

24 LIVE PERIWINKLES
16 LARGE SEA SCALLOPS, WITHOUT ROE
32 SMALL JAPANESE WHITE TURNIPS
8 SPRIGS YOUNG SAMPHIRE
2 PUNNETS MUSTARD CRESS, TRIMMED

Place the live periwinkles into a bucket filled with water and plenty of ice for 20 minutes. This will send them into a coma, which is a more humane way of treating them and also relaxes the meat. Meanwhile, place a large pot of salted water on the stovetop and bring to the boil. Remove the periwinkles from the iced water and place them in the boiling water for 1 minute, then remove and place them straight back into the iced water to stop the cooking process.

With a thin metal skewer, hook and remove the meat from the shells. Discard the intestines, cut the piece of meat in half vertically and remove the red mouth section. Put the periwinkles aside to be reheated later. Cut each scallop in half horizontally.

Trim the green stalks from the white turnips, leaving 5 mm (¼ inch) of stem attached. Lightly peel the turnips and blanch them in boiling salted water for 1 minute, then refresh in iced water. Break the samphire into 2 cm (¾ inch) long sections.

stone pot rice

210 G (7½ OZ/1 CUP) SUSHI RICE
40 ML (1¼ FL OZ) GRAPESEED OIL

Wash the rice three times in cold water. Cook the rice with an equal quantity of cold water in a rice cooker. When the rice is cooked, remove half the rice to a bowl, cover and leave at room temperature for no more than 1 hour before serving.

Continue to cook the other half of the rice left in the rice cooker. Add a couple of tablespoons of water and cook for a further 10 minutes. The aim is to overcook this part of the rice. Take half of the overcooked rice while it is still warm, place it between two sheets of silicone paper and, using a large heavy rolling pin, squash and roll the rice out. You want to roll the rice very, very thinly, to about a 1 mm (1⁄16 inch) thickness. Leave the rice between the sheets of silicone paper and use scissors to cut out a circle of rice and silicone paper to fit the diameter of a non-stick frying pan. You will need two rice sheets for this dish, about 20 cm (8 inches) in diameter.

Heat the rice and silicone paper circle over medium–low heat in the pan for 1 minute, then turn it over and cook for a further 1 minute. The rice should now be slightly firmer and drier. Peel away both sheets of silicone paper. Add 20 ml (½ fl oz) of grapeseed oil to the pan and fry the rice sheet for a further 1–2 minutes on each side until crispy and very lightly golden brown. Repeat for the second rice sheet, using the remaining 20 ml (½ fl oz) of oil. Remove from the pan and cool completely.

Take one rice sheet and, with a sharp knife, finely chop the sheet into small pieces. Tear the other sheet into 2 cm (¾ inch) rough shards. Store the shards and chopped rice in separate airtight containers until required.

to finish and plate

Remove the fish from the oven and allow to cool at room temperature for 10 minutes before breaking the crust with a blunt knife and peeling away the seaweed from the fish. Gently peel the skin off the fish and portion the fish into eight rectangles, using a sharp knife to cut the fish away from the bone. Lift the fish off the bone using a palette knife and cover with a clean kitchen cloth; keep warm. (Try to ensure you remove as many fine bones from the fish as possible when you are removing the flesh.)

Divide the fish glaze between two saucepans. In one pan, gently poach the sea scallops and reheat the periwinkles, baby turnips and samphire. In the other pan, add the reserved sushi rice and gently reheat. Add the mustard cress and finely chopped crispy rice to the rice mixture. Place three or four spoonfuls of the hot rice mixture on each plate. Place one portion of snapper on each plate and ladle the scallops, periwinkles, turnips and samphire around the fish. Garnish with the crispy rice shards and serve immediately.

SERVES 8

salad of west australian marron, lime crème fraîche and seaweed jelly

Marrons are a native Western Australian freshwater crayfish, larger and more highly prized than the Eastern freshwater yabbie. They have a subtle flavour and a crisp, juicy texture. Marrons are mostly farmed and are exported to many countries. In this salad I have combined poached marrons with the fresh citrus flavour of lime crème fraîche and the gentle aniseed flavour of baby fennel. This is offset by the saltiness of the seaweed jelly and samphire, and the peppery heat of the nasturtiums. In this salad I also use a rare Japanese vegetable called hasuimo, which is a type of green taro stem and resembles a vegetable version of an Aero bar.

ingredients

8 X 150–200 G (5½–7 OZ) LIVE MARRONS
8 BABY FENNEL BULBS
16 SMALL BULB SPRING ONIONS (SCALLIONS)
3 LEBANESE (SHORT) CUCUMBERS
1 STEM HASUIMO
16 SMALL SHOOTS WARRIGAL GREENS
16 SPRIGS FENNEL TIPS
32 SAMPHIRE TIPS
8 PEA FLOWERS
16 WHITE CHINESE KALE FLOWERS
32 SMALL NASTURTIUM LEAVES
100 ML (3½ FL OZ) EXTRA VIRGIN OLIVE OIL
FINE SEA SALT

method

Place the live marrons into a large bucket filled with water and plenty of ice for 20 minutes. This will send them into a coma, which is a more humane way to treat them and causes less stress to the flesh. Meanwhile, place a large pot of salted water on the stovetop and bring to the boil. Remove the marrons from the iced water and pierce their heads with a small sharp knife. This will kill the marron. Immediately place the marrons into the boiling water and cook for 8 minutes. Remove from the pot and cool at room temperature for 10 minutes, then refrigerate until they are cold.

Trim and discard any damaged outside layers of the fennel bulbs. Blanch in boiling salted water for 1 minute and refresh in iced water. Do the same with the spring onions. Put aside.

Peel the cucumbers, then use a 5 mm (¼ inch) Parisienne scoop (or melon baller) to scoop out 32 balls of cucumber. Peel the hasuimo and finely slice it. Wash and drain the Warrigal greens, fennel tips, samphire tips, flowers and nasturtium leaves.

seaweed jelly balls

500 ML (17 FL OZ/2 CUPS) STILL MINERAL WATER
1 TEASPOON WHITE TEA LEAVES
5 CM (2 INCH) SQUARE PIECE DRIED KONBU SEAWEED
5 CM (2 INCH) SQUARE OF TOASTED NORI SEAWEED
1 TABLESPOON DRIED WAKAME SEAWEED
25 ML (1 FL OZ) WHITE SOY SAUCE
4 SHEETS TITANIUM GELATINE
FINE SEA SALT

Prepare the seaweed jelly balls 6 hours in advance.
Put the mineral water in a small saucepan and bring
to the boil. Remove the pan from the heat and add
the white tea and dried seaweeds and infuse for
20 minutes. Add the white soy sauce, then strain
through a fine sieve, reserving the liquid. Return the
liquid to a clean saucepan and discard the seaweed.

Bring the seaweed-infused liquid to the boil,
then immediately remove from the heat. Meanwhile,
soak the gelatine sheets in cold water until softened.
Squeeze the excess water from the gelatine and
add to the hot liquid. Stir to dissolve the gelatine,
then taste and check for seasoning. If needed, add
a little sea salt (take care not to add too much, as
the white soy sauce is quite salty). Allow the liquid to
cool but not set.

Take eight 25 cm (10 inch) squares of plastic
wrap and place them over eight coffee cups, leaving
a dip in the middle of the plastic. Place 20 ml (½ fl oz)
of the cool seaweed-infused liquid into the dip in
the plastic. Carefully lift up the four corners of the
plastic wrap and twist them together to form a liquid
ball. Keep twisting, then tie a knot to form a tight ball.
Repeat this process until you have eight seaweed
jelly balls. Refrigerate the jelly balls for 5–6 hours,
or until completely set.

lime crème fraîche

1 TAHITIAN LIME
250 G (9 OZ) CRÈME FRAÎCHE
FINE SEA SALT

To make the lime crème fraîche, finely zest the lime
using a microplane. Wrap the zest in a small purse
of muslin cloth and tie the neck of the purse tightly
with kitchen string. Blanch the zest in boiling water
for 30 seconds, then refresh in iced water. Gently
squeeze the muslin to remove excess water. Remove
the zest from the muslin. Place the crème fraîche in
a bowl and add the blanched zest, all the juice from
the lime and a pinch of sea salt. Whisk together until
soft peaks form. Place the lime crème fraîche in the
refrigerator until needed.

to finish and plate

Shell the marron tails using a sharp knife or a pair of kitchen scissors. Slice each marron tail into three
sections. Shell the marron claws using a small hammer or the back of a knife to gently crack the shells. Brush
the marron with a small amount of extra virgin olive oil and season with sea salt. Arrange the marron on each
plate with three quenelles of lime crème fraîche. Dress and season all the vegetable components with extra
virgin olive oil and sea salt and place randomly on the serving plates. Use a small pair of scissors to cut the
knot from the jelly balls and carefully peel away the plastic wrap. Place one jelly ball in the centre of each
plate. Arrange the fennel sprigs, nasturtiums, Warrigal greens, samphire tips and flowers around the plate,
and serve immediately.

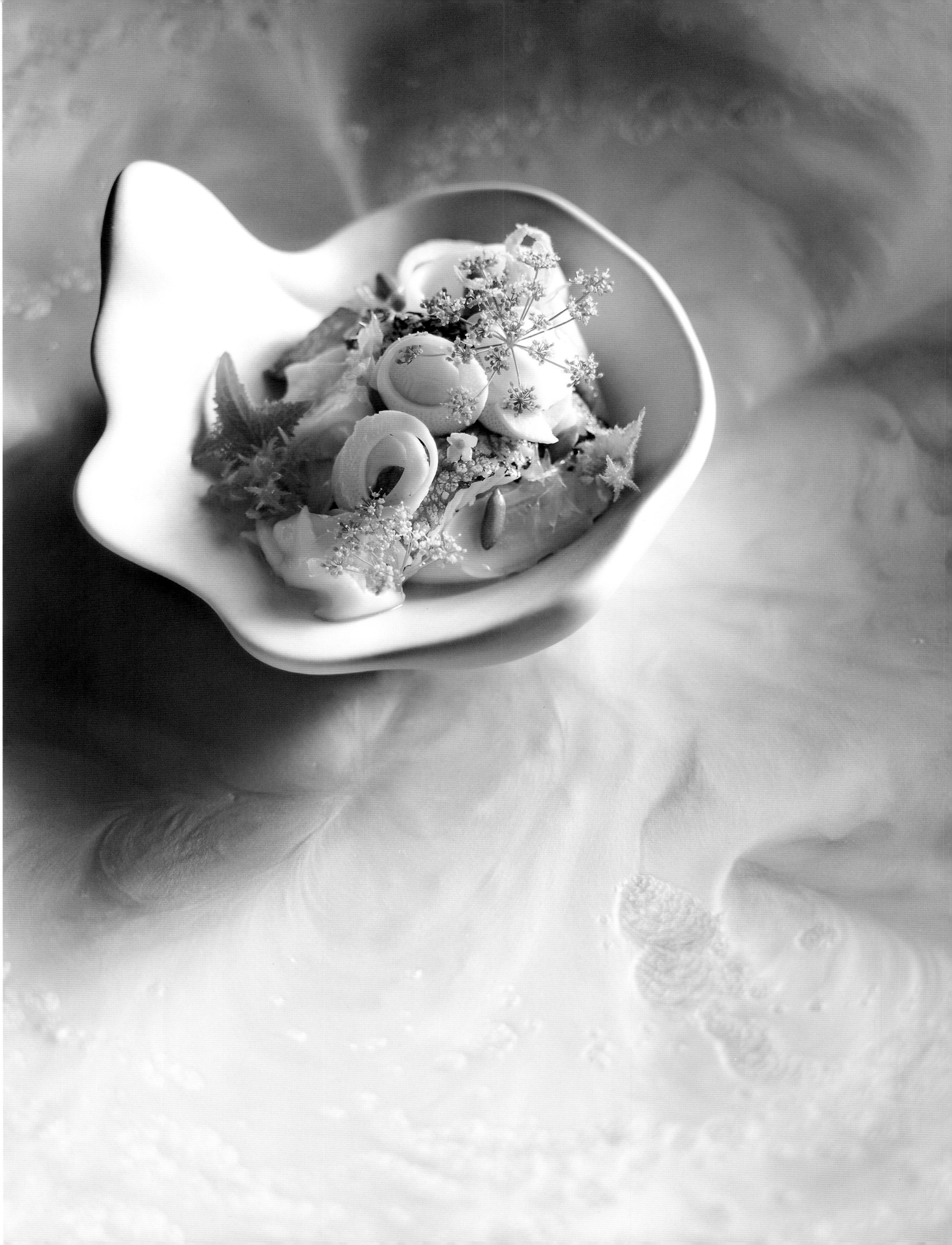

SERVES 8

salad of mud crab with young coconut, palm heart, sour mexican cucumbers and lime

Mud crab really is a luxurious and delicate meat and, in my opinion, has the best flavour of all the crabs available in Australia. You need to buy the crabs live and prepare them on the same day you make the salad. We chill all live seafood in plenty of iced water before cooking it, as the iced water will send most seafood to sleep. It is the most humane way to cook live seafood and has the added benefit of reducing stress in the meat. The crab is paired with fresh palm heart and young coconut flesh. Palm heart has only recently become available in Australia; it has a fantastic crisp texture and a flavour that's a little reminiscent of sweet corn. The salad is rounded out by the use of crisp white cucumbers and a rather rare miniature sour Mexican cucumber. A simple lime vinaigrette adds a good acid balance to this textural and very refreshing summer salad.

ingredients

2 X 1 KG (2 LB 4 OZ) LIVE MALE MUD CRABS
1 FRESH PALM HEART
16 WHITE CUCUMBERS
2 FRESH YOUNG COCONUTS
3 TAHITIAN LIMES
FINE SEA SALT
150 ML (5 FL OZ) GRAPESEED OIL
64 MINIATURE SOUR MEXICAN CUCUMBERS
8 CUCUMBER FLOWERS
8 SMALL CUCUMBER TENDRILS
16 SPRIGS FLOWERING CORIANDER (CILANTRO)

method

Place the live mud crabs into a bucket filled with water and plenty of ice for 15 minutes. This will send them into a coma, which is a more humane way of treating them. Meanwhile, place a large pot of salted water on the stovetop and bring to the boil. Remove the crabs from the iced water and plunge into the boiling water. Simmer over medium heat for 10 minutes, then remove the crabs and place on a tray. Cool for 10 minutes at room temperature, then refrigerate the crabs until they are cold (minimum 2 hours). I allow them to cool so their juices are absorbed back into the flesh. If you crack them as soon as they come out of the pan, you will lose a lot of the precious juice and flavour.

Once the crabs have cooled, crack the bodies, legs and claws and remove as much meat as you can. Try to keep the meat in large chunks, especially from the claws. Place the crabmeat in a bowl and cover with plastic wrap while you assemble the rest of the ingredients.

Peel the palm heart to expose the central core, then slice into 2 mm (1/16 inch) thin discs. Cut the white cucumbers lengthways into 3 mm (1/8 inch) thin slices. Crack the fresh coconuts with a heavy cleaver — you can reserve the coconut water and use it for a refreshing drink. Using a spoon, scoop the young translucent milky flesh from the inside of the coconut and cut into thick strips. Peel one of the limes and segment the flesh. Break the segments apart with your fingers and place them in a small bowl. Squeeze the juice from the other two limes into a small bowl — you will need 30 ml (1 fl oz) of lime juice. Add a pinch of sea salt to the lime juice and whisk in the grapeseed oil. This will form a simple vinaigrette. Place the lime pieces into the dressing and mix well.

to finish and plate

Lightly season the mud crab meat with sea salt. Dress the crab, palm heart, white cucumbers and coconut flesh with the lime vinaigrette. Assemble an even amount of all the ingredients in each serving bowl. Garnish with sour Mexican cucumbers, cucumber flowers and tendrils, and coriander flowers. Serve immediately.

SERVES 8

warm salad of swordfish belly and octopus with artichoke aïoli and chilli threads

Swordfish belly has a high intermuscular fat content, like the toro from tuna. Here I serve it with some assertive flavours to cut through the fat: rocket, chilli, artichoke and slow-cooked tomatoes. The roasted wild Italian mountain radicchio adds a wonderful crispy bitterness to the salad. Use good quality extra virgin olive oil to poach the octopus and swordfish belly as it really adds a wonderful flavour to the dish. The octopus suckers are surprisingly tender when gently poached.

ingredients

ARTICHOKE AÏOLI (BASIC RECIPES, PAGE 268)
1 X 10 CM (4 INCH) SQUARE OF SWORDFISH BELLY
COARSE SEA SALT
2 TENTACLES FROM A LARGE 4 KG (8 LB) OCTOPUS
32 TINY CHERRY TOMATOES
10 G (¼ OZ) CASTER (SUPERFINE) SUGAR
FINE SEA SALT
300 ML (10½ FL OZ) EXTRA VIRGIN OLIVE OIL
16 STEMS OF PRESERVED WILD ITALIAN MOUNTAIN
    RADICCHIO
10 G (¼ OZ) KOREAN FINE-CUT CHILLI THREADS
32 ROCKET (ARUGULA) FLOWERS
1 PUNNET ROCKET (ARUGULA) SPROUTS, TRIMMED
24 ONION CHIVE FLOWERS
16 SPRIGS WILD FLOWERING SORREL

method

Make the artichoke aïoli and refrigerate until required. Trim the tough outside sinews from the swordfish belly and slice into 16 x 3 mm (⅛ inch) thin slices. Put the slices in the refrigerator until required. With some coarse sea salt, scrub the octopus tentacles under running water. Place the tentacles on a board and use a small sharp knife to cut around the suckers. You will need four large suckers per dish (32 suckers in total). Refrigerate until needed.

Preheat the oven to 80°C (175°F/Gas ¼). Bring a saucepan of water to the boil and have some iced water standing by. Blanch the cherry tomatoes in boiling water for 10 seconds, then immediately refresh in the iced water. Peel the tomatoes once they have cooled. Place the tomatoes on a baking tray lined with silicone paper, sprinkle with the sugar and sea salt and drizzle with 30 ml (1 fl oz) of the extra virgin olive oil. Place the tomatoes in the oven and dry them for about 20 minutes. This will help to intensify their flavour.

Soak the preserved mountain radicchio in cold water for 10 minutes, repeating this process three times to help remove the preserving vinegar. Dry the radicchio well on a clean kitchen cloth. Add 20 ml (½ fl oz) of extra virgin olive oil to a large non-stick frying pan, heat on high and pan-roast the radicchio for 1 minute, four pieces at a time. The aim is to get the radicchio well roasted and crispy.

to finish and plate

Heat the remaining 250 ml (9 fl oz/1 cup) of extra virgin olive oil in a saucepan. Make sure the oil has at least a 4 cm (1½ inch) depth. Heat the oil to 68°C (154°F) and maintain that temperature. Working in two batches, poach the octopus suckers in the oil for 2–3 minutes, or until the suckers turn opaque. Keep the octopus covered in a warm place while you poach the swordfish. The swordfish belly will only need 1 minute in the oil and you will need to cook it in two or three batches. Do not overcrowd the saucepan. The swordfish belly will also turn opaque and will be just cooked. Do not overcook the swordfish belly; it has a high fat content like tuna belly and can be consumed as sashimi. Here we are just warming it through and slightly cooking it.

Place a small spoonful of artichoke aïoli in the centre of each serving plate and spread it out a little. Season the swordfish and octopus suckers with a little sea salt and place the swordfish belly on top of the artichoke aïoli. Arrange four octopus suckers around each plate and top the swordfish with some roasted radicchio and fine chilli threads. Place the slow-cooked cherry tomatoes around the salad and garnish with rocket flowers, rocket sprouts, chive flowers and flowering wild sorrel.

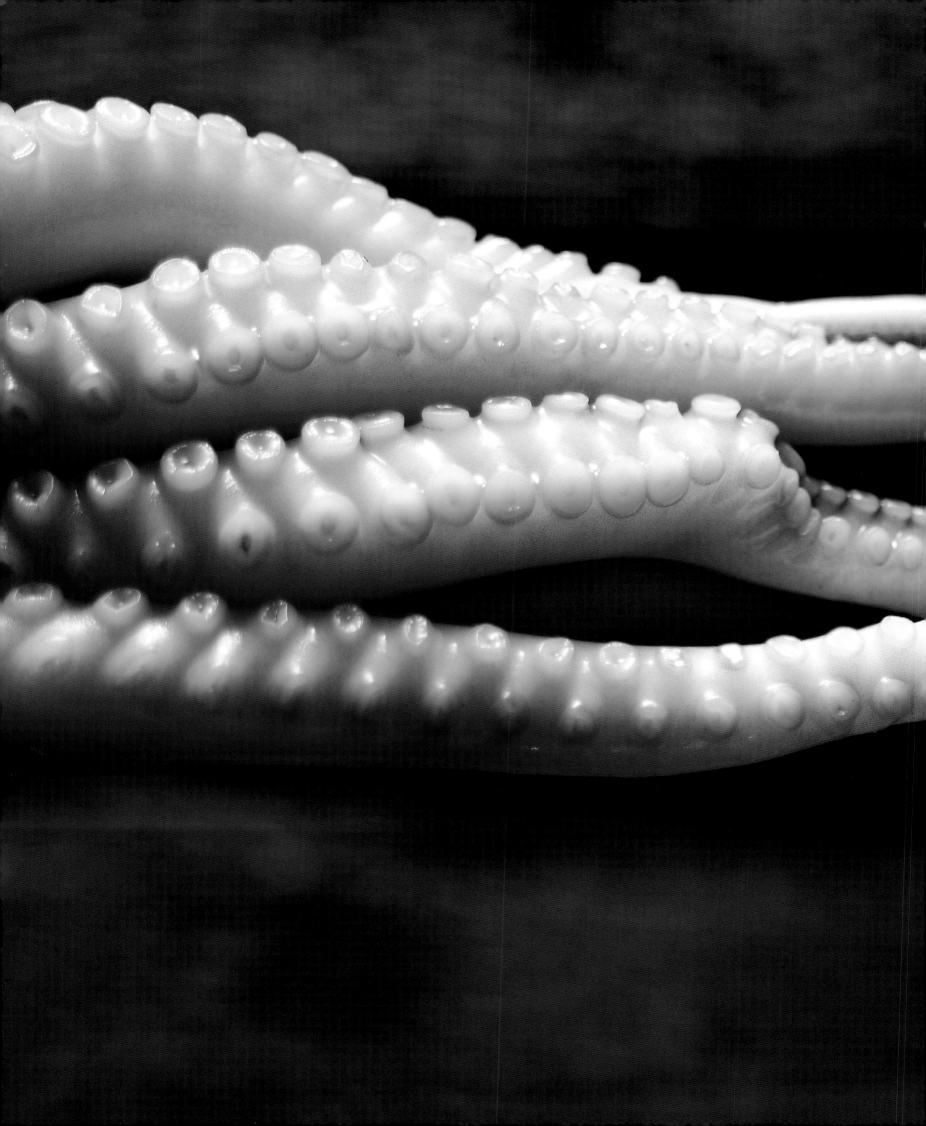

SERVES 8

gently poached south australian squid, octopus and roasted squid consommé

The textures and flavours of this dish are in harmony. The idea of this dish is to have a spoonful of the lush garlic custard, silky squid and intense roasted squid consommé in your mouth all at once — it's a real textural treat. The visual beauty of this dish only adds to the whole experience; the flowers used here are just as important for their scent and flavour as they are for their visual impact. The red core radish originates in China. I discovered this radish about five years ago and now have it grown for Quay at Berridale farm in the Blue Mountains of New South Wales. When blanched it has a mild flavour and the most beautiful colour. This dish sums up all my culinary goals — texture, flavour and beauty.

ingredients

10 X 200 G (7 OZ) WHOLE SOUTHERN SQUID
1 X 500 G (1 LB 2 OZ) OCTOPUS
COARSE SEA SALT
8 RED CORE RADISHES
24 SMALL CHERRY BELLE RADISHES
1 LITRE (35 FL OZ/4 CUPS) CLARIFIED BUTTER
    (BASIC RECIPES, PAGE 264)
FINE SEA SALT
16 SWEET VIOLETS
16 NATIVE VIOLETS
24 ROSEMARY FLOWERS
24 SOCIETY GARLIC FLOWERS
24 RADISH FLOWERS
16 PEA FLOWERS

method

Remove the tentacles, head and intestines from the squid. Reserve the tentacles and discard the head and intestines. Cut the squid tubes in half lengthways and spread them out on the work surface. With a clean kitchen cloth, rub off all the skin, then use a sharp knife to cut the squid into 20 even rectangles. Reserve all the trimmings. Use a sharp, flexible filleting knife to cut the squid horizontally into six thin layers, about 1 mm (1/16 inch) thin. Each squid rectangle should yield six to seven strips. Each strip is then cut into 1 cm (1/2 inch) thick ribbons. This is a highly skilled technique. If you find it too difficult, the squid rectangles could simply be julienned into fine strips.

Remove the legs from the octopus. With some coarse sea salt, scrub the octopus tentacles under running water. Slice the legs across into very fine discs (when these discs are heated in the butter, they will curl up). Refrigerate the squid ribbons and octopus until required.

Peel the red core radishes and slice into 1 mm (1/16 inch) thin discs. Leave eight cherry belle radishes whole, but cut the remaining in half and put aside.

garlic custard

20 G (3/4 OZ) UNSALTED BUTTER
3 SMALL GARLIC CLOVES, ROUGHLY CHOPPED
380 ML (13 FL OZ) MILK
FINE SEA SALT
1 WHOLE EGG
3 EGG YOLKS

Melt the butter in a small saucepan and add the chopped garlic. Gently sweat the garlic in the butter but do not allow it to colour. Add the milk and bring the milk to the point just before simmering (about 90°C/195°F). Remove the pan from the heat and allow the garlic to infuse into the milk for about 15 minutes. Strain the milk and discard the garlic. Season the milk with sea salt to taste.

Place the whole egg and egg yolks in a stainless-steel bowl. When the milk has cooled, whisk the milk onto the eggs. Place the egg and milk mixture into eight 50 ml (1¾ fl oz) ceramic ramekins. At Quay we use small round ceramic dishes, like a dariole mould but with a curved base. Cover the ramekins tightly with plastic wrap and refrigerate until needed.

roasted squid consommé

500 G (1 LB 2 OZ) CHICKEN WINGS
500 G (1 LB 2 OZ) SQUID TRIMMINGS
50 ML (1¾ FL OZ) GRAPESEED OIL
100 G (3½ OZ) UNSALTED BUTTER
1 SMALL BROWN ONION, DICED
2 CARROTS, DICED
2 WHITE CELERY STALKS (INNER STALKS), DICED
300 ML (10½ FL OZ) SAKE
250 G (9 OZ) CHICKEN BREAST MEAT
100 G (3½ OZ) SQUID TRIMMINGS, EXTRA
1 GARLIC CLOVE
6 EGG WHITES

Chop the chicken wings into small pieces using a cleaver. Slice the squid trimmings roughly and keep the tentacles whole.

Heat the grapeseed oil in a heavy-based pan. When the pan is hot, add the chicken wings and squid trimmings and pan-roast the wings and squid until they are nicely browned. Add the butter, half the onion, half the carrot and half the celery and continue to brown for another 4–5 minutes. Use a wooden spoon to stir continuously until all the ingredients are well coloured. Add the sake and reduce over high heat until almost all the liquid has evaporated. Add 3 litres (105 fl oz/12 cups) of water and simmer over low heat for 2½ hours. Strain the stock through a sieve, and remove any fat from the surface with a ladle. You should have 1.5 litres (52 fl oz/6 cups) of stock remaining. Place the stock into a clean pot and allow to cool.

Meanwhile, to make a raft for the consommé, put the chicken and extra squid trimmings in a food processor. Add the garlic and the remaining onion, carrot and celery and process until finely chopped.

Lightly whisk the egg whites by hand until you have very soft peaks, then fold the egg whites through the chicken and vegetable mixture.

Place the cooled stock over medium heat. Vigorously whisk the raft into the stock until well incorporated, stirring occasionally to make sure the raft is not sticking to the bottom of the pot. Allow the stock to come close to boiling point, then turn the heat down to the lowest possible setting; you want the stock to be barely simmering under the raft. Do not stir the raft again at this point. Cook on low heat for 30 minutes. Make a hole in the raft to check that it is fully cooked and that the stock is clear, then cook for a further 10 minutes. The raft will clarify and enrich your stock.

Remove the pot from the heat and set aside for 20 minutes. Carefully ladle the consommé into a sieve lined with a double layer of muslin cloth, making sure you don't break up the raft too much. Once the stock is strained, you should have a clear, pure and intensely flavoured squid consommé. The consommé will be reheated just before serving.

to finish and plate

Put the clarified butter in a saucepan, allowing the butter to have a depth of at least 10 cm (4 inches). Heat the butter to 75°C (165°F) and place a small stainless-steel basket in the butter. Alternatively, use a small strainer so that you can quickly remove the squid and octopus once they are cooked.

Set a steamer up and bring the water to the boil. Reseal the plastic wrap on the garlic custards so they are airtight. Place the custards in the steamer and steam over high heat for about 10 minutes, or until just set. Meanwhile, reheat the roasted squid consommé. Blanch the radishes in boiling water for 1 minute. Line each serving bowl with a ring of red core radish discs and keep the cherry belle radishes warm.

Poach the squid strips and sliced octopus tentacles in the clarified butter. Do this in at least three or four batches so the squid cooks evenly. The squid and octopus will take about 1 minute to cook in the butter. The squid will turn opaque and the octopus will curl when cooked. Remove the squid and octopus from the butter and drain well on a clean kitchen cloth. Season with sea salt.

When the custards are ready, remove them from the steamer and remove the plastic. Use a round soup spoon to remove the custards from the ramekins. Place a custard in the middle of each serving bowl and top with the squid and octopus. Arrange the halved cherry belle radishes on top, adding one whole radish to each dish, and garnish evenly with the flowers. Pour the consommé into a small serving jug. Pour the hot consommé onto the squid at the table, in front of your guests.

SERVES 8

cylinders

This is a novel way to serve sashimi tuna and kingfish. They are served accompanied with smoked eel brandade, red core radishes, horseradish cream and egg white pearls.

smoked eel brandade

70 G (2½ OZ) SMOKED EEL MEAT
200 ML (7 FL OZ) MILK
70 G (2½ OZ) WHITE FLESHED FISH, SUCH AS BLUE
    EYE, SNAPPER OR COD
60 G (2¼ OZ) UNSALTED BUTTER, SOFTENED
40 ML (1¼ FL OZ) EXTRA VIRGIN OLIVE OIL
JUICE OF ½ LEMON
60 G (2¼ OZ) MASHED POTATO
FINE SEA SALT
30 G (1 OZ) CRÈME FRAÎCHE
500 ML (17 FL OZ/2 CUPS) GRAPESEED OIL
100 ML (3½ FL OZ) STRAINED EGG WHITE

To make the smoked eel brandade, first make sure the smoked eel flesh is boneless and skinless. Put the milk in a pan and bring to the boil, then remove the pan from the heat and add the smoked eel. Leave the eel to marinate in the warm milk for 10 minutes, then strain the eel and discard the milk. Steam the white fish until it flakes.

Put the eel and fish in a small bowl. Using a fork, mash them together with 30 g (1 oz) of softened butter. Drizzle over 20 ml (½ fl oz) of extra virgin olive oil and the lemon juice, mixing with the fork as you go. Add the mashed potato and mix well. Add the remaining 30 g (1 oz) of butter and 20 ml (½ fl oz) of extra virgin olive oil and mix well. Season to taste with sea salt. Allow the mixture to cool, then fold in the crème fraîche. Place the mixture in the refrigerator for at least 1 hour.

Take some of the mixture in the palm of your hand and roll it into an 8 cm (3¼ inch) long cylinder; you will need eight cylinders. You may have some mixture leftover, which you can use elsewhere.

To make the egg white pearls, put the grapeseed oil in a small saucepan and heat to 70°C (155°F). Using an eye dropper, drop the strained egg white into the oil, drop by drop, in rapid succession. When you have about 30 egg white droplets, stop and gently stir them around. They need about 1 minute in the oil

to fully set. Carefully sieve out the egg white pearls using a fine strainer and place the pearls on a metal tray. Repeat this process several times, maintaining the oil temperature at about 70°C (155°F), until you have a sufficient amount of egg white pearls to coat eight cylinders of brandade mixture.

To coat the cylinders, lay a 20 cm (8 inch) square of plastic wrap on the work surface. Place a few teaspoons of egg white pearls in the middle and spread them out in a single layer so they form an 8 cm (3¼ inch) square. Place a cylinder of brandade at one end of the egg white pearls and carefully roll the cylinder, with the aid of the plastic, so that the cylinder is completely covered in egg white pearls. Twist both ends of the plastic to form a bon bon. Repeat this process to cover all eight cylinders. Place the brandade cylinders in the refrigerator for a minimum of 2 hours before serving.

radish cylinders

8 LARGE RED CORE RADISHES
30 G (1 OZ) FRESH HORSERADISH
150 G (5½ OZ) CRÈME FRAÎCHE

Peel the red core radishes and cut out cylinders from the radishes using a 2.5 cm (1 inch) round pastry cutter. Slice the cylinders into 1 mm (1/16 inch) thin slices. Blanch the radish slices in boiling salted water for 10 seconds, then refresh in iced water. Drain the radishes on a clean kitchen cloth.

Peel and finely grate the horseradish, then add to the crème fraîche and whisk until firm peaks form.

Lay a 20 cm (8 inch) square of plastic wrap on the work surface. Overlap the radish slices slightly to form an 8 cm (3¼ inch) square in the middle of the plastic. Using a piping bag, pipe a thin strip of horseradish cream at the closest end of the square. With the aid of the plastic, roll the radishes into a thin cylinder. Completely wrap the cylinder in the plastic wrap and twist at both ends to form a bon bon. Place the radish cylinders in the refrigerator for a minimum of 2 hours before serving.

kingfish and tuna cylinders

500 G (1 LB 2 OZ) SASHIMI-GRADE MIDDLE-CUT
    KINGFISH FILLET
500 G (1 LB 2 OZ) SASHIMI-GRADE MIDDLE-CUT
    YELLOWFIN TUNA
200 ML (7 FL OZ) WHITE SOY SAUCE

Slice the fish into 8 cm (3¼ inch) square blocks and then slice into thin strips, about 2 mm (1/16 inch) thick and 1.5 cm (5/8 inch) wide. Briefly marinate the strips in the white soy sauce for 5 seconds, then drain on a clean kitchen cloth. The white soy sauce will season the fish perfectly.

To make the kingfish and tuna cylinders, lay a 20 cm (8 inch) square of plastic wrap on the work surface. Lay the slices of kingfish or tuna in the middle of the plastic to form an 8 cm (3¼ inch) square, very slightly overlapping each slice. You will need approximately six strips to complete the square. With the aid of the plastic, roll the fish into a tight cylinder. Completely wrap the cylinder in the plastic wrap and twist at both ends to form a bon bon. Repeat this process until you have eight kingfish and eight tuna cylinders. Place the fish cylinders in the refrigerator for a minimum of 1 hour before serving.

to finish and plate

50 ML (1¾ FL OZ) GRAPESEED OIL
24 SPRIGS ELDERFLOWER BUDS
40 CHIVE FLOWERS
16 SPRIGS BRONZE FENNEL
16 SPRIGS CELERY FLOWER

Carefully unwrap all the cylinders and brush a little grapeseed oil onto the radish and fish cylinders. Arrange one of each cylinder in the centre of each serving plate. Allow 10–15 minutes before serving for the cylinders to come back to room temperature. Before serving, garnish with elderflower buds, chive flowers, fennel and celery flowers.

SERVES 8

butter-poached murray cod with shaved pearl oyster, cucumber and vongole juices

Murray cod is a native Australian freshwater fish and, in my opinion, the king of freshwater fish. It has firm, sweet white flesh and a delicate flavour. Here I use a butter-poaching method to cook the fish gently — it imparts a little of the butter flavour without the fish actually absorbing too much butter. The butter is just a gentle cooking medium and because of its density it doesn't dilute the fish's natural flavour. I serve the Murray cod with an oyster-infused custard, pearl meat and special miniature white cucumbers, which are especially grown for this dish.

ingredients

500 G (1 LB 2 OZ) CHICKEN WINGS, CHOPPED
20 ML (½ FL OZ) GRAPESEED OIL
300 G (10½ OZ) VONGOLE, SHELLS WELL SCRUBBED
1 WHITE CELERY STALK (INNER STALK), FINELY
    CHOPPED
½ BUNCH GREEN SPRING ONIONS (SCALLIONS),
    WHITE PART ONLY, FINELY CHOPPED
1 SMALL GARLIC CLOVE, FINELY CHOPPED
1 SMALL KNOB YOUNG GINGER, FINELY CHOPPED
200 ML (7 FL OZ) DRY SAKE
20 G (¾ OZ) JAPANESE GLUTINOUS RICE
WHITE SOY SAUCE, TO TASTE
2 X 800 G (1 LB 12 OZ) WHOLE MURRAY CODS
16 PIECES PEARL OYSTER MEAT, THAWED
32 MINIATURE WHITE CUCUMBERS
32 GARLIC CHIVE FLOWER BUDS
32 SPRIGS ELDERFLOWER BUDS
50 G (1¾ OZ) PACKET BLACK MOSS
OYSTER CUSTARD (BASIC RECIPES, PAGE 268)
1 LITRE (35 FL OZ/4 CUPS) CLARIFIED BUTTER
    (BASIC RECIPES, PAGE 264)

method

To make the vongole juices, start by sautéing the chicken wings in a heavy-based pot with the grapeseed oil until lightly brown. Add the vongole and sauté for a further 2 minutes. Add the celery, spring onion, garlic and ginger and sauté for 1 minute. Deglaze with the sake and reduce until the sake has almost evaporated. Add 1.5 litres (52 fl oz/6 cups) of water and simmer for 15 minutes. Use a ladle to remove any scum that comes to the surface. Remove the vongole shells with tongs. Add the rice to the pot and simmer very gently for 30 minutes. Strain the liquid through a fine sieve and discard the solids. The liquid should be slightly thickened from the rice and you should have about 500 ml (17 fl oz/2 cups) left. If you have more, reduce the liquid over high heat until you have this amount. Season to taste with white soy sauce; 1–2 teaspoons should be adequate. Put the vongole juices aside until required.

Fillet and remove the skin from the Murray cod. Cut two even portions from each fillet and remove any bones with fine tweezers. You should have eight oblong portions of Murray cod, about 120 g (4¼ oz) each. Cover the fish and refrigerate until required.

Slice each piece of pearl oyster meat into five fine slices, depending on the thickness of your pearl meat. If you can't find pearl oyster meat, you can use fresh sea scallops. Put the pearl oyster meat in a bowl, cover and refrigerate until required.

Wash the miniature cucumbers and cut half of them in half lengthways. Blanch the garlic chive flower buds in boiling salted water for 10 seconds, then refresh in iced water. Peel the outer casing of the buds away, exposing the small bud heads inside. Put aside until required. Wash the elderflower buds and put aside. Finely pull apart the threads of black moss and put aside. Make the oyster custard.

Heat the clarified butter in a bain-marie until the butter reaches 68°C (154°F). Submerge the cod fillets in the butter and poach for 10–12 minutes, or until slightly opaque and cooked through. Remove the cod to a baking tray lined with silicone paper. Lightly season the fish and keep warm.

to finish and plate

Preheat the oven to 220°C (425°F/Gas 7). While the cod is cooking, set a steamer up and bring the water to the boil. Give the oyster custard a stir and reseal the plastic wrap so it is airtight. Place the custard in the steamer over high heat for 10 minutes, or until the custard is set. Bring the vongole juices back to boiling point, add the whole and halved white cucumbers and sliced pearl oyster meat and simmer for 1–2 minutes.

Flash the fish in the oven for 1 minute. Place 2–3 teaspoons of oyster custard on each plate. Arrange an even amount of white cucumber and pearl meat on each plate, place the cod on top and garnish with garlic chive and elderflower buds and threads of black moss. Spoon over any excess juices and serve immediately.

SERVES 8

mud crab congee

This dish is a textural treat. It differs from the traditional Chinese congee in the use of a Japanese crushed glutinous (or sticky) rice called 'domyojiko', which gives a denser, stickier consistency than regular long-grain rice. The rice is then topped with a light, slightly thickened broth containing the sweet juicy crabmeat, creating a wonderful combination of textures.

ingredients

1.5 KG (3 LB 5 OZ) LIVE MUD CRAB (PREFERABLY MALE, WITH LARGE CLAWS)

3.5 LITRES (122 FL OZ) CHICKEN STOCK (BASIC RECIPES, PAGE 262)

70 G (2½ OZ) PEELED GINGER, SLICED

70 G (2½ OZ) GREEN SPRING ONIONS (SCALLIONS), FINELY SLICED

160 G (5¾ OZ) JAPANESE CRUSHED GLUTINOUS RICE

30 G (1 OZ) CARROT, SLICED

30 G (1 OZ) WHITE CELERY STALK (INNER STALK), SLICED

60 G (2¼ OZ) JAPANESE WHOLE GLUTINOUS RICE

FINE SEA SALT

1 PUNNET MUSTARD CRESS, TRIMMED

1 PUNNET SPRING ONION (SCALLION) SPROUTS, TRIMMED

24 GARLIC CHIVE BUDS

24 PEA FLOWERS

method

Place the live mud crab into a bucket filled with water and plenty of ice for 15 minutes. This will send the crab into a coma, which is a more humane way of treating it. Meanwhile, place a large pot of salted water on the stovetop and bring to the boil. Remove the crab from the iced water and plunge into the boiling water. Reduce the heat to a gentle simmer and cook for 10 minutes. Remove the crab and cool for 10 minutes at room temperature, then refrigerate the crab for 2 hours to cool completely.

Once the crab has cooled, crack the body, legs and claws and remove as much meat as you can. It is desirable to have the meat slightly undercooked, as it will finish cooking when it is reheated in the chicken broth.

While the crab is cooling, put the chicken stock into a saucepan, add 30 g (1 oz) of ginger and 30 g (1 oz) of spring onions and bring to the boil. Take the pan off the heat and allow the ginger and spring onion to infuse for 10 minutes. Strain and keep warm while you cook the rice.

Put the crushed glutinous rice in a small pan and pour in 500 ml (17 fl oz/2 cups) of the infused chicken stock. Put the pan over low heat, stirring occasionally, while adding more infused stock as it is absorbed by the rice. Gently cook out the rice for 30 minutes. It should absorb at least 1.5 litres (52 fl oz/6 cups) in total of the infused stock, leaving you with a thick porridge-like consistency to the rice. Put this aside.

Pour 1.5 litres (52 fl oz/6 cups) of chicken stock into a saucepan. Add the carrot, celery, the whole glutinous rice and the remaining 40 g (1½ oz) of ginger and spring onion and bring to a gentle simmer. Simmer for 25 minutes, then strain the stock, discarding the vegetables and rice. Return the thickened stock to a clean pan and set aside. The starch from the rice will lightly thicken the stock.

to finish and plate

Reheat the crushed congee rice, adding the remaining 500 ml (17 fl oz/2 cups) of chicken stock (the rice should resemble loose porridge). Season with sea salt. Bring the thickened chicken stock back to the boil. Reduce the heat to a simmer, add all the picked crabmeat and gently heat through for about 1 minute. Season with sea salt and add the mustard cress, spring onion sprouts and garlic chive buds. Place a large spoonful of the congee rice in the bottom of each warmed serving bowl and top with the mud crab and broth. Garnish with pea flowers and serve immediately.

SERVES 8

slow braise of sea cucumber, abalone, angasi oyster, pearl oyster and groper cheek

This is a very hearty, textural fish braise using exotic ingredients such as sea cucumber, abalone and pearl oyster. The combination of different textures with a unifying slightly smoky and aniseed fish glaze is what this dish is about.

ingredients

SEA CUCUMBER
4 DEHYDRATED SEA CUCUMBERS
100 ML (3½ FL OZ) SHAOXING RICE WINE

ABALONE
3 X 500 G (1 LB 2 OZ) LIVE GREEN LIPPED ABALONES
COARSE SEA SALT
100 ML (3½ FL OZ) SHAOXING RICE WINE
3–4 THIN SLICES GINGER
500 ML (17 FL OZ/2 CUPS) CHICKEN STOCK
   (BASIC RECIPES, PAGE 262)

8 FRESH BASS GROPER OR HARPUKA CHEEKS
16 UNSHUCKED ANGASI OYSTERS
1 YOUNG WINTER MELON OR HAIRY MELON,
   WITH SMALL SEEDS
500 ML (17 FL OZ/2 CUPS) CHICKEN STOCK
   (BASIC RECIPES, PAGE 262)
16 PIECES PEARL OYSTER MEAT, THAWED

method

To prepare the sea cucumbers, soak them in plenty of cold water for 48 hours. Keep refrigerated and change the water four times. After soaking, place the sea cucumbers in a vacuum bag with the rice wine and 250 ml (9 fl oz/1 cup) of water. Seal in a vacuum sealer and steam in a temperature-controlled combi oven at 85°C (185°F) for 12 hours. After cooking the sea cucumber, it should have swollen to five times its dehydrated size. Split the sea cucumber in half and remove all the innards and grit from the cavity while holding it under cold running water. Using a 3 cm (1¼ inch) round pastry cutter, cut out four discs from each half of the sea cucumber. Refrigerate until required.

Place the live abalones into an iced water bath for 20 minutes, then remove. Shuck the abalones using a large kitchen spoon. Remove all the organs and guts and, with a sharp pair of scissors, trim off the hard external lip. Lightly scrub the abalone meat with coarse sea salt under running water for 1 minute. Place the abalones in a vacuum bag with the rice wine, ginger and chicken stock. Seal the bag and steam in the combi oven at 85°C (185°F) for 8 hours. Once the abalones have cooked, allow to cool. Slice each abalone into 11 slices. Refrigerate until needed.

Clean and peel any sinews away from the groper cheeks and set aside in the refrigerator. Shuck the oysters, reserving and straining any oyster juice into a container with the oysters. Refrigerate until needed.

Peel the winter melon and slice it into 4 cm (1½ inch) thick slices. Using a 2 cm (¾ inch) round pastry cutter, cut out as many cylinders as you can from the flesh; you will need 16 cylinders. Store the winter melon in cold water in the refrigerator.

fish glaze

2 SMALL SNAPPER HEADS, SPLIT IN HALF (ASK YOUR
      FISHMONGER TO DO THIS FOR YOU)
150 ML (5 FL OZ) GRAPESEED OIL
½ BROWN ONION, DICED
1 CARROT, DICED
2 WHITE CELERY STALKS (INNER STALKS), DICED
½ FENNEL BULB, DICED
2 STAR ANISE
1 SMALL KNOB GINGER, FINELY SLICED
½ BUNCH GREEN SPRING ONIONS (SCALLIONS),
      WHITE PART ONLY, SLICED
1 GARLIC CLOVE, SLICED
300 ML (10½ FL OZ) SHAOXING RICE WINE
500 G (1 LB 2 OZ) VONGOLE, SHELLS WELL SCRUBBED
1 LITRE (35 FL OZ/4 CUPS) CHICKEN STOCK
      (BASIC RECIPES, PAGE 262)
10 CM (4 INCH) SQUARE PIECE DRIED KONBU
      SEAWEED
5 G (⅛ OZ) SHAVED DRIED BONITO
4 G (⅛ OZ) XANTANA (FERMENTED CORN STARCH)
WHITE SOY SAUCE, TO TASTE

Remove and discard the eyes and gills from the halved snapper heads, then wash thoroughly under cold running water to remove the excess blood.

In a large saucepan, lightly brown the snapper heads in the grapeseed oil. Add the onion, carrot, celery and fennel and sauté for 1–2 minutes, then add the star anise, ginger, spring onions, garlic and rice wine. Reduce over high heat until all the rice wine has evaporated.

Add the vongole, 1 litre (35 fl oz/4 cups) of water and the chicken stock and simmer over low heat for 2 hours. Skim the stock well with a ladle. Turn the heat right down until there is no movement on the surface of the stock. Add the konbu seaweed and bonito. Remove the pan from the heat and allow to infuse off the heat for 30 minutes. Strain the stock through a sieve lined with muslin cloth. You should have at least 1 litre (35 fl oz/4 cups) of liquid.

Place the stock in a clean saucepan and reduce the liquid until you have 750 ml (26 fl oz/3 cups) of stock left. Add the xantana and whisk well. Simmer

for a further 10 minutes until you are left with 500 ml (17 fl oz/2 cups) of thickened reduced glaze. Taste the glaze and if some seasoning is needed, add some white soy sauce. Strain the glaze through a fine sieve and divide evenly between two saucepans.

to finish and plate

Remove the prepared seafood from the refrigerator. In one saucepan of fish glaze, add the 500 ml (17 fl oz/ 2 cups) of chicken stock and bring to a gentle simmer. Poach the groper cheeks for 3–4 minutes until cooked. Remove the groper cheeks and keep warm. Next poach the pearl oyster meat pieces for 2 minutes, then remove and keep warm. Now add the abalone, reheat for 1 minute, then remove and keep warm. Next add the sea cucumber discs, heat for 1 minute, then remove and keep warm. Lastly add the angasi oysters and their juice, simmer for 1 minute and remove.

While you are poaching all the seafood, bring a saucepan of salted water to the boil and blanch the winter melon discs for 2 minutes, then drain and keep warm. Heat the second saucepan of fish glaze until it reaches boiling point. Arrange all the cooked seafood and winter melon in warmed serving bowls. Ladle over a little of the hot fish glaze and serve immediately.

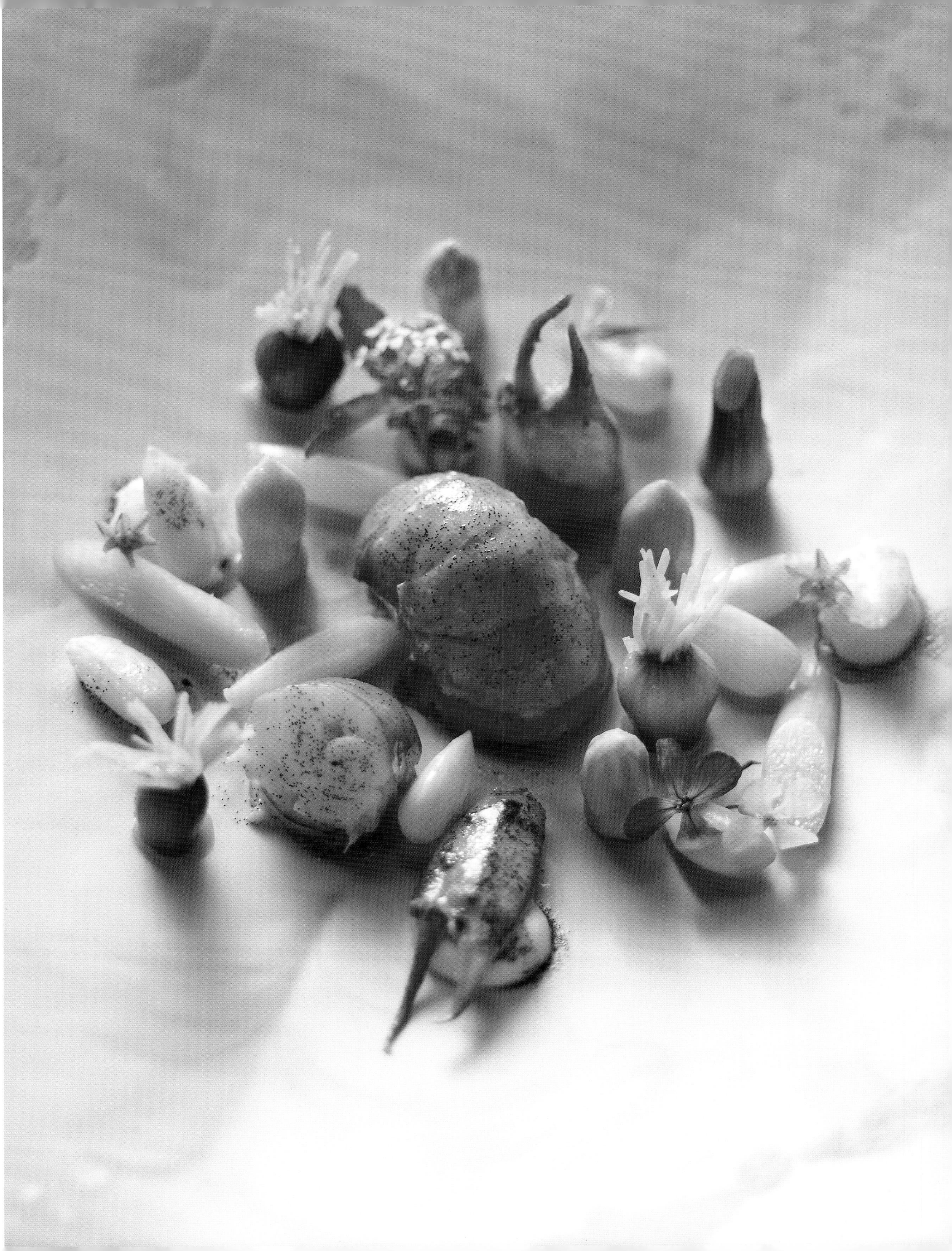

SERVES 8

poached west australian marron with vanilla and star anise butter

This dish makes a perfect warm first course. The subtle flavour of the native Australian freshwater crayfish is enhanced with the vanilla and star anise brown butter. The season for white asparagus occurs at the same time as the green almonds, and I find they make a nice pairing with this marron dish.

ingredients

ALMOND CREAM (BASIC RECIPES, PAGE 265)
54 GREEN IMMATURE ALMONDS WITH JELLY
LEMON JUICE
32 WHITE ASPARAGUS SPEARS
32 PURPLETTE ONIONS
2 STRIPS HASUIMO
8 X 200 G (7 OZ) LIVE MARRONS
100 G (3½ OZ) UNSALTED BUTTER
FINE SEA SALT
8 WATERCRESS FLOWERS
24 RADISH FLOWERS
16 SOCIETY GARLIC FLOWERS

VANILLA AND STAR ANISE BUTTER
150 ML (5 FL OZ) CLARIFIED BROWN BUTTER
  (BASIC RECIPES, PAGE 264)
1 VANILLA BEAN, SPLIT AND SCRAPED
4 STAR ANISE

method

To make the vanilla and star anise butter, warm the clarified brown butter in a saucepan to 70°C (155°F). Add the vanilla bean and seeds to the butter and whisk well. Lightly crush the star anise in a mortar and pestle until just broken up and add to the brown butter. Put aside in a warm place to infuse for about 1 hour. Strain the butter through a fine-mesh metal sieve, with holes large enough to allow the vanilla specks to come through but small enough to stop the star anise and vanilla bean. Discard the star anise and vanilla bean. Put the butter aside until needed. Make the almond cream and refrigerate until needed.

Prepare the green almonds by cutting around the almond with a sharp knife, and levering away the shell with your fingers. Make sure you keep the internal almond whole. Place the internal almonds into water and add a few drops of lemon juice to keep them white. Bring a small saucepan of salted water to the boil. Blanch the almonds for 15 seconds and then refresh immediately in iced water. This will set the jelly inside the almonds and stop them from discolouring. Set the almonds aside.

Peel the white asparagus with a vegetable peeler. Cut the tips from the asparagus to a length of 4 cm (1½ inches) and cut two more lengths from the main body of the spears. With a turning knife, shape the asparagus so they have nice tapered ends. Put aside. Thoroughly clean the purplette onions by washing them under running water, especially the roots. Trim the bulbs off from the stems, leaving 2 cm (¾ inch) of root attached to the bulb. Put aside. Peel the hasuimo and cut on a 45 degree angle into 16 pieces.

Place the live marrons into a large bucket filled with water and plenty of ice for 20 minutes. This will send them into a coma, which is a more humane way of treating them. Meanwhile, place a large pot of salted water on the stovetop and bring to the boil. Remove the marrons from the iced water and pierce their heads with a small sharp knife. This will kill the marron. Immediately place the marrons into the boiling water, then reduce the heat and simmer gently for 8 minutes. Remove from the water and allow to cool naturally for 2 minutes.

Wearing two pairs of plastic gloves to provide some insulation from the heat, remove the tail from the head of the marron with a sharp knife. With a pair of sharp scissors, cut down the inside of the tail. Remove the meat from the shell. Use the back of a knife to crack the claws and remove the meat. Cut the body into two segments and keep warm.

to finish and plate

Preheat the oven to 180°C (350°F/Gas 4). Bring a large pan of salted water to the boil. Blanch the purplette onions and asparagus for 2 minutes. In the last 30 seconds, add the hasuimo, and in the last 10 seconds, add the green almonds, then strain. Melt the butter and brush it liberally over the vegetables, then season with sea salt. Brush the marron pieces liberally with the vanilla and star anise butter. Place the marron on a baking tray lined with silicone paper and reheat in the oven for 1 minute.

Reheat the almond cream in a small saucepan, then place 4 teaspoons of almond cream randomly around each serving plate. Place the marron body and claws on each plate. Arrange four asparagus tips upright on each plate and four purplette onions. Arrange two slices of hasuimo, two asparagus pieces and about seven green almonds on each serving plate. Garnish with the flowers and glaze some of the vegetables and marron with some additional melted vanilla and star anise butter. Serve immediately.

SERVES 8

southern rock lobster with tapioca dumpling, lobster velvet and almond cream

I developed this dish to explore different textures of the lobster. I sometimes serve this dish at Quay with a lobster custard and lobster consommé, which I serve separately. The rich mousseline and tapioca dumpling and poached lobster flesh give the dish its substance, and the light-as-air lobster velvets create a terrific mouthfeel. The technique of whipping egg whites through the mousseline and then poaching the velvet is adapted from a classic Chinese dish that Cheong Liew told me about. Accompanying the dish are poached green almonds, almond cream and lemon confit.

ingredients

YOU WILL NEED 2 X 1 KG (2 LB 4 OZ) WHOLE LIVE LOBSTERS TO MAKE THIS RECIPE

ALMOND CREAM (BASIC RECIPES, PAGE 265)
LEMON CONFIT (BASIC RECIPES, PAGE 269)
32 GREEN ALMONDS

method

Place the live lobsters into a large bucket filled with water and plenty of ice for 20 minutes. This will send the lobsters into a coma, which is a more humane way of treating them. Meanwhile, place a large pot of salted water on the stovetop and bring to the boil. Remove the lobsters from the iced water and pierce their heads with a small sharp knife. This will kill the lobsters. Place the lobsters in the boiling water and blanch for 1 minute, then refresh in plenty of iced water. This will help release the meat from the tail. Remove the heads and legs and reserve them for the lobster jus. With a sharp pair of scissors, cut along the inside of the tail to release the shell. Pull the meat out and cut eight 3 mm (⅛ inch) thick medallions from the thickest part of the tail. Reserve the rest of the flesh for the dumplings and velvet.

Prepare the almond cream and lemon confit, then refrigerate until required.

Remove the green almonds from the husks using a sharp knife. Keep the almond kernels whole and blanch them in a saucepan of boiling salted water for 30 seconds. Remove and refresh in iced water. Drain and refrigerate until required.

lobster jus

2 LOBSTER HEADS, CLEANED, WITH GILLS REMOVED
LEGS FROM 2 LOBSTERS
30 G (1 OZ) UNSALTED BUTTER
20 ML (½ FL OZ) GRAPESEED OIL
½ SMALL BROWN ONION, FINELY DICED
1 CARROT, FINELY DICED
1 WHITE CELERY STALK (INNER STALK), FINELY DICED
1 SMALL FENNEL BULB, FINELY DICED
300 ML (10½ FL OZ) SAUVIGNON BLANC
2 LITRES (70 FL OZ/8 CUPS) CHICKEN STOCK (BASIC RECIPES, PAGE 262)
4 G (⅛ OZ) XANTANA (FERMENTED CORN STARCH)
FINE SEA SALT

Chop the lobster heads into small pieces with a cleaver. Chop the legs. Melt the butter in a saucepan and add the grapeseed oil. Gently sauté the lobster shells, then add the onion, carrot, celery and fennel and sweat for a further 2–3 minutes, being careful not to add any colour. Deglaze with the sauvignon blanc and reduce over high heat until almost all the wine has evaporated. Add the chicken stock and gently simmer for 1½ hours.

Strain the lobster stock through a sieve lined with muslin cloth. Return the liquid to the saucepan and reduce until you have 500 ml (17 fl oz/2 cups) remaining. Add the xantana and whisk well; the stock should thicken to form a lobster jus. Season with sea salt to taste and refrigerate until required.

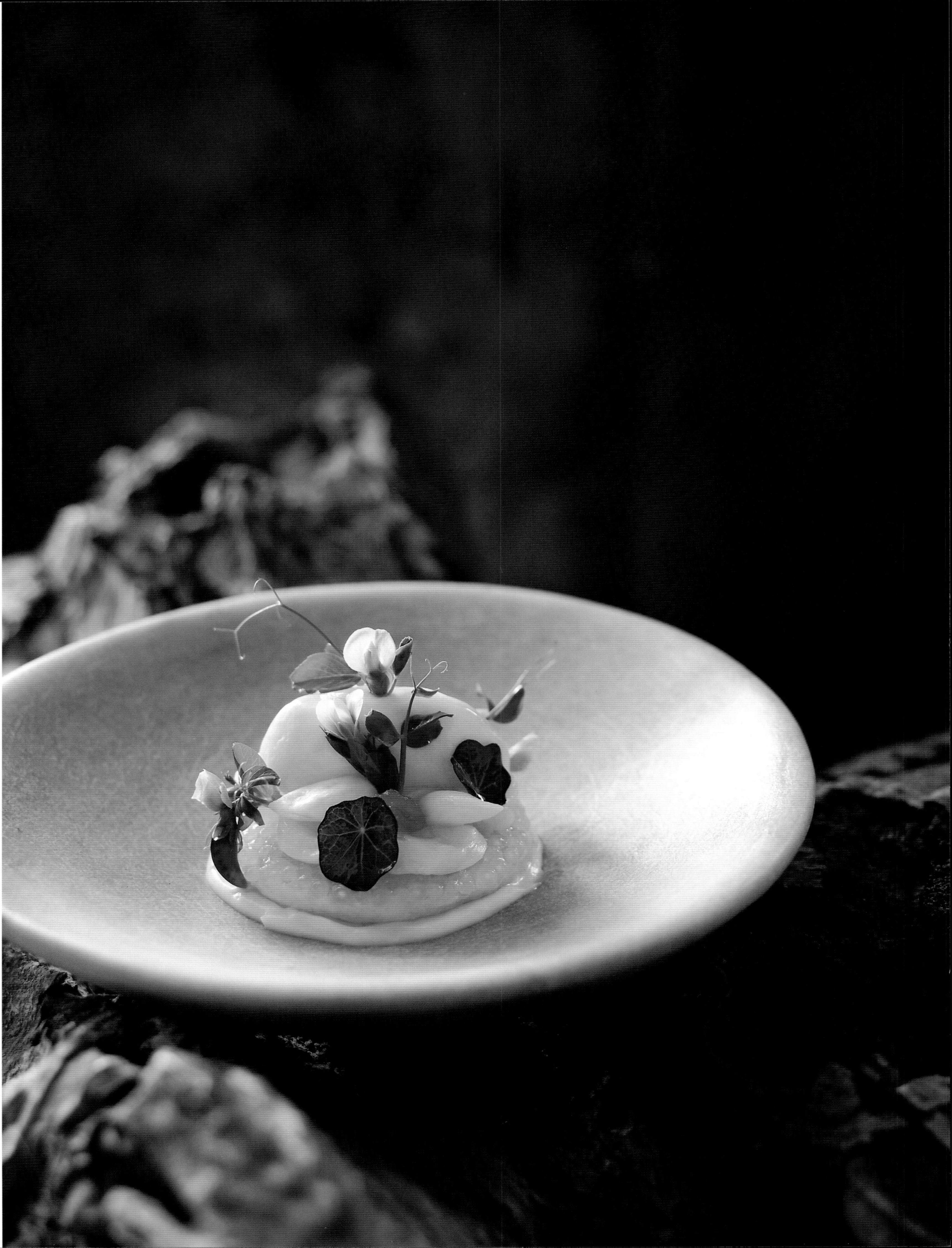

lobster and tapioca dumpling

150 G (5½ OZ) RAW LOBSTER FLESH
1 WHOLE EGG
1 EGG YOLK
100 ML (3½ FL OZ) CREAM (35% FAT)
200 G (7 OZ) FINELY CHOPPED RAW LOBSTER FLESH
¼ TEASPOON FINE SEA SALT
190 G (6¾ OZ) TAPIOCA PEARLS

Put the lobster flesh in a small food processor with the whole egg and egg yolk and process until combined. With the motor running, slowly pour in the cream until you have a smooth lobster mousseline. Remove the mousseline from the food processor and place in a small stainless-steel bowl. Mix in the finely chopped lobster flesh and season with the sea salt. Cover and place the lobster mousseline in the refrigerator to set.

Bring a large pan of water to the boil and add the tapioca. Cook on a high boil for 8–10 minutes, or until the tapioca become opaque, with the smallest dot of undissolved starch remaining in the centre. Strain the tapioca through a fine sieve, then run some cold water over the pearls to cool and stop the cooking process. Place the tapioca on a flat tray and set aside to cool to room temperature.

Tightly wrap a separate tray in plastic wrap. Place an 8 cm (3¼ inch) round pastry cutter on the wrapped tray. Place 3 teaspoons of tapioca in the centre of the cutter and use the back of a spoon to spread the tapioca to form one single layer. Place 2–3 tablespoons of lobster mousseline on top of the pearls. Press down on the mousseline to form a smooth flat surface. The lobster dumpling should be about 3 cm (1¼ inches) thick. Carefully slide the pastry cutter up and away from the dumpling. Clean the cutter and repeat this process until you have eight dumplings in total. Place the tray in the refrigerator to allow the dumplings to set before cooking. This should take at least 3 hours and can be prepared ahead of time if you like.

lobster velvets

200 G (7 OZ) RAW LOBSTER FLESH, CHILLED
1 EGG WHITE
160 ML (5¼ FL OZ) CREAM (35% FAT)
FINE SEA SALT
2 EGG WHITES, EXTRA

To make the mousseline for the velvets, put the lobster flesh into a small food processor. With the motor running, slowly add the egg white, then slowly pour in the cream in a thin stream. The mousseline should become thick and glossy. Season with sea salt, remove from the food processor and place in a small stainless-steel bowl. Refrigerate until required.

to finish and plate

1 LITRE (35 FL OZ/4 CUPS) CLARIFIED BUTTER
  (BASIC RECIPES, PAGE 264)
8 X 3 MM (⅛ INCH) THICK LOBSTER MEDALLIONS
32 FLOWERING PEA SHOOTS
32 NASTURTIUM LEAVES

Put the clarified butter in a large shallow saucepan, allowing the butter to have a depth of 5 cm (2 inches), and heat to 70°C (155°F). Using a palette knife, carefully remove the lobster and tapioca dumplings from the tray and place them in the clarified butter, lobster mousseline side down. At Quay we use a temperature-controlled water bath to maintain the temperature of the butter. At home you will have to adjust the flame on your stove and use a thermometer. Try to maintain the temperature between 70°C (155°F) and 75°C (165°F). The dumplings will take 8–10 minutes to cook. About halfway through the cooking process, top the dumplings with the lobster medallions and continue to cook them together for 4–5 minutes. The lobster flesh will become opaque when ready and the dumpling will become firm.

While the dumplings are cooking, whisk the 2 extra egg whites until soft peaks form. Fold the egg whites through the lobster mousseline so it becomes light. Half-fill a large shallow pan with water and heat to 85°C (185°F). Using 2 tablespoons, form a quenelle of lobster velvet mixture and place into the water bath. Repeat to make eight quenelles in total. Cover with a lid and poach the velvets for about 2 minutes. Reheat the almond cream and lobster jus. Place the green almonds into the lobster jus to warm through.

Place a tablespoon of the warm almond cream in the centre of each serving plate. Spread the cream out with the back of a spoon so it forms a slightly larger disc than the lobster dumpling. Remove the lobster and tapioca dumplings from the pan with a spatula, briefly drain on some kitchen paper and then place on the almond cream. Remove the green almonds from the lobster jus and place around the dumplings. Place a couple of small dabs of lemon confit on the dumpling and glaze the dumpling with a little of the lobster jus. Remove the lobster velvets from the water bath with a slotted spoon. Place the velvets on a flat tray, coat with some lobster jus and then place one on top of each lobster dumpling. Garnish with flowering pea shoots and nasturtium leaves. Serve immediately.

SERVES 8

ginger milk curd, shaved green lipped abalone, white tea and seaweed consommé

Green lipped abalone is one of my favourite ingredients, revered in Japan and China, and enjoyed for its texture more than its flavour. It has a somewhat chewy texture but the aim is to make the abalone tender while retaining just a little resistance. You can achieve this in one of two ways: by slicing the abalone very thinly and cooking it very briefly or by long, gentle cooking. Here I serve the abalone with a ginger-flavoured milk curd and a clean consommé flavoured with white tea and seaweed. With the addition of crisp water chestnuts, white fungi and grated turnip, this is a very textural dish with gentle but distinctive flavours.

ingredients

2 X 400 G (14 OZ) LIVE GREEN LIPPED ABALONES
COARSE SEA SALT
16 FRESH WATER CHESTNUTS
4 GOLF-BALL SIZED WHITE JAPANESE TURNIPS
150 G (5½ OZ) WHITE FUNGI

GINGER MILK CURD
800 ML (28 FL OZ) HOMOGENISED JERSEY MILK
80 G (2¾ OZ) FINELY DICED YOUNG GINGER
FINE SEA SALT
3 ML (¹⁄₁₀ FL OZ) VEGETARIAN RENNET
10 ML (¼ FL OZ) STILL MINERAL WATER

method

Place the live abalones into an iced water bath for 20 minutes, then remove. Shuck the abalones using a large kitchen spoon. Remove all the organs and guts and, with a sharp pair of scissors, trim off the hard external lip. Lightly scrub the abalone meat with coarse sea salt under running water for 1 minute.

For the best results you will need a gear-driven slicing machine. Place each abalone horizontally on the meat slicer and cut into tissue-paper-thin slices. Slicing the abalone so thinly makes it incredibly tender when it's blanched in the consommé. Alternatively, cut the abalone with a very sharp knife vertically, as thinly as possible. Refrigerate the abalone until required.

Peel the water chestnuts with a sharp knife and slice them very thinly using a mandolin. Leave the sliced water chestnuts in water until required. Peel and grate the white turnips on a microplane. Leave them soaking in water until required. Break the white fungi into small pieces and put aside.

seaweed consommé

20 ML (½ FL OZ) GRAPESEED OIL
1 KG (2 LB 4 OZ) CHICKEN WINGS, CHOPPED
250 G (9 OZ) SQUID TRIMMINGS
1 SMALL BROWN ONION, DICED
1 CARROT, DICED
3 WHITE CELERY STALKS (INNER STALKS), 2 DICED AND 1 CHOPPED
500 ML (17 FL OZ/2 CUPS) DRY SAKE
2 LITRES (70 FL OZ/8 CUPS) CHICKEN STOCK (BASIC RECIPES, PAGE 262)
150 G (5½ OZ) CHICKEN BREAST MEAT
10 CM (4 INCH) SQUARE PIECE DRIED KONBU SEAWEED, TORN INTO SMALL PIECES
3 TEASPOONS DRIED WAKAME SEAWEED
3 TEASPOONS WHITE TEA LEAVES
6 EGG WHITES
WHITE SOY SAUCE, TO TASTE

Heat the grapeseed oil in a heavy-based pot. When the pot is hot, add the chicken wings and squid trimmings and sauté until they are nicely browned. Add half the onion, the carrot and diced celery and sauté for a further 2 minutes. Deglaze with the sake and reduce until the sake has almost evaporated. Add the chicken stock and 2 litres (70 fl oz/8 cups) of water and simmer gently over low heat for 2 hours. Strain the stock through a fine sieve lined with muslin cloth, and discard all the solids. Return the stock to the pot and reduce over high heat until you are left with just 2 litres (70 fl oz/8 cups) of liquid.

to finish and plate

Place the reduced liquid into a clean medium-sized pot. The liquid should be to a depth of 15 cm (6 inches) in the pot. Allow the stock to cool.

Meanwhile, to make a raft for the consommé, put the chicken in a food processor with the remaining onion, the chopped celery, konbu seaweed, wakame seaweed and white tea leaves. Process on high for 30 seconds, then transfer the contents to a bowl. In a separate bowl, lightly whisk the egg whites by hand until you have very soft peaks, then fold the egg whites through the processed chicken and vegetable mixture.

Place the cooled stock in the pot over medium heat. Vigorously whisk the raft into the stock until well incorporated, stirring occasionally to make sure the raft is not sticking to the bottom of the pot. Allow the stock to come close to boiling point, then turn the heat down to the lowest possible setting; you want the stock to be barely simmering under the raft. Do not stir the raft again at this point. Cook on low heat for 30 minutes. Make a hole in the raft to check that it is fully cooked and that the stock is clear, then cook for a further 10 minutes. Over this period the stock will clarify, enrich and absorb the flavour of the white tea and seaweeds.

Remove the pot from the heat and set aside for 20 minutes. Carefully ladle the consommé into a sieve lined with a double layer of muslin cloth, making sure you don't break up the raft too much. Season the consommé with white soy sauce to taste.

To make the ginger milk curd, heat the milk in a saucepan until it reaches 70°C (155°F). Add the ginger and allow it to infuse in the milk for 15 minutes. Strain the milk and discard the ginger, then season with sea salt to taste. Have eight Chinese rice bowls ready. Reheat the milk until it reaches 40°C (105°F). In a small bowl, add the rennet to the mineral water. Stir the milk to create a whirlpool action, then add the rennet and water mixture to the milk. Immediately ladle 100 ml (3½ fl oz) of the milk into each rice bowl. You need to do this swiftly, as the milk sets very quickly. Allow the milk to sit in the rice bowls for 2–3 minutes; it should then be set quite firmly.

While the ginger milk curd is setting, place 300 ml (10½ fl oz) of consommé into a saucepan and bring to boiling point. Place the rest of the consommé in another saucepan and heat close to boiling point. Blanch the sliced abalone a few pieces at a time in the boiling consommé. It will only take 5 seconds to cook the abalone. Remove the abalone to a warm plate while you complete the cooking. Drain the water chestnuts and grated white turnip.

Run a small palette knife around the edge of each curd until loosened. Carefully slide a curd into the centre of each warmed serving bowl. Scatter the water chestnuts, grated turnip and white fungi around the ginger curds and place six or seven slices of the abalone on top. Pour the simmering consommé into a serving jug. Serve the ginger curd and abalone to your guests and pour the consommé at the table.

SERVES 8

toro of southern bluefin tuna with radish, pearls, caviar and wasabi flowers

'Toro' is the Japanese term for bluefin tuna belly, which is the most highly prized part of the tuna. The toro has an extremely high fat marbling content — similar to wagyu beef — and is where the tuna stores its energy reserves. The toro literally melts in the mouth and is very expensive. At Quay we use Southern bluefin tuna, which is ranched out of Port Lincoln in South Australia. If you can't find it you could substitute with swordfish belly or yellowfin tuna belly, although these are not as marbled as the bluefin tuna belly. You could of course use any sashimi-grade tuna loin. The wasabi flowers are grown as part of the fresh wasabi industry in Tasmania. They have a subtle heat and combine well with the toro.

red core radish and horseradish cream cylinders

8 LARGE RED CORE RADISHES
30 G (1 OZ) FRESH HORSERADISH
150 G (5½ OZ) CRÈME FRAÎCHE
FINE SEA SALT

Peel the red core radishes and cut out cylinders from the radishes using a 2.5 cm (1 inch) round pastry cutter. Slice the cylinders into 1 mm (1/16 inch) thin slices. Blanch the radish slices in boiling salted water for 10 seconds, then refresh in iced water. Drain the radishes on a clean kitchen cloth.

Peel and finely grate the horseradish, then add to the crème fraîche with a pinch of sea salt. Whisk until firm peaks form.

Lay a 20 cm (8 inch) square of plastic wrap on the work surface. Overlap the radish slices slightly to form a 5 cm (2 inch) square in the middle of the plastic. Using a piping bag, pipe a thin strip of horseradish cream at the closest end of the square. With the aid of the plastic, roll the radishes into a thin cylinder. Completely wrap the cylinder in the plastic wrap and twist at both ends to form a bon bon. Place the radish cylinders in the refrigerator for a minimum of 2 hours before serving.

smoked eel and egg white pearl

35 G (1¼ OZ) SMOKED EEL MEAT
100 ML (3½ FL OZ) MILK
35 G (1¼ OZ) WHITE FLESHED FISH, SUCH AS BLUE EYE, SNAPPER OR COD
30 G (1 OZ) UNSALTED BUTTER, SOFTENED
20 ML (½ FL OZ) EXTRA VIRGIN OLIVE OIL
JUICE OF ¼ LEMON
30 G (1 OZ) MASHED POTATO
FINE SEA SALT
15 G (½ OZ) CRÈME FRAÎCHE
500 ML (17 FL OZ/2 CUPS) GRAPESEED OIL
50 ML (1¾ FL OZ) STRAINED EGG WHITE
8 NATIVE VIOLETS

To make the smoked eel brandade, first make sure the smoked eel flesh is boneless and skinless. Put the milk in a pan and bring to the boil, then remove from the heat and add the smoked eel. Leave the eel to marinate in the warm milk for 10 minutes, then strain the eel and discard the milk. Steam the white fish until it flakes.

Mix the eel and fish in a small bowl. Using a fork, mash them together with 15 g (½ oz) of softened butter. Drizzle over 10 ml (¼ fl oz) of extra virgin olive oil and the lemon juice, mixing with the fork as you go. Add the mashed potato and mix well. Add the remaining butter and olive oil and mix well. Season to taste with sea salt. Allow the mixture to cool, then fold in the crème fraîche. Place the mixture in the refrigerator for at least 1 hour.

Take some of the mixture in the palm of your hand and roll it into balls the size of a marble. You will need eight balls. You may have some mixture leftover, which you can use elsewhere.

To make the egg white pearls, put the grapeseed oil in a small saucepan and heat to 70°C (155°F). Using an eye dropper, drop the strained egg white into the oil, drop by drop, in rapid succession. When you have about 30 egg white droplets, stop and gently stir them around. They need about 1 minute in the oil to fully set. Carefully sieve out the egg white pearls using a fine strainer and place the pearls on a metal tray. Repeat this process several times, maintaining the oil temperature at 70°C (155°F), until you have a sufficient amount of egg white pearls to coat the eight small balls of brandade mixture.

To coat the brandade mixture, take eight 20 cm (8 inch) squares of plastic wrap and place them over eight demi-tasse cups. Place 1 teaspoon of egg white pearls in the middle of the plastic and spread them out so they form a single layer. Place one ball of brandade in the centre. Carefully lift up the four corners of the plastic wrap and twist them together to form a ball, then tie a knot in the plastic. The aim is to coat the brandade balls in the egg white pearls, with the aid of the plastic wrap. When you have eight perfectly covered egg white balls, place them in the refrigerator to set for 30 minutes.

dashi jelly pearl

250 ML (9 FL OZ/1 CUP) STILL MINERAL WATER
6 G (⅕ OZ) SHAVED DRIED BONITO
6 G (⅕ OZ) DRIED KONBU SEAWEED
25 ML (¾ FL OZ) LIGHT SOY SAUCE
10 ML (¼ FL OZ) MIRIN
2 SHEETS TITANIUM GELATINE

To make the dashi stock, put the mineral water in a small saucepan and bring to the boil. Remove the pan from the heat and add the bonito, konbu seaweed, light soy sauce and mirin. Infuse for 20 minutes, then strain the liquid through a sieve lined with muslin cloth into a clean pan. Reheat the dashi stock to 70°C (155°F). Meanwhile, soak the gelatine sheets in cold water until softened. Squeeze the excess water from the gelatine and add to the warm dashi. Stir to dissolve the gelatine. Allow the mixture to cool completely at room temperature; be careful not to let the dashi set.

Take eight 20 cm (8 inch) squares of plastic wrap and place them over eight demi-tasse cups, leaving a dip in the middle of the plastic. Add 10 ml (¼ fl oz) of the dashi stock, then carefully lift up the four corners of the plastic wrap and twist them together to form a liquid ball. Tie a knot in the plastic so the liquid jelly is completely sealed. Repeat this process until you have eight balls. Place in the refrigerator to set for 2 hours before serving.

seaweed and white tea jelly, wasabi and chive flower pearl

250 ML (9 FL OZ/1 CUP) STILL MINERAL WATER
1 X 10 CM (4 INCH) SQUARE SHEET DRIED KONBU
   SEAWEED
5 G (⅛ OZ) DRIED WAKAME SEAWEED
1 X 15 CM (6 INCH) SHEET TOASTED NORI SEAWEED
1½ TEASPOONS WHITE TEA LEAVES
20 ML (½ FL OZ) WHITE SOY SAUCE
2 SHEETS TITANIUM GELATINE
16 INDIVIDUAL WASABI FLOWERS
8 GARLIC CHIVE BUD FLOWERS

Put the mineral water in a saucepan and bring to the boil. Add the dried seaweeds, white tea leaves and white soy sauce, then remove the pan from the heat. Infuse for 20 minutes, then strain the liquid through a sieve lined with muslin cloth into a clean saucepan. Reheat the infused liquid to 70°C (155°F). Meanwhile, soak the gelatine sheets in cold water until softened. Squeeze the excess water from the gelatine and add to the warm liquid. Stir to dissolve the gelatine. Allow the mixture to cool completely at room temperature; be careful not to let it set.

Take eight 20 cm (8 inch) squares of plastic wrap and place them over eight demi-tasse cups, leaving a dip in the middle of the plastic. Add 10 ml (¼ fl oz) of the cooled mixture, then place two wasabi flowers and one garlic chive bud in the liquid. Carefully lift up the four corners of the plastic wrap and twist them together to form a liquid ball. Tie a knot in the plastic so the liquid jelly is completely sealed. Repeat this process until you have eight balls. Place in the refrigerator to set for 2 hours before serving.

tapioca, horseradish cream and silver leaf pearl

100 G (3½ OZ) PEARL TAPIOCA
30 G (1 OZ) FRESH HORSERADISH
150 G (5½ OZ) CRÈME FRAÎCHE
FINE SEA SALT
2 X 10 CM (4 INCH) SQUARE SHEETS PURE SILVER LEAF

Cook the tapioca in boiling water for 10 minutes, or until the tapioca become opaque and the smallest pinprick of white is visible in the centre. Drain the tapioca and spread them out on a flat plate or tray.

Peel and finely grate the horseradish, then add to the crème fraîche with a pinch of sea salt. Whisk until firm peaks form. Place in the refrigerator.

Take eight 20 cm (8 inch) squares of plastic wrap and place them over eight demi-tasse cups. Place 1 teaspoon of the tapioca in the middle of the plastic and spread them out so they form a single layer. Place 1 teaspoon of horseradish crème fraîche in the centre of the tapioca and then carefully lift up the four corners of the plastic wrap and twist them together. Tie a knot in the plastic. The aim is to coat the horseradish cream in the tapioca, with the aid of the plastic wrap. Repeat this process until you have eight balls. Place in the refrigerator to set for 1 hour before serving. Cut the sheets of silver leaf into quarters.

to finish and plate

1 X 1 KG (2 LB 4 OZ) BELLY OF BLUEFIN TUNA (TORO)
100 ML (3½ FL OZ) WHITE SOY SAUCE
30 G (1 OZ) AQUACULTURE STURGEON CAVIAR
8 BUNCHES WASABI FLOWER HEADS

Cut the toro into 16 slices, 10 cm (4 inch) long. Briefly marinate the toro slices in the white soy sauce for a maximum of 5 seconds (this is enough time to perfectly season the toro), then drain on a clean kitchen cloth. Place two slices of toro on each serving plate. Remove all the pearls and cylinders from the refrigerator. Use a small pair of scissors to cut and remove the plastic from the pearls and cylinders. Attractively arrange one of each type of pearl and one cylinder on each plate. Place a piece of silver leaf on top of the tapioca pearl to cover. Use a pair of tweezers to insert a violet into each smoked eel and egg white pearl. Top the radish and horseradish cream cylinder with a spoonful of the caviar. Place a bunch of fresh wasabi flowers on top of each piece of toro. Serve immediately.

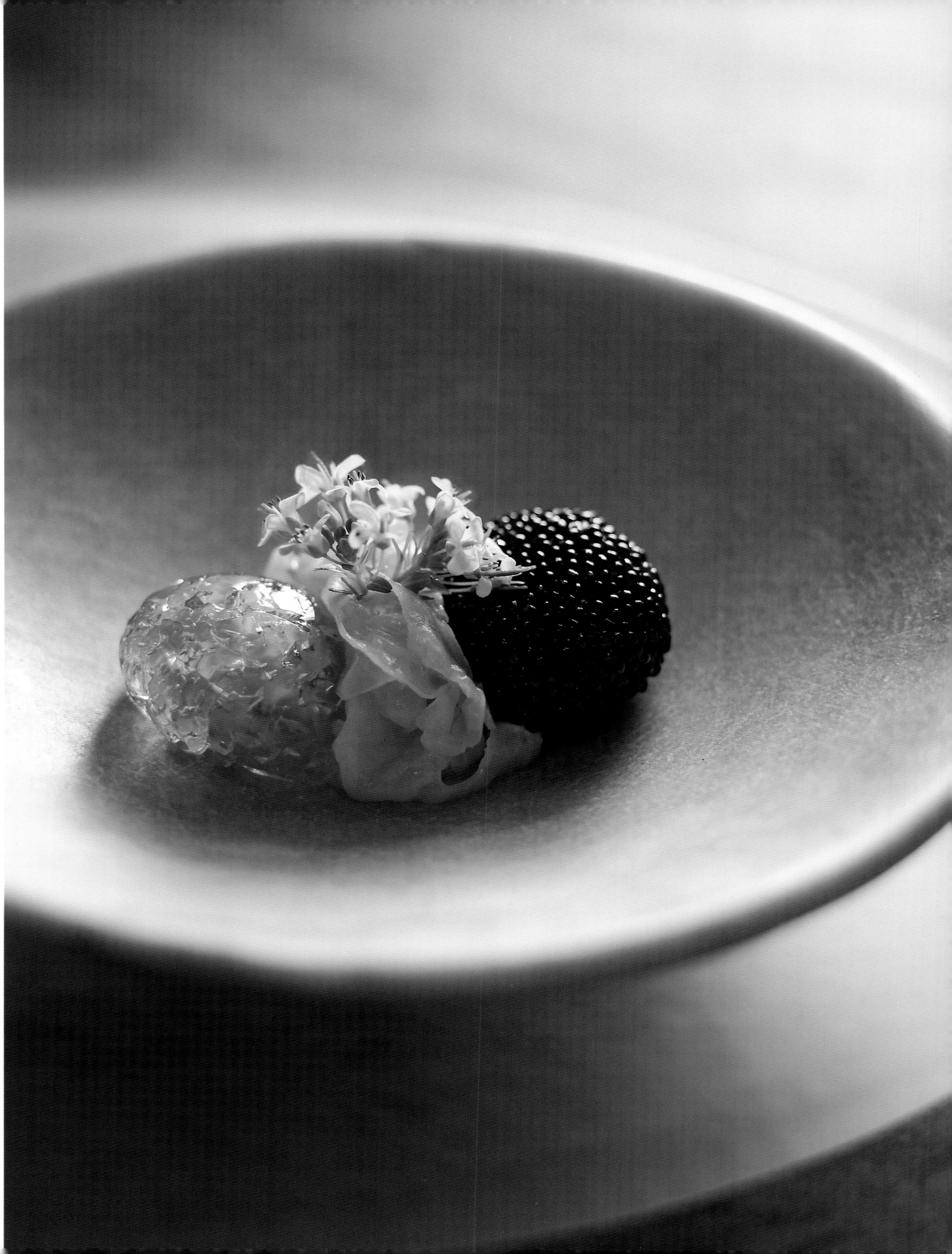

SERVES 8

caviar pearl with scallop, pearl oyster and white tea jelly

This dish is extremely elegant and beautiful to eat. The burst of briny sea flavour from the caviar is tempered by the lushness of the crème fraîche and sashimi sea scallop. The pearl meat is an absolute delicacy and has a texture similar to abalone when it is shaved thinly and cooked gently. The jelly is crystal clear and you can see the oyster cream through the middle — this is a technique I developed for desserts, which I've applied here in savoury form.

ingredients

OYSTER CREAM (BASIC RECIPES, PAGE 265)
24 SMALL PIECES PEARL OYSTER MEAT, THAWED
8 LARGE SEA SCALLOPS, WITHOUT ROE
100 ML (3½ FL OZ) WHITE SOY SAUCE
80 G (2¾ OZ) CRÈME FRAÎCHE
160 G (5½ OZ) AQUACULTURE STURGEON CAVIAR
1 LITRE (35 FL OZ/4 CUPS) GRAPESEED OIL
FINE SEA SALT
8 BUNCHES WASABI FLOWER HEADS

WHITE TEA AND SEAWEED JELLY BALLS
400 ML (14 FL OZ) STILL MINERAL WATER
1 TEASPOON WHITE TEA LEAVES
1 X 10 CM (4 INCH) SQUARE SHEET DRIED KONBU SEAWEED
1 TEASPOON DRIED WAKAME SEAWEED
40 ML (1¼ FL OZ) WHITE SOY SAUCE
3 SHEETS TITANIUM GELATINE

method

Make the oyster cream. To make the white tea and seaweed jelly, put the mineral water in a saucepan and bring to the boil. Add the white tea and dried seaweeds, then remove the pan from the heat and put aside to infuse for 2 minutes exactly. Strain the liquid through a fine sieve lined with muslin cloth and discard the solids. Season the infusion with the white soy sauce (it must be white soy sauce), bring back to the boil and remove from the heat. Meanwhile, soak the gelatine sheets in cold water until softened. Squeeze the excess water from the gelatine and add to the hot liquid. Stir to dissolve the gelatine. Pour the liquid jelly into a flat stainless-steel tray with 1 cm (½ inch) deep sides and place in the refrigerator to set for 1 hour.

To prepare the jelly balls, dice the set jelly into 5 mm (¼ inch) cubes. Take eight 20 cm (8 inch) squares of plastic wrap and place them over eight coffee cups. Put 2 teaspoons of jelly in the middle of the plastic and make a small well in the centre of the jelly. Put 1 teaspoon of oyster cream in the well, then top with 1 more teaspoon of jelly. Carefully lift up the four corners of the plastic wrap and twist them tightly together to form a ball of jelly, with the oyster cream contained in the centre. Tie a knot in the plastic. Repeat this process until you have eight balls. Place in the refrigerator to set for 2 hours before serving.

Meanwhile, with a sharp knife, shave each piece of pearl oyster meat into several 1 mm (¹⁄₁₆ inch) thin slices. Put aside. Dice the white scallop meat into

1 cm (½ inch) cubes. Marinate the scallop meat in the white soy sauce for a maximum of 5 seconds. The white soy will season and lightly cook the scallops. Drain on kitchen paper, then place in a bowl. Lightly whisk the crème fraîche until it forms soft peaks and fold it through the scallops. Form eight balls (the size of a large marble) with the scallop mixture, using the same method as for the jelly balls. Place in the refrigerator for 30 minutes to set.

Line eight coffee cups with 20 cm (8 inch) squares of plastic wrap, but this time pull the plastic taut against the edge of the cups. Put 20 g (¾ oz) of caviar on top of the plastic and evenly spread the caviar out to form a 7 cm (2¾ inch) circle, making sure there are no gaps. Unwrap the set scallop balls and place them in the middle of the caviar. Carefully lift up the four corners of the plastic to encase the scallop balls in caviar. Twist the plastic together tightly at the base of the ball to ensure the caviar sticks to the scallop and crème fraîche mixture. Carefully unwrap the plastic wrap and place the caviar pearls in the refrigerator for just 10 minutes before serving.

Put the grapeseed oil in a small saucepan, to a depth of 10 cm (4 inches), and heat the oil to 70°C (155°F). Cook the shaved pearl oyster meat in the oil for 20–30 seconds until it turns opaque. Remove from the oil, drain on a clean kitchen cloth and lightly season with sea salt. Allow 5 minutes for the pearl oyster meat to cool to room temperature.

to finish and plate

Place a caviar pearl to the right hand side, just off centre, of each serving plate. Place a teaspoon of the remaining oyster cream in the centre of each plate. Top the oyster cream with the shaved pearl oyster meat. Carefully unwrap the white tea and seaweed jelly balls and place on the other side of the pearl meat. Garnish the pearl oyster meat with a wasabi flower head and serve.

SERVES 8

bass groper with a brioche crust, scallops, periwinkles, green tea and wakame broth

Bass groper is a delicate-tasting fish with a firm, meaty white flesh, and is caught in the waters of eastern Australian and in New Zealand. Interesting textural counterpoints to the fish are the firm, slightly chewy periwinkles — which aren't used very much these days — and the Japanese vegetable hasuimo, which is a green shoot from the taro. Hasuimo has a crisp cell-like structure that absorbs flavours well.

ingredients

1 KG (2 LB 4 OZ) LIVE PERIWINKLES
16 LARGE SEA SCALLOPS, WITHOUT ROE
1 YOUNG WINTER MELON OR HAIRY MELON, WITH SMALL SEEDS
2 STEMS HASUIMO
8 PEA FLOWERS
8 CUCUMBER TENDRILS

method

Place the live periwinkles into a large bucket filled with water and plenty of ice for 20 minutes. This will send them into a coma, which is a more humane way of treating them and also relaxes the meat. Meanwhile, place a large pot of salted water on the stovetop and bring to the boil. Remove the periwinkles from the water and place them in the boiling water for 1 minute, then remove and place them straight back into the iced water to stop the cooking process. With a thin metal skewer, hook and remove the meat from the shells. Discard the intestines, cut the piece of meat in half vertically and remove the red mouth. Slice each scallop in half horizontally so that each piece is about 5 mm (¼ inch) thick. Refrigerate the seafood until required.

Peel the winter melon and cut into 5 cm (2 inch) thick slices. Using a 4 cm (1½ inch) round pastry cutter, cut out cylinders from the centre of each slice (this will include the fine edible seeds), then finely slice each disc into 1 mm (1⁄16 inch) thin slices. Store the winter melon in cold water in the refrigerator until required.

Peel the hasuimo and slice into 2 cm (¾ inch) thick discs, then cut these in half to form semicircles. Put aside.

parsley and fennel butter

2 SMALL BUNCHES PARSLEY
200 G (7 OZ) UNSALTED BUTTER, SOFTENED
20 SMALL SALTED CAPERS
20 FENNEL SEEDS
1 BUNCH CHIVES
FINE SEA SALT

Chop the parsley very finely and place in a clean kitchen towel; squeeze to remove as much juice as possible. Discard the juice and add the chopped parsley to the butter. Wash the capers well to remove the salt, chop finely and add to the butter.

Put the fennel seeds in a dry frying pan over medium heat and roast until lightly coloured. Remove the seeds and chop very finely, then add to the butter. Slice the chives very finely and add to the butter. Mix the butter well and season to taste with sea salt. Leave at room temperature until required.

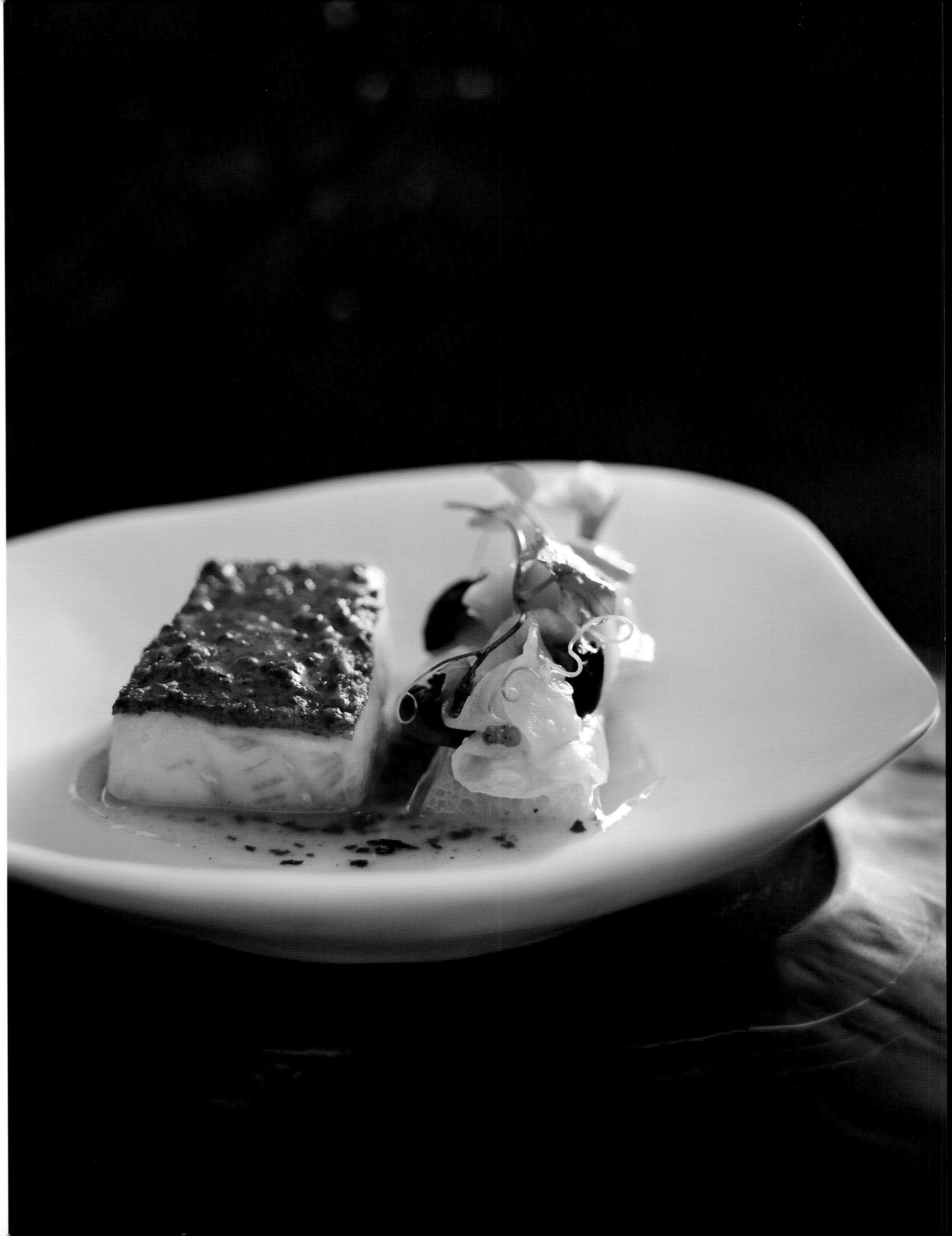

brioche with fish

½ LOAF GOOD QUALITY BRIOCHE
200 ML (7 FL OZ) CLARIFIED BUTTER (BASIC RECIPES,
    PAGE 264)
8 X 150 G (5½ OZ) OBLONG PORTIONS OF BASS
    GROPER (OR HARPUKA, BLUE EYE OR COD)
10 ML (¼ FL OZ) GRAPESEED OIL

Slice the brioche into 2 mm (1⁄16 inch) thick slices.
A slicing machine is useful to achieve this or a steady
hand with a sharp bread knife. You will need eight
slices of brioche. Lay the brioche on a chopping
board. Brush the slices well with clarified butter.

Place each portion of fish on top of the brioche
square and, using a sharp knife, cut down the sides
of the fish through the brioche. Discard the excess
brioche. Slide a spatula under the brioche and turn
it over with the fish. The clarified butter should
have helped the brioche to adhere to the fish. Now
brush the top side of the brioche with the butter.
Essentially you should have a thin tile of brioche
stuck to the top of your fish. Put aside until required.

green tea and wakame broth

1 KG (2 LB 4 OZ) SNAPPER HEADS, SPLIT IN HALF
    (ASK YOUR FISHMONGER TO DO THIS FOR YOU)
60 ML (2 FL OZ/¼ CUP) GRAPESEED OIL
1 FENNEL BULB, DICED
1 SMALL ONION, DICED
1 CARROT, DICED
1 WHITE CELERY STALK (INNER STALK), DICED
10 G (¼ OZ) PEELED GINGER, SLICED
200 ML (7 FL OZ) DRY SAKE
1 LITRE (35 FL OZ/4 CUPS) CHICKEN STOCK
    (BASIC RECIPES, PAGE 262)
1 X 10 CM (4 INCH) SQUARE SHEET DRIED KONBU
    SEAWEED
2 G (1⁄16 OZ) DRIED WAKAME SEAWEED
1 TEASPOON GOOD QUALITY JAPANESE GREEN
    LEAF TEA

Remove and discard the eyes and the gills from the
halved snapper heads, then wash thoroughly under
running water to remove the excess blood.

In a large pan, lightly brown the snapper heads
in the grapeseed oil. Add the fennel, onion, carrot,
celery and ginger and sweat for a few minutes, then
add the sake and reduce until almost all the sake
has evaporated. Add the chicken stock and 1 litre
(35 fl oz/4 cups) of water and simmer very gently
for 1½ hours. You should be left with 1 litre (35 fl oz/
4 cups) of liquid. Add the konbu seaweed to the
liquid, then remove the pan from the heat and infuse
for 30 minutes. Strain the liquid through a fine sieve
lined with a double layer of muslin cloth. Use a ladle
to remove any fat from the surface. Return the fish
broth to a small clean saucepan and reduce by half,
then refrigerate until required. Finely chop the
wakame and green tea leaves and set aside.

to finish and plate

Preheat the oven to 180°C (350°F/Gas 4). To cook the brioche with fish, heat a large non-stick ovenproof frying
pan and add the grapeseed oil. Place the fish in the pan, brioche side down, and allow to colour for 1 minute,
or until the brioche is golden brown. Turn the fish over and place in the oven for 5 minutes, or until the fish is
cooked through. Meanwhile, heat half of the fish broth in one saucepan and the other half in another saucepan.
In one pan, gently poach the periwinkles and scallops for 2 minutes. In the other pan of broth, add the chopped
wakame and green tea and gently reheat. Blanch the hasuimo slices and winter melon in boiling salted water,
then drain and put aside. Remove the fish from the oven and check that it is cooked correctly. Top the brioche
with the softened parsley and fennel butter and allow it to melt with the residual heat from the fish.

Place a piece of fish on the left side of each plate (choose a plate that is slightly concaved so it holds the
green tea and wakame broth), then construct a nice pile of periwinkles, scallops, hasuimo and winter melon
next to the fish. Garnish with pea flowers and cucumber tendrils and pour a small amount of the green tea
and wakame broth around the dish. Serve immediately.

SERVES 8

poached sea scallops, lettuce hearts, periwinkles, oyster cream and scallop velvet

This is a very elegant and clean-tasting seafood dish. The gentle texture of sea scallops contrasts with the more robust texture of the periwinkles, and the crisp texture of lettuce hearts and cucumbers works well with the luscious scallop velvet and oyster cream. The intensity of the roasted scallop consommé with its crisp acid balance highlights the gentle seafood flavours.

ingredients

16 LIVE PERIWINKLES

16 LIVE SEA SCALLOPS IN THE SHELL, OR FRESHLY
     SHUCKED SCALLOPS

24 BUTTER LETTUCES, WITH ROOTS ATTACHED

8 MINIATURE WHITE CUCUMBERS

16 ASIAN RADISH PODS

24 SOUR MEXICAN CUCUMBERS

2 HEADS WHITE GARLIC CHIVE FLOWERS

OYSTER CREAM (BASIC RECIPES, PAGE 265)

1 LITRE (35 FL OZ/4 CUPS) SPRING ONION AND
     GINGER OIL (BASIC RECIPES, PAGE 264)

50 G (1¾ OZ) UNSALTED BUTTER

FINE SEA SALT

method

Place the live periwinkles and scallops into a large bucket filled with water and plenty of ice for 20 minutes. This will send them into a coma, which is a more humane way of treating them and also relaxes the meat. Meanwhile, place a large pot of salted water on the stovetop and bring to the boil.

Remove the scallops and shuck them. Remove the white meat, then slice the white meat across the scallop into 3 slices, each about 4 mm (⅛ inch) thick. Remove the periwinkles from the iced water, place them in the boiling water and cook for 1 minute, then remove and place them straight back into the iced water to stop the cooking process. With a thin metal skewer, hook and remove the meat from the shells. Discard the intestines, cut the piece of meat in half vertically and remove the red mouth section. Refrigerate the seafood until required.

Remove all the leaves from the butter lettuce cores and trim the roots from the cores using a sharp knife. Peel back the core using your hands until you have exposed the bright green under flesh of the lettuce heart. Place the lettuce hearts in cold water until required. Peel the miniature cucumbers until all you are left with are the small seeds attached to the core. You can use a turning knife to do this. Place in cold water until required. Trim the Asian radish pods away from their stems and set aside the sour Mexican cucumbers and garlic chive flowers. Make the oyster cream.

scallop velvets

200 G (7 OZ) FRESH SEA SCALLOP MEAT,
     WITHOUT ROE, CHILLED

1 EGG WHITE

200 ML (7 FL OZ) CREAM (35% FAT)

FINE SEA SALT

2 EGG WHITES, EXTRA

1 LITRE (35 FL OZ/4 CUPS) CHICKEN STOCK
     (BASIC RECIPES, PAGE 262)

To make the scallop mousseline for the velvets, put the chilled scallop flesh into a small food processor. Add the egg white and begin to process. With the motor running, slowly pour the cream in a thin continuous stream onto the scallops. Once all the cream is combined with the scallops, season the mousseline with sea salt, remove from the food processor and store in the refrigerator. The scallop velvets will be finished just before serving.

scallop consommé

2 SNAPPER HEADS, SPLIT IN HALF (ASK YOUR
 FISHMONGER TO DO THIS FOR YOU)

100 ML (3½ FL OZ) GRAPESEED OIL

2 KG (4 LB 8 OZ) CHICKEN WINGS, CHOPPED

500 G (1 LB 2 OZ) SQUID TRIMMINGS

500 G (1 LB 2 OZ) SEA SCALLOP TRIMMINGS OR SMALL
 SEA SCALLOPS

4 SMALL FENNEL BULBS, 3 DICED AND 1 CHOPPED

4 WHITE CELERY STALKS (INNER STALKS), DICED

½ BROWN ONION, DICED

250 G (9 OZ) UNSALTED BUTTER

2 GARLIC CLOVES, DICED

200 ML (7 FL OZ) GOOD QUALITY APPLE VINEGAR

750 ML (26 FL OZ) BOTTLE DRY UNOAKED
 CHARDONNAY

3 LITRES (105 FL OZ/12 CUPS) CHICKEN STOCK
 (BASIC RECIPES, PAGE 262)

1 KG (2 LB 4 OZ) VONGOLE, SHELLS WELL SCRUBBED

2 SMALL CHICKEN BREASTS, SKIN REMOVED

FINE SEA SALT

10 EGG WHITES

Remove and discard the eyes and gills from the halved snapper heads, then wash thoroughly under running water to remove the excess blood. Pan-roast the snapper heads in a large saucepan with the grapeseed oil until lightly coloured. Add the chicken wings, squid trimmings and sea scallops and cook until the chicken wings and seafood are well coloured. Add three diced fennel bulbs to the pan along with the celery, onion and butter. Continue to pan-roast the ingredients in the butter until everything is golden brown, stirring and scraping the base of the pan with a wooden spoon to make sure the ingredients are not sticking. Add the garlic and deglaze with the apple vinegar until almost all the vinegar has evaporated. Stir and scrape well so that all the brown bits on the bottom of the pan are dissolved. Add the wine and reduce until almost all the wine has evaporated, then add the chicken stock and 2 litres (70 fl oz/8 cups) of water and bring to simmering point. Reduce the heat until the liquid is barely moving and cook over low heat for 2 hours. Do not remove the butter from the surface of the stock at this point, as the flavour of the butter will infuse with the stock.

After 2 hours, add the vongole to the stock, then add the remaining bulb of chopped fennel. Remove the pan from the heat and allow all the ingredients to infuse for 30 minutes. Carefully strain the stock through a fine strainer and discard the solids. Now you can remove any oil or butter from the surface of the stock with a small ladle. Strain the stock through a sieve lined with muslin cloth into a clean pot and allow to cool.

Meanwhile, to make a raft for the consommé, put the chicken and a few pinches of salt in a food processor and process until finely chopped. Lightly whisk the egg whites by hand until you have very soft peaks, then fold the egg whites through the processed chicken.

Place the cooled stock in the pot over medium heat. Vigorously whisk the raft into the stock until well incorporated, stirring occasionally to make sure the raft is not sticking to the bottom of the pot. Allow the stock to come close to boiling point, then turn the heat down to the lowest possible setting; you want the stock to be barely simmering under the raft. Do not stir the raft again at this point. Cook on very low heat for 30 minutes. Make a hole in the raft to check that it is fully cooked and that the stock is clear, then cook for a further 10 minutes.

Remove the pot from the heat and set aside for 20 minutes. Carefully ladle the consommé from the pot into a sieve lined with a double layer of muslin cloth, making sure you don't break up the raft too much. You should have a crystal clear, intensely flavoured roasted scallop consommé. Taste and adjust the seasoning if required. Keep the consommé in the refrigerator until required.

to finish and plate

Gently reheat the oyster cream. Heat the spring onion and ginger oil in a small pan until it reaches 70°C (155°F). Put the chicken stock in a large shallow pan with a fitted lid and heat to 80°C (175°F). Place a third pan on the stove filled with salted water and bring to the boil.

To finish the scallop velvets, whisk the extra 2 egg whites in a clean bowl until soft peaks form. Place 4 tablespoons of the scallop mousseline into a separate bowl and add one-third of the whisked egg whites. Mix the egg white and mousseline together thoroughly, then gently fold through the remaining egg whites. Lift the lid from the hot chicken stock and place 1 shallow tablespoon of scallop and egg white mixture into the stock. Repeat to make eight scallop velvets in total, then replace the lid and gently poach for 2 minutes. Meanwhile, reheat the consommé. Place the lettuce hearts in the boiling water and 30 seconds later add the sour Mexican cucumbers, the white cucumbers and radish pods. Blanch for 30 seconds, then remove and drain. Melt the butter and brush it over the vegetables, then season with sea salt. Poach the sea scallops and periwinkles in the ginger oil for about 30 seconds. Remove with a slotted spoon and season with sea salt.

To assemble, place a poached scallop velvet in the centre of each serving bowl. Top with slices of scallop and periwinkles, lettuce hearts, cucumbers and radish pods. Add a few dots of oyster cream and garnish with garlic chive flowers. Serve immediately to your guests and pour the hot consommé at the table.

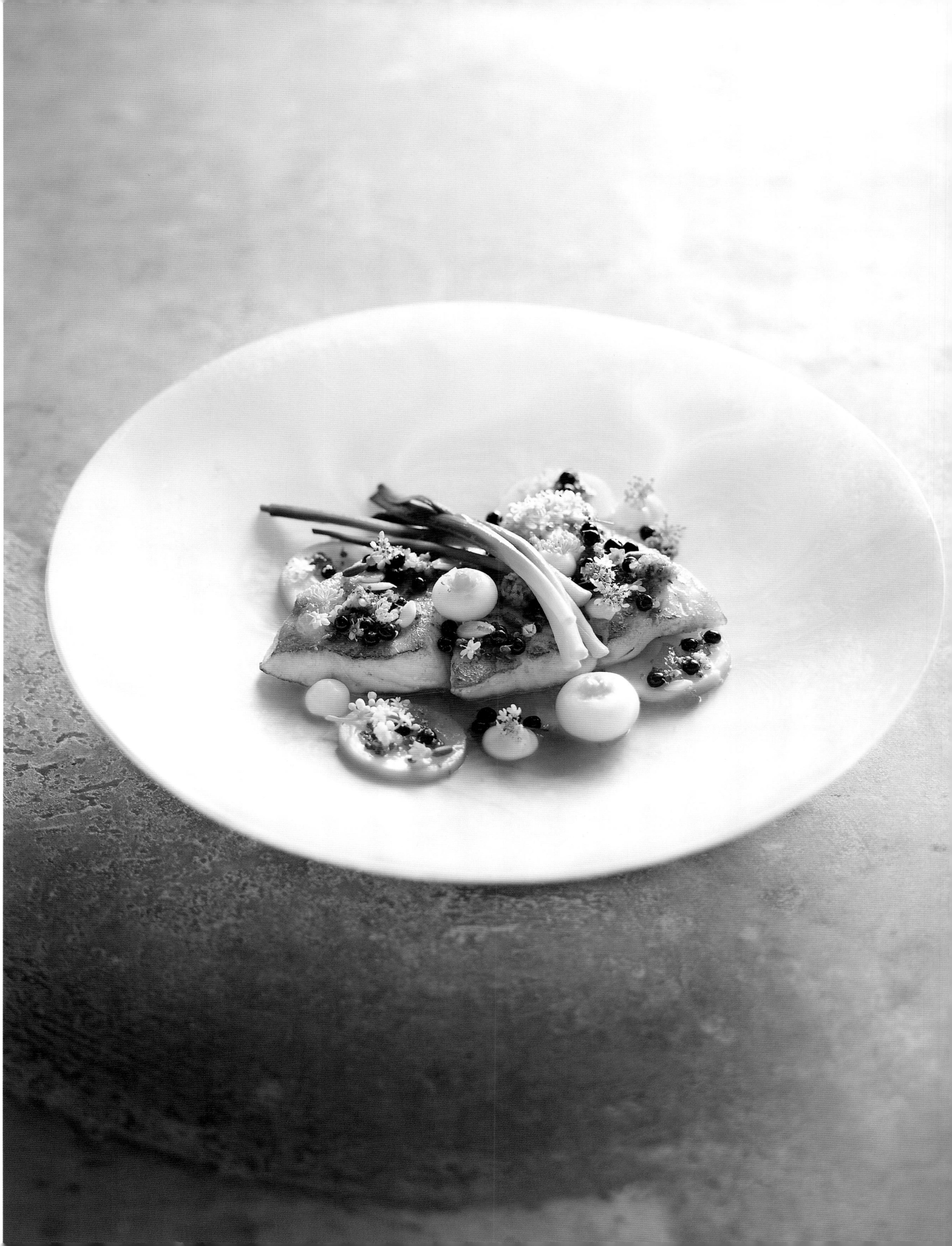

SERVES 8

john dory with summer squash, elderberries and lemon confit

This is a pan-roasted fish dish with flavours from late summer. The coriander and fennel flowers perfume the dish, the lemon confit cuts through the richness of the brown butter and the ripe elderberries add a sweet note. I like to use baby turnips, very young leeks and the core of the summer squash for the vegetable components, because they are not too dominant and allow the fish to shine.

ingredients

100 G (3½ OZ) DRIED CHICKPEAS
8 X 200 G (7 OZ) JOHN DORY FILLETS
1 TEASPOON CUMIN SEEDS
½ TEASPOON CORIANDER SEEDS
50 G (1¾ OZ) UNSALTED BUTTER
2 FRENCH SHALLOTS, FINELY DICED
½ GARLIC CLOVE, FINELY DICED
12 G (½ OZ/1 CUP) FLAT-LEAF PARSLEY, FINELY CHOPPED
1 EGG, LIGHTLY BEATEN
FINE SEA SALT
100 ML (3½ FL OZ) GARLIC CREAM (BASIC RECIPES, PAGE 265)
2 TEASPOONS LEMON CONFIT (BASIC RECIPES, PAGE 269)
150 ML (5 FL OZ) CLARIFIED BROWN BUTTER (BASIC RECIPES, PAGE 264)
50 G (1¾ OZ) RED QUINOA
40 VERY YOUNG BABY LEEKS
16 BABY KABU (WHITE) TURNIPS
8 YELLOW BUTTON SQUASH
2 TEASPOONS WINTER MELON SEEDS
1 TABLESPOON RIPE ELDERBERRIES
1 TEASPOON DRIED FENNEL POLLEN
2 ELDERFLOWER HEADS, SEPARATED
4 CORIANDER (CILANTRO) FLOWER HEADS, SEPARATED
4 FENNEL FLOWER HEADS, SEPARATED
32 FLOWERING BABY SOUR MEXICAN CUCUMBERS

method

Soak the chickpeas in cold water overnight, then drain. Boil the chickpeas in water for 30 minutes. Meanwhile, remove the skin from the John Dory fillets using a sharp knife. Trim the edges of the fish and remove any sinews. Place the fillets in the refrigerator until required.

Put the cumin and coriander seeds in a dry frying pan over medium heat and roast until lightly coloured. Remove from the pan and finely chop. Heat 30 g (1 oz) of butter in a frying pan and lightly sauté the shallots and garlic, without colouring. Add the chopped seeds to the pan and put aside.

Drain the cooked chickpeas, place them in a food processor and process until they are finely chopped. Add the shallot, garlic, cumin, coriander and parsley and process until combined. Transfer the chickpea mixture to a bowl, add the egg and mix through, then season to taste with sea salt.

Form the mixture into eight small patties and refrigerate until required. These will be pan-fried and crumbled closer to serving.

Prepare the garlic cream, lemon confit and clarified brown butter. Boil the red quinoa in water for 4–5 minutes, then drain and put aside. Top, tail and wash the baby leeks. Wash the baby turnips and trim the leaves so there is only 5 mm (¼ inch) of green stem showing. Using a 3 cm (1¼ inch) round pastry cutter, punch a hole through the middle of each button squash. Trim away any remaining yellow skin and slice the squash into 4 mm (⅛ inch) thick discs; you will need 32 slices.

to finish and plate

Gently reheat the garlic cream. Pan-fry the chickpea patties until golden brown. Allow to cool slightly and then crumble the patties. Lightly season the John Dory. In two large non-stick frying pans, pan-roast the fish in 50 ml (1¾ fl oz) of clarified brown butter. The fish should take no more than 2 minutes to cook, then drain and set aside. While the fish is cooking, gently heat the remaining 100 ml (3½ fl oz) of clarified brown butter in a small saucepan. Add the lemon confit, red quinoa, winter melon seeds and elderberries. Blanch the leeks, turnips and squash in a saucepan of boiling water for 1 minute, then drain. Melt the remaining 20 g (¾ oz) of butter and brush it over the vegetables, then season with sea salt.

Place four slices of squash on each serving plate. Add four dabs of garlic cream near the squash and place the fish on top. Sprinkle over the crumbled chickpea mixture. Place 2 tablespoons of the brown butter mixture over the top of the fish, sprinkle with fennel pollen and add the elderflowers, coriander flowers, fennel flowers and baby Mexican cucumbers. Finish the dish with the baby leeks and turnips. Serve immediately.

SERVES 8

toro of southern bluefin tuna with jamón ibérico de bellota and egg white pearl flowers

The toro and jamón have a very similar amount of interspersed fat content, giving each ingredient a very similar, rich mouthfeel. This is the reason for putting these two seemingly diverse ingredients together: they play off each other well. Their flavours are rounded out with a little heat from the juniper and horseradish cream, nasturtiums, peppery watercress and radish. The smokiness of the egg white, eel and celeriac flowers and the nuttiness of the hazelnuts really complement the flavours of the toro and jamón. There is a logic to this dish that defies its list of ingredients; a sense of harmony and balance within the diversity.

ingredients

100 ML (3½ FL OZ) GRAPESEED OIL
2 G (1⁄16 OZ) BONITO FLAKES
10 ML (¼ FL OZ) WHITE SOY SAUCE
1 X 1 KG (2 LB 4 OZ) BELLY OF BLUEFIN TUNA (TORO)
24 HAZELNUTS
24 SLICES OF JAMÓN IBÉRICO DE BELLOTA
8 BABY CHERRY BELLE RADISHES
16 NASTURTIUM LEAVES
8 NASTURTIUM BUDS
24 WATERCRESS BLOOMS WITH LEAVES
24 RADISH FLOWERS

method

Heat the grapeseed oil in a pan over low heat until it reaches about 40°C (105°F). Add the bonito and white soy sauce and stir well, then remove the pan from the heat and allow to infuse for 10 minutes. Pass the oil through a fine sieve lined with muslin cloth, discard the solids and reserve the oil. Put aside to cool.

Trim and slice the toro into 32 strips, about 2 mm (1⁄16 inch) thin, 10 cm (5 inches) long and 2 cm (¾ inch) wide. Place the toro in the refrigerator.

Preheat the oven to 180°C (350°F/Gas 4). Place the hazelnuts on a baking tray and roast in the oven for 10 minutes, or until lightly brown. Remove the hazelnuts from the oven and rub them in a kitchen cloth to remove as much skin as possible, then split them with a small sharp knife and put aside. Roll the freshly sliced jamón into cylinders. Trim the cherry belle radishes, leaving some leaves on.

juniper and horseradish cream

20 DRIED JUNIPER BERRIES
50 ML (1¾ FL OZ) CREAM (35% FAT)
10 G (¼ OZ) FINELY GRATED FRESH HORSERADISH
100 G (3½ OZ) CRÈME FRAÎCHE
FINE SEA SALT

Preheat the oven to 180°C (350°F/Gas 4). Put the juniper berries on a baking tray and lightly roast in the oven. Remove and roughly crush them with a mortar and pestle. Place the crushed juniper berries in a small pan with the cream. Heat the cream until simmering, reduce slightly, then remove the pan from the heat and allow to infuse for 15 minutes. Pour the cream through a fine sieve lined with muslin cloth and set aside.

Fold the grated horseradish into the crème fraîche and season with a little sea salt to taste. Lightly whip the crème fraîche until soft peaks form. Dilute the crème fraîche with the cold juniper berry cream and stir well. You should have the consistency of a light cream that can be spread out on a plate but will still hold its form. Refrigerate until required.

egg white and smoked eel pearl flowers

70 G (2½ OZ) SMOKED EEL MEAT

200 ML (7 FL OZ) MILK

70 G (2½ OZ) WHITE FLESHED FISH, SUCH AS BLUE EYE, SNAPPER OR COD

60 G (2¼ OZ) UNSALTED BUTTER, SOFTENED

40 ML (1¼ FL OZ) EXTRA VIRGIN OLIVE OIL

JUICE OF ½ LEMON

60 G (2¼ OZ) MASHED POTATO

FINE SEA SALT

30 G (1 OZ) CRÈME FRAÎCHE

500 ML (17 FL OZ/2 CUPS) GRAPESEED OIL

100 ML (3½ FL OZ) STRAINED EGG WHITE

1 CELERIAC

To make the smoked eel brandade, first make sure the smoked eel flesh is boneless and skinless. Put the milk in a pan and bring to the boil, then remove the pan from the heat and add the smoked eel. Leave the eel to marinate in the warm milk for 10 minutes, then strain the eel and discard the milk. Steam the white fish until it flakes.

Put the eel and fish in a small bowl. Using a fork, mash them together with 30 g (1 oz) of softened butter. Drizzle over 20 ml (½ fl oz) of extra virgin olive and all the lemon juice, mixing with the fork as you go. Add the mashed potato and mix well. Add the remaining 30 g (1 oz) of butter and 20 ml (½ fl oz) of extra virgin olive oil and mix well. Season to taste with sea salt. Allow the mixture to cool, then fold in the crème fraîche. Place the mixture in the refrigerator for at least 1 hour.

Take some of the mixture in the palm of your hand and roll into balls the size of a small marble. You will need 16 balls. You may have some mixture leftover, which you can use elsewhere.

To make the egg white pearls, put the grapeseed oil in a small saucepan and heat to 70°C (155°F). Using an eye dropper, drop the strained egg white into the oil, drop by drop, in rapid succession. When you have about 30 egg white droplets, stop and gently stir them around. They need about 1 minute in the oil to fully set. Carefully sieve out the egg white pearls using a fine strainer and place the pearls on a flat metal tray. Repeat this process several times, maintaining the oil temperature at about 70°C (155°F), until you have a sufficient amount of egg white pearls to coat the balls of brandade.

To cover the brandade mixture with the egg white pearls, first line 16 demi-tasse cups with 12 cm (4½ inch) squares of plastic wrap. Place 1 teaspoon of egg white pearls in the middle of the plastic and spread them out so they form a single layer. Place a ball of brandade in the centre. Carefully lift up the four corners of the plastic wrap and twist them together to form a ball, then tie a knot in the plastic. The aim is to coat the brandade balls in the egg white pearls, with the aid of the plastic wrap. When you have 16 perfectly covered balls, place them in the refrigerator until required.

Peel the celeriac and cut into 3 cm (1¼ inch) thick slices. Using a 2 cm (¾ inch) round pastry cutter, cut out cylinders from the celeriac. Use a mandolin to slice the cylinders into 1 mm (¹⁄₁₆ inch) thin discs. You will need 96 discs (six discs per flower, for a total of 16 flowers). Blanch the celeriac discs in boiling water for 10 seconds and refresh in iced water. Dry the discs thoroughly.

Lay 15 cm (6 inch) squares of plastic wrap over 16 demi-tasse cups, leaving a slight dip in the middle of the plastic. Place six overlapping discs of celeriac

in the centre of the plastic to form a small circle. Place an egg white and smoked eel pearl in the centre and pull each corner of the plastic together so the slices of celeriac come up to the sides of the pearl. With your fingers, pinch the base so the celeriac petals stick to the pearl. Refrigerate in the demi-tasse cups for 1 hour.

to finish and plate

Trace two lines of juniper and horseradish cream on each serving plate. Place two dabs of the juniper and horseradish cream on the plates. Unwrap the celeriac and smoked eel pearl flowers and place two pearl flowers on the two dabs of cream on each plate. Briefly marinate the toro slices in the bonito and white soy oil. Each strip of toro should stay in the marinade for only 5 seconds. Drain the strips on a clean kitchen cloth and then place four strips on each plate. Intersperse the strips of toro with three cylinders of jamón. Garnish with hazelnuts, radishes, nasturtium leaves and buds, and the flowers. Serve immediately.

the land

I try wherever possible to buy my meat and poultry directly from
the farmer who produces it, or I use specialist providores who
search far and wide for the finest breeders and growers. I like to
buy free-range animals that have been bred by passionate farmers
in humane conditions, with an emphasis on breeds that are grown
for their flavour and eating qualities rather than how quickly or
cost-efficiently they grow. The best meat will yield the best results.

SERVES 8

blackmore's pure-bred wagyu beef fillet sous vide with morels and bone marrow

Wagyu is a specialised Japanese breed of beef often referred to as Kobe beef. The meat is naturally marbled with fat, producing an incredible mouthfeel. David Blackmore is a pioneer of wagyu genetics in Australia and produces some of the best wagyu in the country. His meat has a 9+ marble score (a method of rating the meat devised by the Japanese), which is the highest achievable marble score in Australia. I like to cook the fillet sous-vide style, which makes an incredibly tender meat even more so.

ingredients

4 YEARLING MARROW BONES, CUT INTO 8 CM (3¼ INCH) LONG SECTIONS (ASK YOUR BUTCHER TO DO THIS FOR YOU)
165 G (5¾ OZ) UNSALTED BUTTER
30 G (1 OZ) PEELED FRESH WASABI ROOT, FINELY GRATED
FINE SEA SALT
32 FRESH OR DRIED MORELS
1 KG (2 LB 4 OZ) DAVID BLACKMORE WAGYU FILLET (CENTRE CUT), MARBLE SCORE 9+
550 ML (19 FL OZ) REDUCED VEAL STOCK (GLAZE) (BASIC RECIPES, PAGE 263)
80 BABY SPINACH LEAVES
16 RED MARBLE ONIONS
10 ML (¼ FL OZ) OLIVE OIL
8 WASABI FLOWER HEADS

method

Put the marrow bones under cold running water for 30 minutes, then soak in a container of cold water for 2 hours. This will help remove any excess blood from the marrow. Remove the marrow from the bones by pushing it out with your finger. Soak the marrow in cold water for a further 2 hours. Put aside until ready to poach.

To make wasabi butter, soften 100 g (3½ oz) of butter in a bowl. Add the grated wasabi and a pinch of sea salt and whip together. Put aside until needed.

Brush the fresh morels well to remove any grit and set aside. If using dried morels, soak them in 300 ml (10½ fl oz) of warm water for 1 hour. Strain the morel soaking liquid through a sieve lined with a double layer of muslin cloth to remove any dirt, reserving the liquid. Transfer the strained liquid to a small saucepan and reduce it down to 40 ml (1¼ fl oz). Reserve the reduced liquid. Thoroughly wash the soaked morels in five or six changes of cold water to be sure you have removed all the dirt and grit, remove the stems, then return the morels to

the reduced liquid and allow them to soak until needed. This will ensure you have maximum flavour and no grit in your dried morels.

Trim the wagyu fillet of any visible sinews. Place in a large vacuum bag with 300 ml (10½ fl oz) of the veal glaze and seal in a vacuum sealer. Using a temperature-controlled water bath set at 65°C (150°F), poach the beef for 40 minutes. This should achieve a medium-rare cooked meat. Allow the beef to rest for 10 minutes in the bag.

Meanwhile, preheat the oven to 180°C (350°F/ Gas 4). Remove the stalks from the spinach leaves. Wash and dry the spinach. Top and tail the red marble onions and place on a large square of silicone paper. Drizzle with the olive oil and sprinkle with sea salt. Wrap the onions in the silicone paper to form a parcel and place in the oven for 10–15 minutes, depending on size, until the onions are tender.

to finish and plate

While the beef is resting, slice the bone marrow into 4 mm (⅛ inch) thick slices and poach in 200 ml (7 fl oz) of veal glaze for a couple of minutes over low heat until the bone marrow is still pink. Sauté the spinach in a shallow frying pan with 40 g (1½ oz) of butter. Season with sea salt and drain on a kitchen cloth. Briefly sauté the morels with 25 g (1 oz) of butter until wilted, then add the remaining 50 ml (1¾ fl oz) of veal glaze and cook for a further minute. Season the mushrooms with sea salt.

Slice the fillet into eight even portions and place on a baking tray. Spoon over some of the veal glaze from the bag, season with sea salt and flash in a 180°C (350°F/Gas 4) oven for 1 minute to bring the beef up to serving temperature. Place each slice of beef in the centre of the serving plate. Top the beef with the sautéed spinach, morels, bone marrow, red marble onions and a spoonful of wasabi butter. Garnish with wasabi flowers and serve.

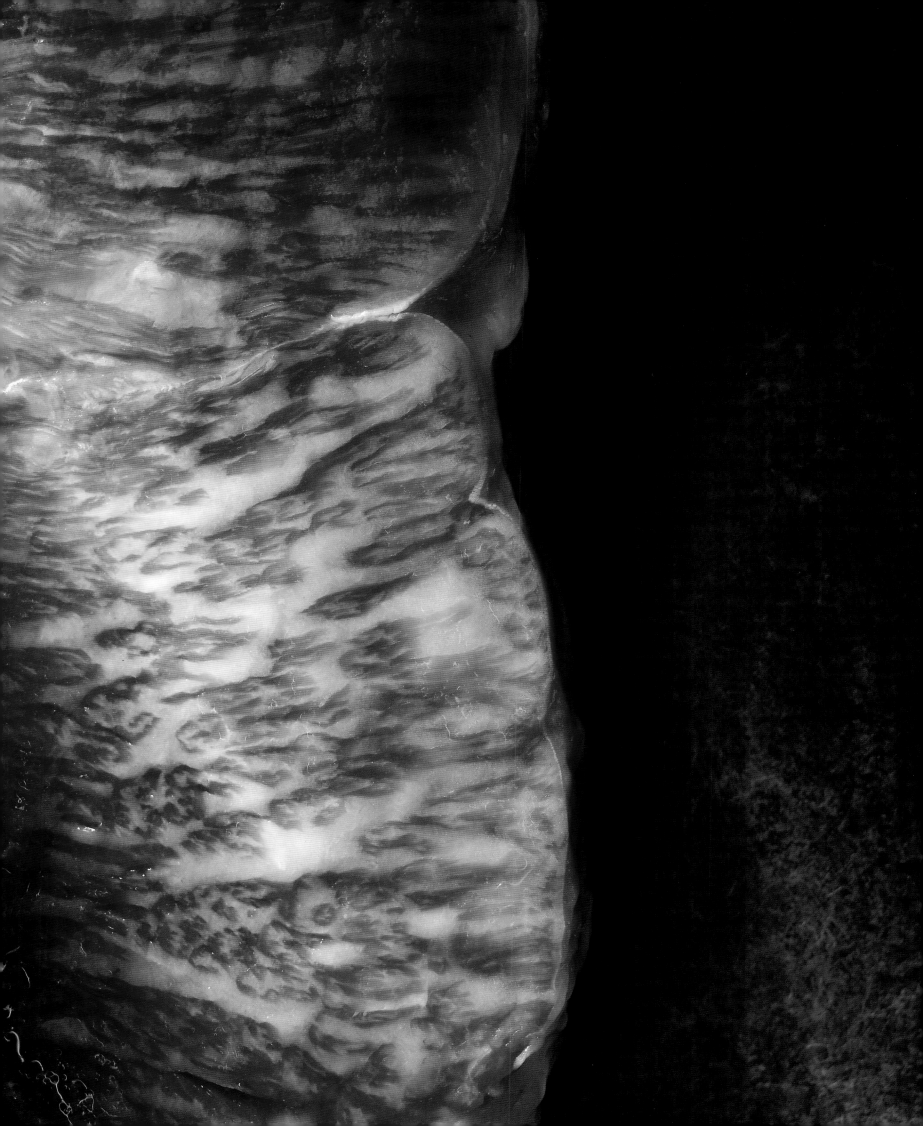

SERVES 8

12 hour slow-braised milk-fed lamb shoulder

Taking a second grade cut of meat, such as the shoulder, and cooking it very slowly will make the meat tender. By applying this principle to a young milk-fed lamb shoulder, the result is an incredibly tender, rich and flavoursome piece of meat. Accompanying the lamb are baby heirloom carrots — the two varieties I've used here are from strains at least 100 years old. The white carrots were developed in Belgium and the red carrots are from Japan. Nasturtiums, capers and Spanish arbequina olives balance the sweetness that comes from the carrots and white carrot cream.

ingredients

3 X 1 KG (2 LB 4 OZ) MILK-FED LAMB SHOULDERS, BONE IN

5 LITRES (175 FL OZ) LAMB STOCK (BASIC RECIPES, PAGE 262)

WHITE CARROT CREAM (RECIPE, PAGE 199)

24 BABY RED HEIRLOOM CARROTS

24 BABY WHITE HEIRLOOM CARROTS

16 DUTCH CARROTS

4 TABLESPOONS SMALL SALTED CAPERS

40 ARBEQUINA OLIVES

100 G (3½ OZ) UNSALTED BUTTER

FINE SEA SALT

100 G (3½ OZ) CLARIFIED BROWN BUTTER (BASIC RECIPES, PAGE 264)

8 SMALL CLUSTERS NASTURTIUM LEAVES

8 NASTURTIUM BUDS

8 SPRIGS OKRA SHOOTS

32 PINK ROSEMARY FLOWERS

8 SOCIETY GARLIC FLOWERS

method

To braise the lamb shoulders, preheat the oven to 110°C (225°F/Gas ½). Place the lamb shoulders in a large, deep ovenproof container and submerge them completely in the lamb stock. Place in the oven and cook for 11 hours, making sure the lamb is completely submerged in the stock throughout the cooking process. Alternatively the lamb shoulders can be placed in three vacuum bags, with 500 ml (17 fl oz/ 2 cups) of stock in each, sealed in a vacuum sealer and steamed in a temperature-controlled combi oven at 85°C (185°F) for 11 hours. When the lamb has finished cooking it should literally fall off the bone.

When the lamb is cooked, take it out of the stock and reserve the stock. Carefully remove the bone by twisting it slowly and pulling it from the flesh. Shape each lamb shoulder into three equal portions; try to retain the skin on the surface of each portion. Place the lamb portions into a baking dish. Strain the reserved stock into a saucepan and reduce it by half over high heat. Skim and strain the stock, then pour the reduced stock over the lamb portions, to come at least three-quarters of the way up the portions. Cover and refrigerate the lamb portions and stock until required.

Meanwhile, prepare the carrot purée for the white carrot cream. Put aside until needed.

Peel all the baby carrots. Wash the salted capers in several changes of water to remove the salt. With a sharp knife, remove the stones from the olives.

to finish and plate

Increase the oven temperature to 150°C (300°F/Gas 2). Remove the lamb and reduced stock from the refrigerator, cover with foil and place in the oven for 1 hour to reheat. Once the lamb is completely warmed through, use a slotted spoon to remove the lamb onto a tray lined with silicone paper. Keep the lamb warm. Pour the remaining lamb stock into a saucepan and reduce over high heat until you are left with a rich, sticky glaze, then whisk in 50 g (1¾ oz) of butter. Season the lamb with sea salt and coat the lamb well with the glaze. Return the lamb to the oven to reheat while periodically basting the lamb. Meanwhile, cook the carrots in a saucepan of boiling water until tender, then drain. Melt the remaining 50 g (1¾ oz) of butter and brush it over the carrots, season with sea salt and keep warm.

To finish the white carrot cream, whip the cream until soft peaks form. Reheat the carrot purée, then fold through the whipped cream. Warm the capers and olives in a small saucepan with the brown butter.

Place a spoonful of the white carrot cream to the side of each warmed serving plate. Use a slotted spoon to place the portions of lamb next to the carrot cream. Arrange the carrots on top of the cream and then place a couple of spoonfuls of the capers and olives close by. Add the nasturtium leaves, buds, okra shoots and flowers, and serve.

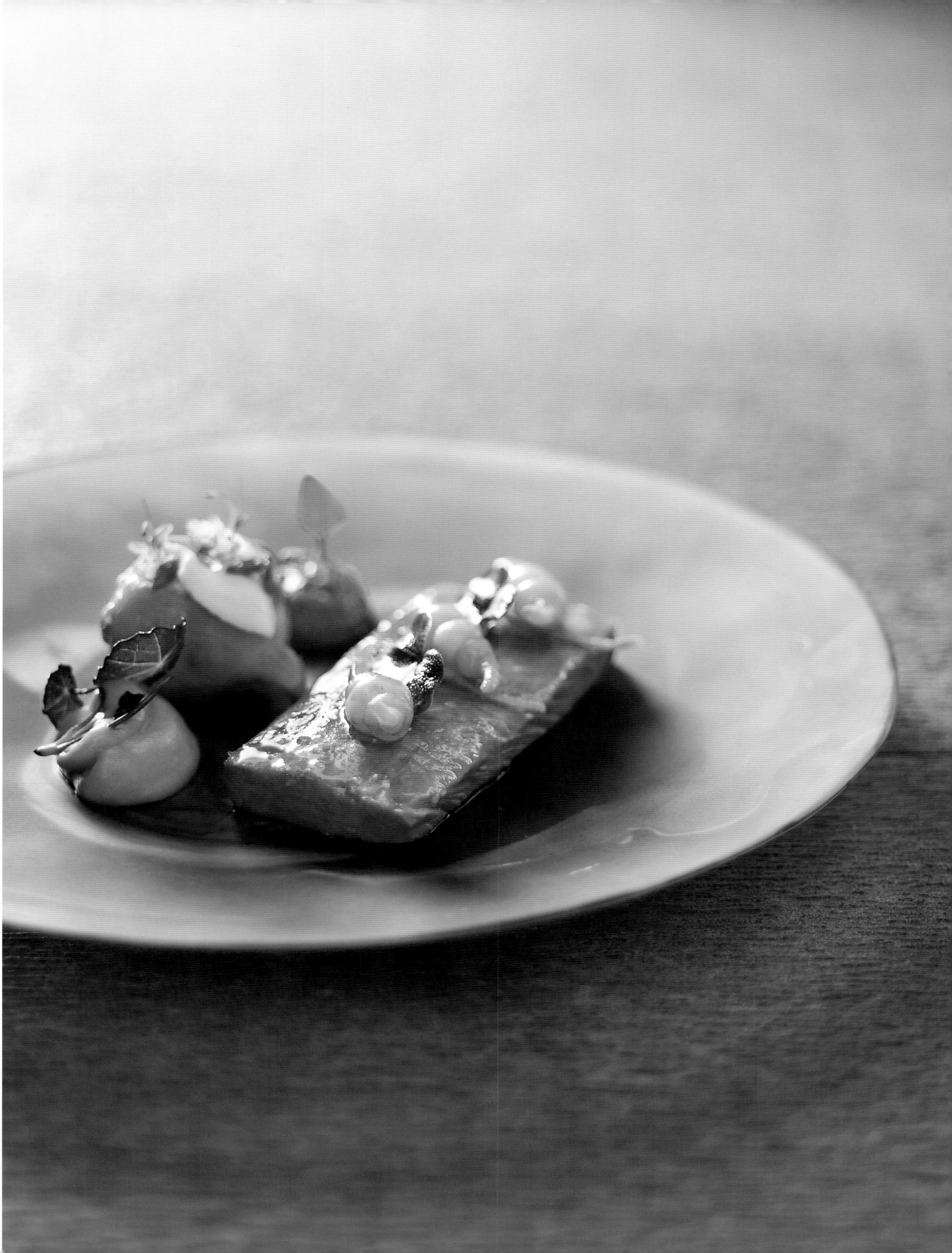

SERVES 8

confit of suffolk lamb loin with chinese, jerusalem and globe artichokes

Suffolk lamb meat has wonderful fat marbling, resulting in a superior taste and tenderness. Suffolk lamb is bred primarily for its meat as opposed to a lot of lamb sold in Australia, which is really a by-product of the wool industry. Here I've cooked the lamb sous-vide style, coated in its own fat. You could conventionally roast the lamb if you like, but the low temperature cooking of the sous vide really adds to the tenderness of the lamb. The lamb is served with three types of artichokes, although each one is a completely different vegetable. Chinese artichokes, also known as crosne, are a rare and hard-to-find vegetable. They have a crisp texture, similar to water chestnuts.

ingredients

8 X 10 CM (4 INCH) SUFFOLK LAMB LOINS (ABOUT 200 G/7 OZ EACH), OFF THE BONE, WITH CAP ON
5 LARGE GLOBE ARTICHOKES
100 ML (3½ FL OZ) EXTRA VIRGIN OLIVE OIL
FINE SEA SALT
4 FRENCH SHALLOTS, DICED
1 WHITE CELERY STALK (INNER STALK), DICED
1 GARLIC CLOVE, DICED
200 G (7 OZ) UNSALTED BUTTER
500 ML (17 FL OZ/2 CUPS) CHICKEN STOCK (BASIC RECIPES, PAGE 262)
8 MEDIUM-SIZED JERUSALEM ARTICHOKES
24 CHINESE ARTICHOKES
LEMON JUICE
20 G (¾ OZ) PINE NUTS
20 G (¾ OZ) SUNFLOWER SEEDS
160 G (5½ OZ) TOMA DELLA ROCCA CHEESE, RIND REMOVED
300 ML (10½ FL OZ) CLARIFIED BUTTER (BASIC RECIPES, PAGE 264)
16 ROSEMARY FLOWERS
16 SPRIGS OKRA SHOOTS
24 NASTURTIUM LEAVES
100 G (3½ OZ) JAR OF ITALIAN HOPS PURÉE
8 SPRIGS WARRIGAL GREENS

method

Remove all of the skin, fat and sinews from the lamb loins. Carefully render the fat by gently heating it in a small saucepan. Strain, discard any solids and cool slightly. Place the trimmed loins in a vacuum bag, add the melted lamb fat and seal in a vacuum sealer. Put aside ready for cooking.

Trim the globe artichoke stems and remove some of the outer leaves. Place in a vacuum bag with the extra virgin olive oil, season with sea salt, then seal tightly to avoid exposure to the air. Steam the artichokes in a temperature-controlled combi oven at 90°C (195°F) for 15–20 minutes, or until tender. Remove the artichokes from the bag and peel the remaining outer leaves away, exposing the heart. Split the heart and remove the choke.

Sweat the shallots, celery and garlic in a pan with 50 g (1¾ oz) of butter, but do not colour. Slice the artichoke hearts and add to the pan. Cover with chicken stock and simmer until almost all the stock has evaporated. Place the contents of the pan into a blender with 50 g (1¾ oz) of butter and a pinch of sea salt and blend on high until very smooth, then pass the purée through a drum sieve. Put the artichoke purée aside.

Steam the Jerusalem artichokes for 10–15 minutes, or until tender but still firm. Peel away the skin with a sharp knife, then cover and refrigerate. To prepare the Chinese artichokes, scrub them with a clean green scourer. This is the best way to remove their fine skin and keep their shape. Rinse well and place them in a container of water with a little lemon juice. Keep them away from the light by wrapping the container in foil, as they oxidise quickly.

Roast the pine nuts and sunflower seeds on a baking tray in a 180°C (350°F/Gas 4) oven until golden. Put aside. Place the cheese in a bowl and lightly mash with a fork. Leave at room temperature.

to finish and plate

Using a temperature-controlled water bath set at 72°C (162°F), poach the lamb for 18–20 minutes. Meanwhile, shallow-fry the Jerusalem artichokes in the clarified butter until golden brown and heated through. Reheat the globe artichoke purée. Blanch the Chinese artichokes for 1 minute, then drain. Melt the remaining 100 g (3½ oz) of butter and brush it over the Chinese artichokes, then season with sea salt. Make a slit in the Jerusalem artichokes and place a teaspoon of the cheese inside. Sprinkle with pine nuts and sunflower seeds and top with two rosemary flowers.

Place the confit lamb loins on the serving plate, then place three Chinese artichokes on top with two sprigs of okra shoots. Place a cheese-filled Jerusalem artichoke next to the lamb, a spoonful of the artichoke purée topped with some nasturtium leaves, then a spoonful of the hops purée topped with a briefly blanched sprig of Warrigal greens. Serve immediately.

SERVES 8

crisp confit of rare breed pig belly with green lipped abalone and silken tofu

I created this dish in 2000 at De Beers restaurant at Whale Beach and it came with me to Quay in 2001. Its first conception was a crisp confit of pork belly with roasted sea scallops. This dish and the chocolate cake became my first signature dishes at Quay. The reviews I received for the pork belly and scallops were incredible, and the dish was soon replicated in restaurants all around Australia, so much so that in 2004 I decided it was time for it to evolve into something new, but I still wanted to maintain the essential essence of the dish. The pork belly is slowly braised in olive oil, cinnamon and star anise for 8 hours until it becomes meltingly tender. It is pressed overnight and then roasted in a hot pan, skin side down, so it becomes incredibly crisp. I decided to marry it with silken tofu and a gentle braise of green lipped abalone, shaved cuttlefish and Japanese mushrooms to provide an even greater textural contrast to the pork belly. This dish will remain one of my classics for a long time to come.

ingredients

250 ML (9 FL OZ/1 CUP) VIRGIN OLIVE OIL
1 CINNAMON STICK, CRUSHED
4 STAR ANISE
1 SMALL BONELESS PIG BELLY (ABOUT 1 KG/2 LB 4 OZ)
    FROM A 30 KG (66 LB) RARE BREED PIG (BERKSHIRE,
    LARGE BLACK OR OTHER TRADITIONAL BREED
    WITH GOOD FAT MARBLING)
1 X 500 G (1 LB 2 OZ) LIVE GREEN LIPPED ABALONE
COARSE SEA SALT
4 X 200 G (7 OZ) WHOLE CUTTLEFISH
500 ML (17 FL OZ/2 CUPS) GRAPESEED OIL
75 G (2½ OZ) PEELED GINGER, SLICED
75 G (2½ OZ) GREEN SPRING ONIONS (SCALLIONS),
    SLICED
1.5 LITRES (52 FL OZ/6 CUPS) CHICKEN STOCK
    (BASIC RECIPES, PAGE 262)
100 ML (3½ FL OZ) WHITE SOY SAUCE

50 G (1¾ OZ) JAPANESE GLUTINOUS RICE
200 G (7 OZ) SHIITAKE MUSHROOMS
100 G (3½ OZ) ENOKI MUSHROOMS
2 X 250 G (9 OZ) PACKETS GOOD QUALITY
    SILKEN TOFU
FINE SEA SALT
20 ML (½ FL OZ) SALT-REDUCED LIGHT SOY SAUCE
10 ML (¼ FL OZ) MIRIN
24 GARLIC CHIVE FLOWERS
1 PUNNET SPRING ONION (SCALLION) SHOOTS,
    TRIMMED

method

To cook the pork belly, start by gently heating the olive oil in a small saucepan to 70°C (155°F). Add the crushed cinnamon and star anise to the oil and heat for 10 minutes, maintaining the oil at 70°C (155°F). Remove the pan from the heat and allow to infuse for 2 hours. Strain the oil through a sieve lined with muslin cloth, discarding the cinnamon and star anise.

Place the pork belly in a large vacuum bag with the infused oil and seal in a vacuum sealer. Steam in a temperature-controlled combi oven at 90°C (195°F) for 12 hours. To achieve a similar result at home, you will need to use 2.5 litres (87 fl oz/10 cups) of infused oil in a very deep metal or ceramic container. Place the belly, skin side up, in the oil, ensuring it is completely submerged. You may need to weight the belly so it doesn't float in the oil (use a stainless-steel cake rack to achieve this). The belly will need to be cooked in a 90°C (195°F/Gas ¼) oven for a minimum of 8 hours.

Once the belly has finished cooking, it will be incredibly soft and tender. Allow to cool slightly.

Line two flat baking trays with plastic wrap and press the pork belly between them, weighted with a stack of plates. Place in the refrigerator overnight.

To prepare the live abalone, place them into an iced water bath for 20 minutes, then remove. Shuck the abalone using a large kitchen spoon. Remove all the organs and guts and, with a sharp pair of scissors, trim off the hard external lip. Lightly scrub the abalone meat with coarse sea salt under running water for 1 minute. Cut the abalone into the thinnest possible strips you can achieve. Next clean and remove the innards from the cuttlefish until you are left with flat strips of the body. Using a sharp knife, cut the cuttlefish into thin slivers. Refrigerate the seafood until required.

To make the ginger and spring onion infused oil, heat the grapeseed oil in a saucepan to 70°C (155°F). Add 25 g (1 oz) of ginger and 25 g (1 oz) of spring onion and heat for 10 minutes, maintaining the oil at 70°C (155°F). Remove the pan from the heat and allow to infuse for 2 hours. Strain the oil through a sieve lined with muslin cloth, discarding the ginger and spring onion. Put the infused grapeseed oil aside until needed.

To make a poaching liquid for the tofu, combine 500 ml (17 fl oz/2 cups) of chicken stock with 50 ml (1¾ fl oz) of white soy sauce. Put aside until needed.

To make the glaze for the pork belly, put the remaining ginger and spring onion in a pan with the remaining 1 litre (35 fl oz/4 cups) of chicken stock, the remaining 50 ml (1¾ fl oz) of white soy sauce and the glutinous rice. Slowly simmer for 30 minutes, or until the stock has reduced by half and the rice is overcooked. The rice will thicken the stock and give you a light natural glaze. Strain through a sieve lined with muslin cloth, reserving 500 ml (17 fl oz/2 cups) of the thickened chicken stock. Discard the solids. Pour the stock into a saucepan and reduce until you are left with 250 ml (9 fl oz/1 cup) of thick, glossy glaze. Put aside.

Slice the shiitake mushrooms into thin slivers and trim the stems of the enoki mushrooms.

to finish and plate

Preheat the oven to 200°C (400°F/Gas 6). Cut the pressed pork belly into 2.5 cm (1 inch) cubes; you will need 24 cubes. Carefully cut the silken tofu into 24 cubes, the same size as the pork belly. Use two large non-stick ovenproof frying pans. Start by heating the pans on the stovetop. Add a small amount of the infused grapeseed oil to each pan, making sure the pans are very hot. Season the pork belly with sea salt and add to the pans; seal all the sides of the pork belly, except the skin. Drain the oil from the pans and put the pork belly cubes back in the pans, skin side down. Place the pans in the oven for about 5 minutes, or until the skin becomes very crisp.

While this is happening, gently heat the tofu squares in the chicken stock and white soy mixture. Remove from the heat and leave the tofu in the liquid until required. Sauté the shiitake mushrooms in a little infused grapeseed oil until lightly browned, then finish the shiitake mushrooms with the soy sauce and mirin. Drain the mushrooms and keep warm. Braise the abalone and cuttlefish slices in the remaining infused grapeseed oil at about 80°C (175°F) for 1–2 minutes, or until they become opaque. Drain the abalone and cuttlefish and keep warm. Blanch the garlic chive flowers and spring onion shoots in boiling salted water for a few seconds. Remove and drain.

You can use a 10 cm (4 inch) diameter flat ring to assist in the assembly of this dish. Remove the hot tofu from the chicken stock with a slotted spoon and place three squares on each warmed plate. Place three of the hot crisp pork belly cubes on the plate. Put a chive flower and a strip of spring onion shoot on each piece of tofu. Place a small pile of shiitake mushrooms in the centre of each plate and strips of the shaved cuttlefish in between the pork belly and tofu squares. Place the slices of abalone on top of the shiitake mushrooms. Reheat the glaze for the pork belly and add the enoki mushrooms. Dress the pork belly and tofu squares with the glaze and enoki mushrooms, remove the circle rings if using, and serve immediately.

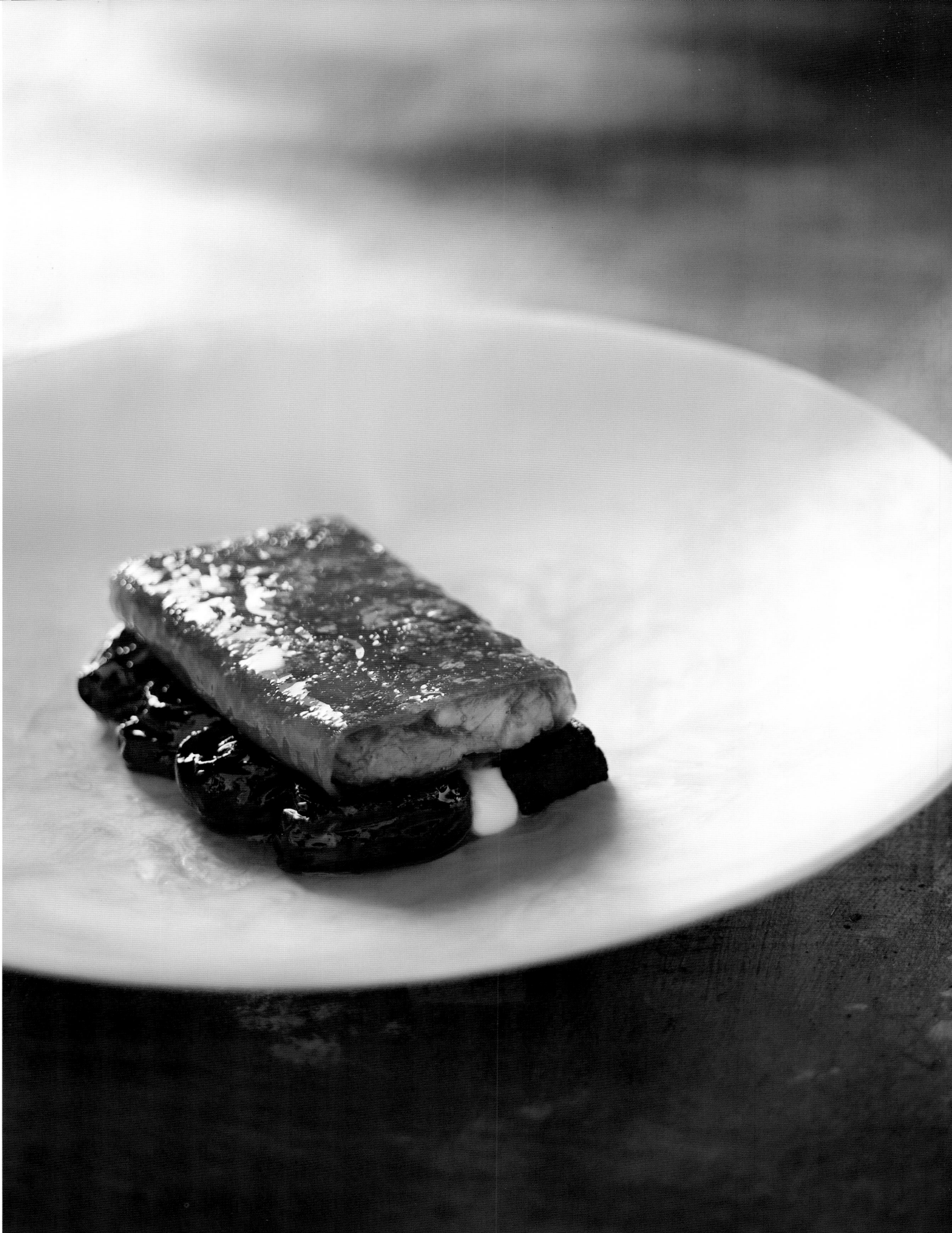

crisp pressed suckling pig with prunes, pedro ximénez sherry vinegar, black pudding and cauliflower cream

This is the same technique that I use for the duck recipe. The suckling pig is accompanied with bittersweet chocolate black pudding, cauliflower cream and macerated prunes — it's a rich, full-flavoured combination.

ingredients

1 WHOLE 10 KG (22 LB) SUCKLING PIG

1 KG (2 LB 4 OZ) PORK BACK FAT, RENDERED AND
    STRAINED TO GIVE 400 ML (14 FL OZ)

FINE SEA SALT

32 UNPITTED PRUNES

100 ML (3½ FL OZ) PEDRO XIMÉNEZ NOBLE SOUR
    VINEGAR

100 ML (3½ FL OZ) PEDRO XIMÉNEZ SHERRY

BITTERSWEET CHOCOLATE BLACK PUDDING
    (BASIC RECIPES, PAGE 268)

CAULIFLOWER CREAM (BASIC RECIPES, PAGE 264)

50 ML (1¾ FL OZ) GRAPESEED OIL

method

Remove the head from the suckling pig carcass and reserve for another use. Cut the rest of the pig into four, dividing it along the spine and then in half forequarter and hindquarter cuts. Place each quarter into a large vacuum bag with 100 ml (3½ fl oz) of the pork back fat spread evenly over each quarter, and seal in a vacuum sealer. Steam in a temperature-controlled combi oven at 70°C (155°F) for 24 hours.

When the pork has finished cooking, cool slightly, then carefully remove from the bags. You need to separate all of the skin from the flesh, being careful not to break the skin. The pork is so soft you can do this with your fingers. I suggest doing this while the pork is still warm, wearing two pairs of plastic gloves. Lay the skin on a flat board and use a blunt knife to scrape away as much fat as possible. The thinner you can get the skin, the crisper the result will be. Next remove all the flesh and fat from the bones. Gently flake the flesh apart using your fingers. Finely chop the soft rendered fat. You need one-third fat to two-thirds flesh. Mix the fat and flesh together well and season with sea salt.

You should have four good sections of thin unbroken skin. Trim the skin to form four rectangles, at least 20 cm (8 inches) long and 14 cm (5½ inches) wide. Place each piece of skin separately, skin side down, on a strip of plastic wrap, about 1 metre (40 inches) in length. Divide the meat into four equal portions. Place a portion of meat in the centre of the skin in a strip 7 cm (2¾ inches) wide, along the length of the skin. Wrap each edge of the skin so it meets in the centre and then tightly wrap the rectangles of pork in the plastic. Place each rectangle between two flat baking trays and weight evenly with a stack of plates. Refrigerate overnight to compress.

Place the prunes in a ceramic bowl and pour over 300 ml (10½ fl oz) of cold water. Leave to soften overnight. Place the prunes in a single layer in a large saucepan. Add the vinegar and sherry and any remaining soaking juices and cook the prunes over low heat for 10–15 minutes, then set aside to cool. Using a sharp knife, make a slit on the side of each prune and remove the stone, trying to keep the prunes as whole as possible. Return to the pan.

Prepare the bittersweet chocolate black pudding. When cool, slice into eight 10 x 2 cm (4 x ¾ inch) oblongs. Prepare the cauliflower purée for the cauliflower cream, and refrigerate until needed.

to finish and plate

Preheat the oven to 200°C (400°F/Gas 6). Remove the pork from the press. Unwrap the rectangles, trim each end so it is straight, then halve each rectangle to give eight smaller rectangles, about 10 cm (4 inches) long and 7 cm (2¾ inches) wide. Heat two non-stick ovenproof frying pans on the stovetop and add a little grapeseed oil to each pan. Add the pork rectangles to the pans and seal them, join side down, for 1 minute, carefully turn them over and immediately place the pans in the oven for 8 minutes. Remove the pans from the oven and carefully turn over the rectangles again; leave in the pan for 2 minutes off the heat. Meanwhile, to finish the cauliflower cream, whip the cream until soft peaks form. Reheat the cauliflower purée, then fold through the whipped cream. Reheat the prunes. Seal the black pudding strips in a hot non-stick frying pan with a little grapeseed oil for 30 seconds on each side. Place a line of cauliflower cream along the centre of each plate. Put a strip of black pudding next to the cream and then place four warmed prunes on the other side of the cream. Carefully place the pork on top of the cream and serve immediately.

SERVES 8

slow-braised pig cheek with celeriac cream and mushrooms

This is a relatively simple recipe for autumn. The earthy flavours of celeriac and mushrooms really complement the texture and flavour of the slow-braised pig cheeks.

ingredients

8 X 200 G (7 OZ) PIG CHEEKS
300 ML (10½ FL OZ) CHICKEN STOCK (BASIC RECIPES, PAGE 262)
500 ML (17 FL OZ/2 CUPS) REDUCED VEAL STOCK (GLAZE) (BASIC RECIPES, PAGE 263)
250 G (9 OZ) SHIITAKE MUSHROOMS
250 G (9 OZ) ENOKI MUSHROOMS
250 G (9 OZ) NAMEKO MUSHROOMS
200 ML (7 FL OZ) DRY VERMOUTH (NOILLY PRAT)
FINE SEA SALT
100 ML (3½ FL OZ) GRAPESEED OIL

method

Prepare the pig cheeks by trimming around the meaty part, leaving a 3 cm (1¼ inch) circumference of fat and skin around the meat. Bring a saucepan of water to the boil and blanch the pig cheeks in the boiling water for only 1 minute. Refresh in iced water and dry well. Place the pig cheeks into two vacuum bags, with 150 ml (5 fl oz) of chicken stock and 50 ml (1¾ fl oz) of veal glaze in each bag. Seal in a vacuum sealer and steam in a temperature-controlled combi oven at 85°C (185°F) for 10 hours. Alternatively, if cooking conventionally, you could use more chicken stock and veal glaze and braise the pig cheeks in a casserole dish with a lid in a 100°C (200°F/Gas ½) oven for 6 hours. Once the pig cheeks have cooked, allow to cool completely, then place them in the refrigerator until required.

Remove all the stalks from the shiitake, enoki and nameko mushrooms and put aside. Put the vermouth in a small saucepan and reduce it down to 30 ml (1 fl oz), then add the remaining 400 ml (14 fl oz) of veal glaze and put aside.

celeriac cream

4 FRENCH SHALLOTS, FINELY CHOPPED
2 WHITE CELERY STALKS (INNER STALKS), FINELY CHOPPED
1 GARLIC CLOVE, FINELY CHOPPED
200 G (7 OZ) UNSALTED BUTTER
1 HEAD CELERIAC
500 ML (17 FL OZ/2 CUPS) CHICKEN STOCK (BASIC RECIPES, PAGE 262)
FINE SEA SALT
150 ML (5 FL OZ) CREAM (35% FAT)

Sweat the shallots, celery and garlic in a frying pan with 100 g (3½ oz) of butter and sauté, being careful not to add any colour. Peel and dice the celeriac into 2 cm (¾ inch) cubes and add to the vegetables. Add the chicken stock and simmer gently until almost all the stock has evaporated. Place the contents of the pan into a blender and blend on high for 1 minute. Add the remaining 100 g (3½ oz) of butter and blend for a further minute. Pass the purée through a drum sieve. Taste and season with sea salt, then put aside.

to finish and plate

Preheat the oven to 180°C (350°F/Gas 4). Remove the pig cheeks from the bags and remove any jellied stock. Trim the cheeks, remove the skin and cut around the fat so that there is only 1 cm (½ inch) of fat surrounding and covering the top of the meat. Season the cheeks with sea salt. Heat 50 ml (1¾ fl oz) of grapeseed oil in an ovenproof saucepan and sauté the cheeks, fat side down, until golden brown. Remove the cheeks and the oil from the pan. Return the cheeks to the pan with 300 ml (10½ fl oz) of the vermouth-enriched veal glaze. Place the saucepan and cheeks into the oven and allow the cheeks to warm through for about 10 minutes.

To finish the celeriac cream, whip the cream until soft peaks form. Reheat the celeriac purée, then fold through the whipped cream. Sauté all the mushrooms in the remaining 50 ml (1¾ fl oz) of grapeseed oil. When the mushrooms are light brown, add the remaining vermouth-enriched veal glaze and reduce until the mushrooms are well glazed. Season with sea salt. Remove the cheeks from the oven and finish reducing the glaze on the stovetop. Spoon the glaze over the cheeks as you go, until the cheeks are well glazed.

Place a spoonful of celeriac cream in the centre of each serving plate and top with a glazed cheek. Place a couple of spoonfuls of mushrooms next to the cheek and serve immediately.

SERVES 8

slow-braised beef tendon with jersey milk curd, shaved truffle and oxtail consommé

This is a highly textural and quite sensual dish to eat. The delicate nature of the Jersey milk curd is an interesting counterpoint to the gelatinous texture of the beef tendon. Both, if prepared correctly, should melt in your mouth. The bittersweet chocolate black pudding earths the dish. All together this dish is a celebration of textures and flavours and is one of my favourites.

ingredients

16 SHORT BEEF TENDONS
1 LITRE (35 FL OZ/4 CUPS) REDUCED VEAL STOCK
    (DEMI-GLAZE) (BASIC RECIPES, PAGE 263)
BITTERSWEET CHOCOLATE BLACK PUDDING
    (BASIC RECIPES, PAGE 268)
2 X 50 G (1¾ OZ) BLACK WINTER TRUFFLES
200 ML (7 FL OZ) REDUCED VEAL STOCK (GLAZE),
    HEAVILY REDUCED (BASIC RECIPES, PAGE 263)
10 ML (¼ FL OZ) GRAPESEED OIL
16 PEA FLOWERS

JERSEY MILK CURD
400 ML (14 FL OZ) HOMOGENISED JERSEY MILK
FINE SEA SALT
2 ML (¹⁄₁₆ FL OZ) VEGETARIAN RENNET

method

To cook the beef tendons the way we do at Quay, place them in a large vacuum bag with the veal demi-glaze and seal in a vacuum sealer. Steam in a temperature-controlled combi oven at 85°C (185°F) for 12 hours. Alternatively, if cooking conventionally, you could use more veal demi-glaze and braise the beef tendons in a casserole dish with a lid in a 90°C (195°F/Gas ¼) oven for a similar time period. Regularly check the stock levels and top up as needed. When the tendons are cooked they should feel very soft. Remove them from the bag and trim away any surrounding meat. Cut each tendon into a 5 cm (2 inch) long cylinder and put aside.

Prepare the bittersweet chocolate black pudding. When completely cool, carefully remove from the bag and dice into 5 mm (¼ inch) cubes; you will need 240 cubes. There will be some black pudding leftover, which you can use elsewhere.

oxtail and prune consommé

1 WHOLE OXTAIL, CHOPPED INTO 2 CM (¾ INCH)
    THICK ROUNDS (ASK YOUR BUTCHER TO DO
    THIS FOR YOU)
20 ML (½ FL OZ) GRAPESEED OIL
1 ONION, DICED
2 CARROTS, DICED
2 WHITE CELERY STALKS (INNER STALKS), DICED
50 G (1¾ OZ) UNSALTED BUTTER
1 GARLIC CLOVE, SQUASHED
250 ML (9 FL OZ/1 CUP) OLOROSO SHERRY
15 UNPITTED PRUNES
3 LITRES (105 FL OZ/12 CUPS) CHICKEN STOCK
    (BASIC RECIPES, PAGE 262)
100 G (3½ OZ) CHICKEN BREAST MEAT
FINE SEA SALT
8 EGG WHITES

In a large pot, sauté the oxtail in grapeseed oil until well browned. Add half the onion, half the carrot, half the celery and the butter. Sauté until the vegetables are golden brown. Add the garlic and then deglaze with the sherry, scraping the bottom of the pot with a wooden spoon while deglazing.

Using a heavy knife or meat cleaver, chop the prunes directly through the stone into four pieces. You want the flavour of the prune stones as well as the prune flesh. Add the prunes to the pot, then add the chicken stock. Simmer for 2½ hours and only skim the stock at the very end of the cooking period, as you want the flavour of the browned butter to permeate through the stock. Strain the stock through a sieve lined with muslin cloth into a clean pot. Remove any surface fat with a ladle. Allow the stock to cool.

to finish and plate

Meanwhile, to make a raft for the consommé, put the chicken in a food processor. Add the remaining onion, carrot and celery and a pinch of salt and process until all the ingredients are finely chopped, then transfer to a bowl. In a separate bowl, lightly whisk the egg whites by hand until you have very soft peaks, then fold the egg whites through the processed chicken and vegetables.

Place the cooled stock in the pot over medium heat. Vigorously whisk the raft into the stock until well incorporated, stirring occasionally to make sure the raft is not sticking to the bottom of the pot. Allow the stock to come close to boiling point, then turn the heat down to the lowest possible setting; you want the stock to be barely simmering under the raft. Do not stir the raft again at this point. Cook on very low heat for 30 minutes. Make a hole in the raft to check that it is fully cooked and that the stock is clear, then cook for a further 10 minutes. The raft will clarify and enrich your stock.

Remove the pot from the heat and set aside for 20 minutes. Carefully ladle the consommé into a sieve lined with a double layer of muslin cloth, making sure you don't break up the raft too much. You should have a crystal clear, well-flavoured oxtail and prune consommé. Taste the consommé and add sea salt if needed.

Have eight warmed serving bowls ready. Cut the truffles into 96 thin slices using a truffle slicer or mandolin, then cut out rounds using 2 cm (¾ inch) and 3 cm (1¼ inch) round pastry cutters. Arrange the truffle discs on one side of the bowl, interchanging the smaller and larger discs to make an interesting pattern. Reserve eight small slices to go on top.

To prepare the Jersey milk curds, you will need eight small round-bottomed ceramic ramekins of at least 50 ml (1¾ fl oz) capacity. Warm the milk to 40°C (105°F) and season with sea salt to taste. Stir the milk with a spoon to create a whirlpool effect. This will ensure an even distribution of rennet. While the milk is swirling, use an eye dropper to drop the rennet into the milk. Immediately ladle the milk into the ramekins and place the ramekins in a warm part of the kitchen. The curd should set within 1 or 2 minutes.

Reheat the oxtail and prune consommé. Put the tendons in a saucepan with the reduced veal glaze and heat through. Seal the black pudding cubes in a hot non-stick frying pan with the grapeseed oil for 30 seconds on each side, then arrange the black pudding cubes at the edge of the truffles. Using a round soup spoon, carefully scoop out the Jersey milk curds and place one curd in the centre of each bowl. Top with a slice of truffle. Put two pieces of tendon next to the curd and top each tendon with a pea flower. Place the oxtail and prune consommé in a jug. Serve the dish to your guests and carefully pour a portion of consommé at the table.

masterstock chicken with jellyfish, scallop, eggplant and lily bud salad

A masterstock is a deeply flavoured stock used for poaching poultry and pork. It has its origins in Chinese cuisine and the word refers to the fact that the stock can go on forever; in fact, there are stocks in Chinese restaurants that have been passed on from generation to generation. The stock needs to be topped up with ingredients and used every day for this to happen, its flavour and intensity developing over the years. This is impossible to do at home, but you can make a stock with similar flavours using the ingredients given here. For this recipe, I've paired the masterstock chicken with a classic jellyfish salad. Don't be put off by the idea of eating jellyfish — it has virtually no flavour and is used more for its textural properties and for the fact that it absorbs the other flavours in the dish. It is available in Chinese supermarkets; all you need to do is simply rinse and soak the jellyfish in a couple of changes of water and it's ready to use. I add roasted sesame seeds, black fungi, enoki and shiitake mushrooms, along with lily buds and water chestnuts to the salad, and accompany the chicken with steamed eggplant and sea scallops. This salad is a real textural treat and makes a perfect summer first course.

ingredients

230 ML (7¾ FL OZ) GRAPESEED OIL

10 G (¼ OZ) PEELED GINGER, FINELY SLICED

10 G (¼ OZ) GREEN SPRING ONION (SCALLION), WHITE PART ONLY, FINELY SLICED

2 LARGE EGGPLANTS (AUBERGINES)

JUICE OF ½ LEMON

FINE SEA SALT

16 DEHYDRATED LILY BUDS

100 G (3½ OZ) PACKET SALTED DEHYDRATED JELLYFISH

100 G (3½ OZ) ENOKI MUSHROOMS

100 G (3½ OZ) BLACK FUNGI MUSHROOMS

100 G (3½ OZ) SHIITAKE MUSHROOMS

10 ML (¼ FL OZ) MIRIN

15 ML (½ FL OZ) SALT-REDUCED SOY SAUCE

4 FRESH WATER CHESTNUTS

1 PUNNET SPRING ONION (SCALLION) SHOOTS, TRIMMED

4 LARGE SEA SCALLOPS, WITHOUT ROE

50 ML (1¾ FL OZ) WHITE SOY SAUCE

1 PUNNET SHISO, TRIMMED

1 PUNNET BABY CORIANDER (CILANTRO), TRIMMED

2 TEASPOONS WHITE SESAME SEEDS, ROASTED

4 WASABI FLOWER HEADS

method

Heat 100 ml (3½ fl oz) of grapeseed oil in a small saucepan to 70°C (155°F). Add the ginger and spring onion and infuse over very low heat for 2 minutes. Strain the oil and discard the ginger and spring onions. This oil will be used to dress the salad just before serving.

Preheat the oven to 180°C (350°F/Gas 4). To prepare the eggplants, peel and cut them into quarters. Remove the seeds from each quarter and trim the flesh into an 8 x 3 cm (3¼ x 1¼ inch) baton. Combine the lemon juice and 100 ml (3½ fl oz) of grapeseed oil and brush the eggplant batons liberally with the oil and lemon mixture. Lightly season the eggplant batons with sea salt and wrap them into an airtight parcel with silicone paper. Bake the eggplant in the oven for 10–12 minutes, or until just tender. Refrigerate the eggplant until required.

Soak the lily buds in cold water for 1 hour, then peel away the outer leaves to expose the bright centre leaves. Drain and put aside until required. To prepare the jellyfish and remove the salt, soak in several changes of cold water, leaving them to soak for 10 minutes each time. Drain and put aside.

Trim the enoki so you are left with just the small caps. Break apart the black fungi mushrooms with your fingers and thinly slice the shiitake. Heat the remaining 30 ml (1 fl oz) of grapeseed oil in a frying pan and sauté the shiitake mushrooms until lightly browned. Add the enoki tops, mirin and salt-reduced soy sauce. Stir to combine, then add the black fungi mushrooms. Stir a couple of times, then transfer all the mushrooms and cooking juices to a plate and allow to cool.

Peel the water chestnuts and briefly blanch them in boiling water for 30 seconds. Refresh in iced water and then thinly slice on a mandolin. Briefly blanch the trimmed spring onion shoots in boiling water for 10 seconds and then refresh in iced water.

masterstock poached chicken

2 LITRES (70 FL OZ/8 CUPS) CHICKEN STOCK
   (BASIC RECIPES, PAGE 262)
3 LITRES (105 FL OZ/12 CUPS) WATER
1 LITRE (35 FL OZ/4 CUPS) SHAOXING RICE WINE
200 G (7 OZ) YELLOW ROCK SUGAR
200 ML (7 FL OZ) DARK SOY SAUCE
100 G (3½ OZ) PEELED GINGER, SLICED
1 BUNCH GREEN SPRING ONIONS (SCALLIONS),
   WHITE PART ONLY
5 STRIPS DRIED MANDARIN PEEL
5 STAR ANISE
3 GARLIC CLOVES
100 G (3½ OZ) CASSIA BARK
1 X 1.6 KG (3 LB 8 OZ) FREE-RANGE CHICKEN

To make the masterstock poaching liquid, combine all the ingredients, except the chicken, in a large pot. Bring to the boil, skimming the surface if necessary, then reduce the heat to very low and cook for 2 hours. Take the pot off the heat and strain the liquid through a sieve lined with muslin cloth. Discard the solids and return the liquid to a clean saucepan large enough to poach the chicken.

To prepare the chicken for poaching, remove the legs and reserve them for another use or to make a stock. Cut away the backbone, leaving the two breasts attached to the crown. Bring the masterstock to the boil and carefully lower the chicken breast crown into the masterstock, ensuring the chicken is completely submerged. Gently simmer for 12 minutes, then remove the pan from the heat and allow the chicken to cool in the pan at room temperature. When cool, refrigerate the chicken in the stock until required. (You could cook the chicken 1 day in advance.)

To assemble the salad, remove the chicken from the stock and cut the breasts from the bone. Peel the skin from the breasts and slice each diagonally into four. The chicken should be just cooked through and slightly pink in colour, but not fleshy.

to finish and plate

Slice each sea scallop into six thin slices. Briefly marinate the scallops in the white soy sauce for 5 seconds, then remove and drain on a clean kitchen cloth. Do this just before you are ready to assemble the dish.

Coat the sliced masterstock chicken with some ginger and spring onion oil. Lightly season with sea salt and place in the centre of each serving plate. Place an eggplant baton next to the chicken, leaving a small gap between them. Lightly dress the jellyfish, mushrooms, scallops, water chestnuts, lily buds and spring onion shoots with the ginger and spring onion oil, and lightly season. Arrange all the ingredients attractively between the chicken and the eggplant. Garnish with shiso leaves, coriander, roasted sesame seeds and wasabi flowers. Serve immediately.

SERVES 8

gently poached partridge breast with chestnuts, walnuts, truffle custard and mushroom consommé

This is one of my favourite winter dishes where the season for partridge, truffles and chestnuts fortuitously arrives at the same time. The combination of the tender partridge breasts, warm truffle custard, rich chestnut cream and the crunch of walnuts combine as a beautiful textural contrast and a marriage of great flavours.

ingredients

TRUFFLE CUSTARDS (BASIC RECIPES, PAGE 268)
4 X 500 G (1 LB 2 OZ) PARTRIDGES
3 LITRES (105 FL OZ/12 CUPS) CHICKEN STOCK
 (BASIC RECIPES, PAGE 262)
120 G (4¼ OZ) FINE SEA SALT
1 LITRE (35 FL OZ/4 CUPS) CLARIFIED BUTTER
 (BASIC RECIPES, PAGE 264)
¼ BROWN ONION, DICED
½ CARROT, DICED
½ WHITE CELERY STALK (INNER STALK), DICED
24 FRESH CHESTNUTS
16 FRESH WALNUTS
1 X 40 G (1½ OZ) BLACK WINTER TRUFFLE
16 FLOWERING PEA SHOOTS

method

Prepare the truffle custards and refrigerate. Prepare the partridges by removing the crowns (the two breasts on the bone) from the legs. Reserve the legs for the glaze. Heat 2 litres (70 fl oz/8 cups) of chicken stock with the sea salt (creating a brine) to 70°C (155°F). Place the four crowns of partridge in the hot brine and maintain the temperature at 70°C (155°F) for 20 minutes. Remove and allow the partridge crowns to cool. Cooking in this salted stock has the dual effect of perfectly seasoning and tenderising the meat. The breasts will be cooked to a perfect medium at this stage and will be reheated in clarified butter before serving. Refrigerate the partridge crowns until needed.

To make a partridge glaze, brown the partridge legs in a heavy-based saucepan with 50 ml (1¾ fl oz) of clarified butter. Add the onion, carrot and celery and sauté, then add the remaining 1 litre (35 fl oz/ 4 cups) of chicken stock and simmer slowly for 2 hours. Strain the stock into a small saucepan and reduce the liquid until you have 100 ml (3½ fl oz) of thick, glossy partridge glaze.

Score a cross in the top of each chestnut and steam for 15 minutes. While warm, peel the outer and inner skins of the chestnuts with a small knife. Put aside. Preheat the oven to 180°C (350°F/Gas 4). Shell the walnuts (you should have 32 halves), place on a baking tray and roast in the oven for 8–10 minutes. When cool enough to handle, use the point of a sharp knife to scrape away the skin, as the skin can be a little bitter.

chestnut cream

400 G (14 OZ) FRESH CHESTNUTS
4 FRENCH SHALLOTS, FINELY DICED
1 WHITE CELERY STALK (INNER STALK), FINELY DICED
1 GARLIC CLOVE, FINELY DICED
60 G (2¼ OZ) UNSALTED BUTTER
1 LITRE (35 FL OZ/4 CUPS) CHICKEN STOCK
 (BASIC RECIPES, PAGE 262)
50 ML (1¾ FL OZ) CREAM (35% FAT)

Preheat the oven to 160°C (315°F/Gas 2–3). Score a cross in the top of each chestnut, place on a baking tray and roast in the oven for 15 minutes; the chestnuts will begin to open. When cool enough to handle, peel the chestnuts. You should yield 200 g (7 oz) of peeled chestnuts.

Sweat the shallots, celery and garlic in a saucepan with 30 g (1 oz) of butter, being careful not to brown the vegetables. Add the chestnuts and chicken stock and simmer rapidly for 20–30 minutes until almost all the stock has evaporated, leaving behind very soft and slightly wet chestnuts.

Place the chestnuts and vegetables into a blender with any remaining liquid in the pan. Add the remaining 30 g (1 oz) of butter and blend on high to form a smooth purée. Return the chestnut purée to a small saucepan and put aside until needed.

chestnut mushroom consommé

500 G (1 LB 2 OZ) CHESTNUT MUSHROOMS
4 FRENCH SHALLOTS, DICED
2 CARROTS, DICED
2 WHITE CELERY STALKS (INNER STALKS), DICED
1 GARLIC CLOVE, DICED
100 G (3½ OZ) UNSALTED BUTTER
200 G (7 OZ) SHIITAKE MUSHROOMS
6 EGG WHITES
FINE SEA SALT

Preheat the oven to 70°C (155°F/Gas ¼). Line two baking trays with silicone paper, spread the chestnut mushrooms in a single layer on the trays and place in the oven for a minimum of 4 hours until the mushrooms are completely dry. This will intensify the flavour of the mushroom stock.

Sweat the shallots, half the carrot, half the celery and the garlic in a saucepan with the butter, being careful not to brown the vegetables. Add 2 litres (70 fl oz/8 cups) of water and bring to a rapid simmer. Add the dried mushrooms, reduce the heat and gently simmer for 4 hours. The liquid should reduce by half. Skim the surface well and remove any fat. Strain the mushroom stock through a sieve lined with muslin cloth into a clean pan and allow to cool.

Meanwhile, to make a raft for the consommé, put the shiitake mushrooms and remaining carrot and celery in a food processor, pulse for 30 seconds, then transfer to a bowl. In a separate bowl, lightly whisk the egg whites by hand until you have very soft peaks, then fold the egg whites through the processed vegetables.

Place the cooled stock in the pan over medium heat. Vigorously whisk the raft into the stock until well incorporated, stirring occasionally to make sure the raft is not sticking to the bottom of the pan. Allow the stock to come close to boiling point, then turn the heat down to the lowest possible setting; you want the stock to be barely simmering under the raft. Do not stir the raft again at this point. Cook on very low heat for 30 minutes. Make a hole in the raft to check that it is fully cooked and that the stock is clear, then cook for a further 10 minutes. The raft will clarify and enrich your stock.

Remove the pan from the heat and set aside for 20 minutes. Carefully ladle the consommé into a sieve lined with a double layer of muslin cloth, making sure you don't break up the raft too much. You should have about 600 ml (21 fl oz) of chestnut mushroom consommé. Taste the consommé and add sea salt if needed. This recipe will give you more than required, so enjoy the remaining consommé in another dish.

to finish and plate

Place the remaining 950 ml (32 fl oz) of clarified butter in a small pan and heat to 70°C (155°F). Remove the partridge breasts from the crowns with a sharp knife, leaving the skin on each breast. Submerge the breasts in the warmed clarified butter and maintain the heat at 70°C (155°F). The breasts will take 7–8 minutes to warm through and finish cooking. The butter imparts a beautiful flavour, as well as being a stable and dense cooking medium, so there is no dilution of flavour from the meat. At the same time, place the truffle custards in a steamer for 8–10 minutes, or until just set. Heat the partridge glaze and add the walnuts and chestnuts to the glaze to heat through. Reheat 350 ml (12 fl oz) of the chestnut mushroom consommé.

To finish the chestnut cream, whip the cream until soft peaks form. Reheat the chestnut purée, then fold through the whipped cream. Place a spoonful of chestnut cream in the centre of each serving bowl. Using a round soup spoon, carefully scoop out the truffle custard from each mould and place on the chestnut cream. Place three chestnuts and four walnuts around the custards. Remove the partridge from the clarified butter and peel the skin from the breasts. Place each breast on top of the custard. Slice eight thin slices of black truffle and place a slice on each breast. Spoon over 2 tablespoons of chestnut mushroom consommé and arrange two flowering pea shoots on either side of the breast. Serve immediately.

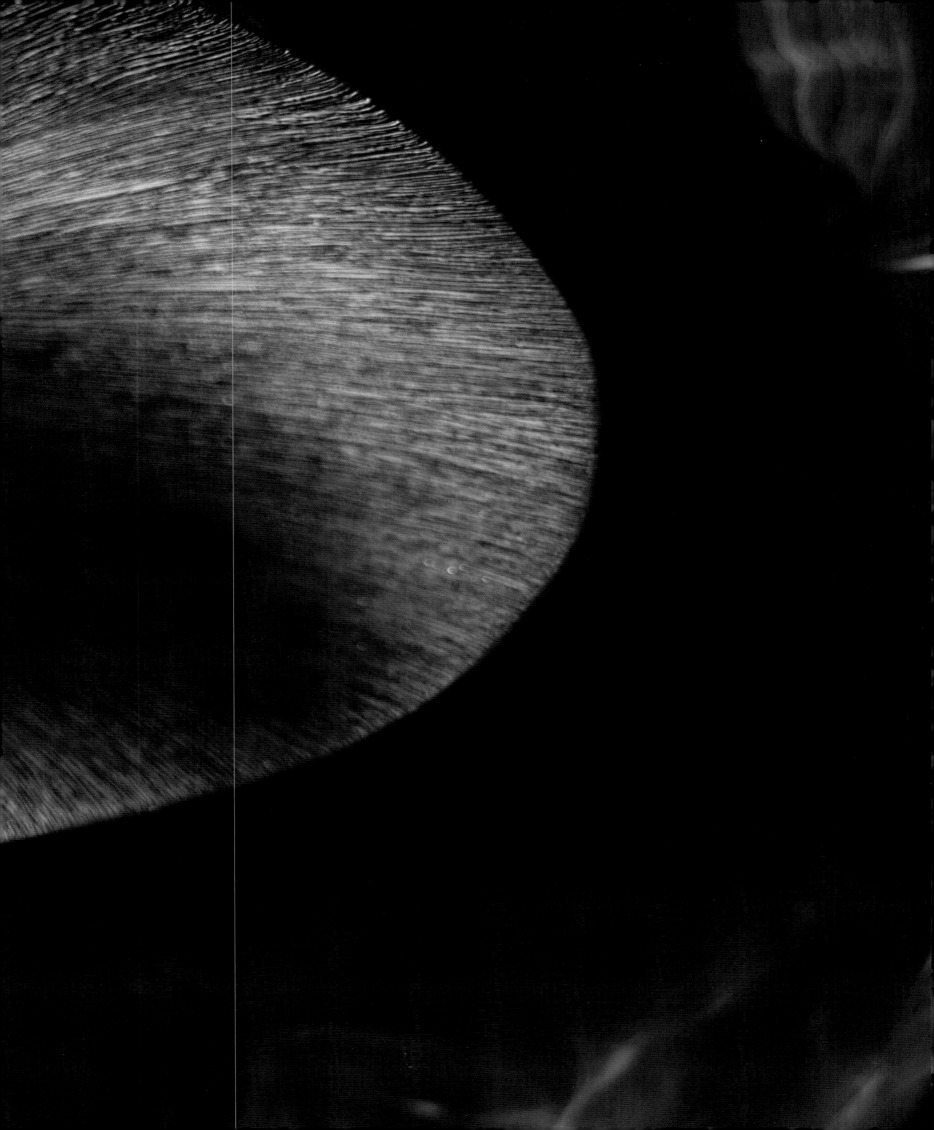

SERVES 8

crisp pressed cinnamon spiced duck confit

This is a technique I developed 10 years ago, where I'm able to serve a duck confit that is boneless and completely wrapped in its own crispy skin. The flavour of cinnamon marries beautifully with duck, and the use of vegetables and sea scallops provides a nice textural contrast. The sweetness of scallops works incredibly well with duck, taking inspiration from the Cantonese idea of serving seafood and meats together, and it's a combination I like to use in my cooking. The garlic scapes are a seasonal rarity, only available in late spring. They are the flower pods from hardneck, cool-climate garlic. They have a wonderful crisp texture and mild garlic flavour.

ingredients

2 X 2 KG (4 LB 8 OZ) PEKING DUCKS
8 LITRES (280 FL OZ) OLIVE OIL
1 CINNAMON STICK
FINE SEA SALT
32 BABY KABU (WHITE) TURNIPS
16 GARLIC SCAPES
1 YOUNG WINTER MELON OR HAIRY MELON,
    WITH SMALL SEEDS
2 STEMS HASUIMO
16 GARLIC CHIVE BUDS
16 SMALL BULB SPRING ONIONS (SCALLIONS)
4 HEADS OF VERY YOUNG GARLIC
50 ML (1¾ FL OZ) GRAPESEED OIL
8 LARGE SEA SCALLOPS, WITHOUT ROE

method

The Peking ducks are a breed of duck not to be confused with the roasted Chinese duck speciality. To prepare the ducks, make a slit in the neck and, with a bicycle pump, pump as much air into the duck as possible to try to release the duck skin from the flesh. You can also use a long metal spoon handle to release the skin from the flesh, being careful not to rip the skin. This process is important to help remove the skin from the duck once it is cooked. You can sometimes purchase ducks called pumpy ducks from Asian butchers, where this process has already been applied.

Preheat the oven to 110°C (225°F/Gas ½). Place the olive oil in a very large, deep baking tray, large enough to hold and submerge the two whole ducks. This recipe would be difficult to attempt in a domestic oven, as most domestic ovens won't accommodate such a large container. In the restaurant kitchen we use a large stainless-steel gastronorm container.

Remove the neck, wings and drumstick portion from the legs with a sharp knife. Place the body of the ducks, breast side up, in the oil so that the ducks are completely covered by the oil when pressed down. They will float on the oil. Put the ducks in the oven and cook for 2 hours, then carefully turn the ducks over and cook for a further 2½ hours. The oil should not boil at any stage (maintain the oil at about 90–95°C/195–203°F). The ducks will lightly brown all over and be very soft by the end of the cooking process. Carefully remove the baking tray of oil and ducks from the oven and cool at room temperature for 1 hour. Carefully remove the ducks from the oil.

Place the ducks on a large chopping board and, with a sharp knife, make an incision through the skin all around the side of the ducks. Using your hands, carefully peel off the top half of the skin and put aside. Turn the duck over and peel off the bottom half of the skin, being careful not to tear or rip the skin. Place the skins on a board and remove any fat or flesh that is still stuck to the skin. You should end up with four paper-thin pieces of duck skin. Square off the duck skin edges with a sharp knife, leaving yourself with four oblongs of duck skin, about 18 cm (7 inches) long and 12 cm (4½ cm) wide. Put the skins aside.

Grind the cinnamon stick into a fine powder using a spice grinder. Remove all of the flesh from the duck carcass. Shred the flesh with your fingers and season with sea salt and the powdered cinnamon. Add a little of the cooking oil to the duck flesh to moisten and form the duck flesh into four oblongs, 18 cm (7 inches) long, 4 cm (1½ inches) wide and about 2 cm (¾ inch) thick.

Roll out a long wide sheet of plastic wrap, place one duck skin at the closest end of the plastic wrap, skin side down. Place an oblong of the duck flesh in the middle and fold the duck skin to form a parcel. Carefully wrap up the duck parcel tightly, fold over the ends of the plastic wrap and continue to roll until you have achieved 5 to 6 layers of plastic wrap. Repeat this process with all the duck skins. You will have four tightly wrapped duck oblongs. Place the ducks between two flat baking trays and weight with a stack of plates. Place the duck press in the refrigerator so the ducks sit under weight for a minimum of 6 hours.

duck and garlic juices

1 KG (2 LB 4 OZ) DUCK BONES
500 G (1 B 2 OZ) CHICKEN WINGS
100 ML (3½ FL OZ) GRAPESEED OIL
1 SMALL BROWN ONION, DICED
1 CARROT, DICED
2 WHITE CELERY STALKS (INNER STALKS), DICED
8 MATURE SMALL GARLIC CLOVES, SLICED
250 ML (9 FL OZ/1 CUP) DRY SAKE
1 LITRE (35 FL OZ/4 CUPS) CHICKEN STOCK
   (BASIC RECIPES, PAGE 262)
3 G (¹⁄₁₀ OZ) XANTANA (FERMENTED CORN STARCH)
30 ML (1 FL OZ) WHITE SOY SAUCE
FINE SEA SALT

Prepare the vegetables. Peel and halve the baby turnips and trim the garlic scapes. Peel the winter melon and slice into 1 cm (½ inch) thick slices. Using a 2 cm (¾ inch) round pastry cutter, cut out 24 discs from the winter melon. Peel the hasuimo and slice diagonally into 1 cm (½ inch) thick slices. Trim the chive buds so they are about 4 cm (1½ inches) in length. Peel and halve the bulb spring onions. Peel and separate the heads of garlic to give you 24 small garlic cloves. Blanch the garlic cloves in two changes of boiling salted water for 1 minute each time.

To make the duck and garlic juices, sauté the duck bones and chicken wings together in a heavy-based pan with the grapeseed oil. When the bones are lightly browned, add the onion, carrot, celery and garlic. Lightly brown the vegetables and then deglaze with the sake. Allow the sake to reduce almost completely, then add the chicken stock and 1 litre (35 fl oz/4 cups) of water. Slowly simmer and skim the stock for 2½ hours. Strain the stock through a sieve lined with a double layer of muslin cloth. Remove any fat from the surface.

Return the stock to a small saucepan and reduce the liquid until you have 500 ml (17 fl oz/2 cups) remaining. Whisk in the xantana, whisking until the liquid is lightly thickened, then season with the white soy sauce. Taste and season with sea salt if required. Put the duck and garlic juices aside until needed.

to finish and plate

Preheat the oven to 240°C (475°F/Gas 8). Unwrap the duck parcels and trim each end with a sharp knife. Cut each parcel in half to give you eight portions of duck. Heat two large non-stick ovenproof frying pans on the stovetop and add 25 ml (1 fl oz) of grapeseed oil to each. When the pans are very hot, add the duck portions and seal them, join side down, for 1 minute until golden brown. Turn the ducks over with a spatula, then place the frying pans into the oven for 5–6 minutes. Remove the pans from the oven and mop up any released oil with kitchen paper. Turn the ducks over — the skins should feel very crisp and be a deep golden brown colour. If not, turn the ducks back over and return the pans to the hot oven for a few more minutes.

While the ducks are cooking, blanch the vegetables in a large pan of boiling salted water until tender. Add the turnips and spring onions first, followed by the winter melon. Lastly, add the hasuimo, garlic scapes, garlic cloves and garlic chives. Strain all the vegetables into a colander. Reheat the duck and garlic juices in a small saucepan. Cut the scallops in half horizontally. Add the scallops to the duck and garlic juices and poach for 1 minute, then add all the vegetables and coat well with the thickened juices.

Using a slotted spoon, divide the scallops and vegetables among eight serving bowls. Top them with a spoonful of the juices, place the crisp duck on top and serve immediately.

SERVES 8

free-range chicken with truffle and early spring vegetables

This dish is my interpretation of the French classic, 'chicken in half mourning'. I make this dish in very early spring when there are fresh truffles still available, but you could use preserved truffles or even some preserved truffle butter instead. I like to serve this chicken with radishes, peas and onions, but you can use any spring vegetables you like.

ingredients

2 X 50 G (1¾ OZ) BLACK WINTER TRUFFLES
275 G (9¾ OZ) UNSALTED BUTTER
FINE SEA SALT
4 X 1.6 KG (3 LB 8 OZ) FREE-RANGE CHICKENS
GARLIC CREAM (BASIC RECIPES, PAGE 265)
250 G (9 OZ) FRESH PEAS IN THE POD
8 PERENNIAL LEEKS
8 RED MARBLE ONIONS
8 GREEN SPRING ONIONS (SCALLIONS)
8 RED KALE LEAVES
½ SMALL SAVOY CABBAGE
16 SMALL CHERRY BELLE RADISHES, LEAVES INTACT
12 SMALL CHERRY BELLE RADISHES, EXTRA, TRIMMED
    AND HALVED
32 SMALL FRENCH BREAKFAST RADISHES, LEAVES
    REMOVED
24 PEA FLOWERS
8 FLOWERING PEA SHOOTS

method

Scrub the truffles with a brush and wipe with a cloth to remove any traces of dirt. Peel the truffles with a sharp knife. You can use the peelings in a truffle stock or infuse in an oil (keep the oil in the fridge and use within 2 weeks). Finely grate 30 g (1 oz) of truffle using a microplane and add to 225 g (8 oz) of butter. Season with sea salt and put aside.

To prepare the chickens, place a chicken on a chopping board with the backbone facing up. With a sharp knife, cut the skin lengthways down the backbone. Using your hands, gently ease the skin from the chicken, going around the legs first and pulling the skin to the top of each leg. Cut the skin from the leg with a knife, leaving only the smallest hole. Using your fingers, continue to remove the skin from around the breast and pull back the breast until you reach the wing tips. Pull the skin back over the wing tips as far as possible, using a knife to cut and release the skin from the wing tips. Reserve the skin, then remove the breasts from the bird and reserve. The rest of the carcass and legs can be used to make a chicken stock if you like. Repeat for each bird.

Spread the chicken skin out on a flat board, skin side down. Trim the skin into a large oblong, cutting off any rough edges. You should have an oblong about 30 x 24 cm (12 x 9½ inches). Remove any excess fat from the skin with a knife, being very careful not to break the skin. Spread out a length of plastic wrap on the work surface, about 70 cm (27½ inches) long and 45 cm (17½ inches) wide. Remove the chicken skin from the board and place it on top of the plastic, up from the bottom edge, skin side down. Slice eight thin slices of truffle and arrange two rows of truffles across the top two-thirds of the skin. Place two chicken breasts horizontally on top of the truffles, with the two points of the chicken breasts overlapping slightly in the centre to give an even thickness. Open up the fillet on each breast and use a knife to make a small incision down the length of each breast, being careful not to cut through the breast. Place 30 g (1 oz) of softened truffle butter down the length of each incision and fold the fillets over the butter. Roll the chicken breasts in its skin until it is rolled into a cylinder. The sliced truffle should now be showing through the thin skin. Next, tightly roll the chicken in the plastic wrap, to give you at least three layers of plastic around the chicken. Tighten each end of the excess plastic by holding it as you roll to form a sausage shape. Now roll in a second layer of plastic wrap just as you have done before. Tie a tight knot in each end of the plastic. Your chicken should now be watertight. Repeat this process for each chicken and refrigerate for a minimum of 4 hours before cooking.

Meanwhile, make the garlic cream and put aside until needed. Shell the peas and trim the leeks, onions, kale and cabbage ready for blanching.

to finish and plate

Using a temperature-controlled water bath set at 68°C (154°F), submerge the chicken cylinders and cook for 40 minutes, then remove and put aside for 5 minutes. Meanwhile, reheat the garlic cream by whisking over low heat, adding some extra milk if necessary. Cook all the vegetables in boiling salted water, starting with the leeks and onions, then the radishes, peas, cabbage and kale. Cook until tender, then drain. Melt the remaining 50 g (1¾ oz) of butter and brush it over the vegetables, then season with sea salt. Remove each chicken from its plastic wrap, trim the ends and slice into four. Check that the chicken is cooked sufficiently; flash the chicken in a medium oven if necessary. Arrange two slices of chicken, some vegetables and garlic cream on each serving plate. Top each chicken slice with one additional slice of truffle and place smaller pieces of truffle around the plate. Garnish with the pea flowers and shoots. Serve immediately.

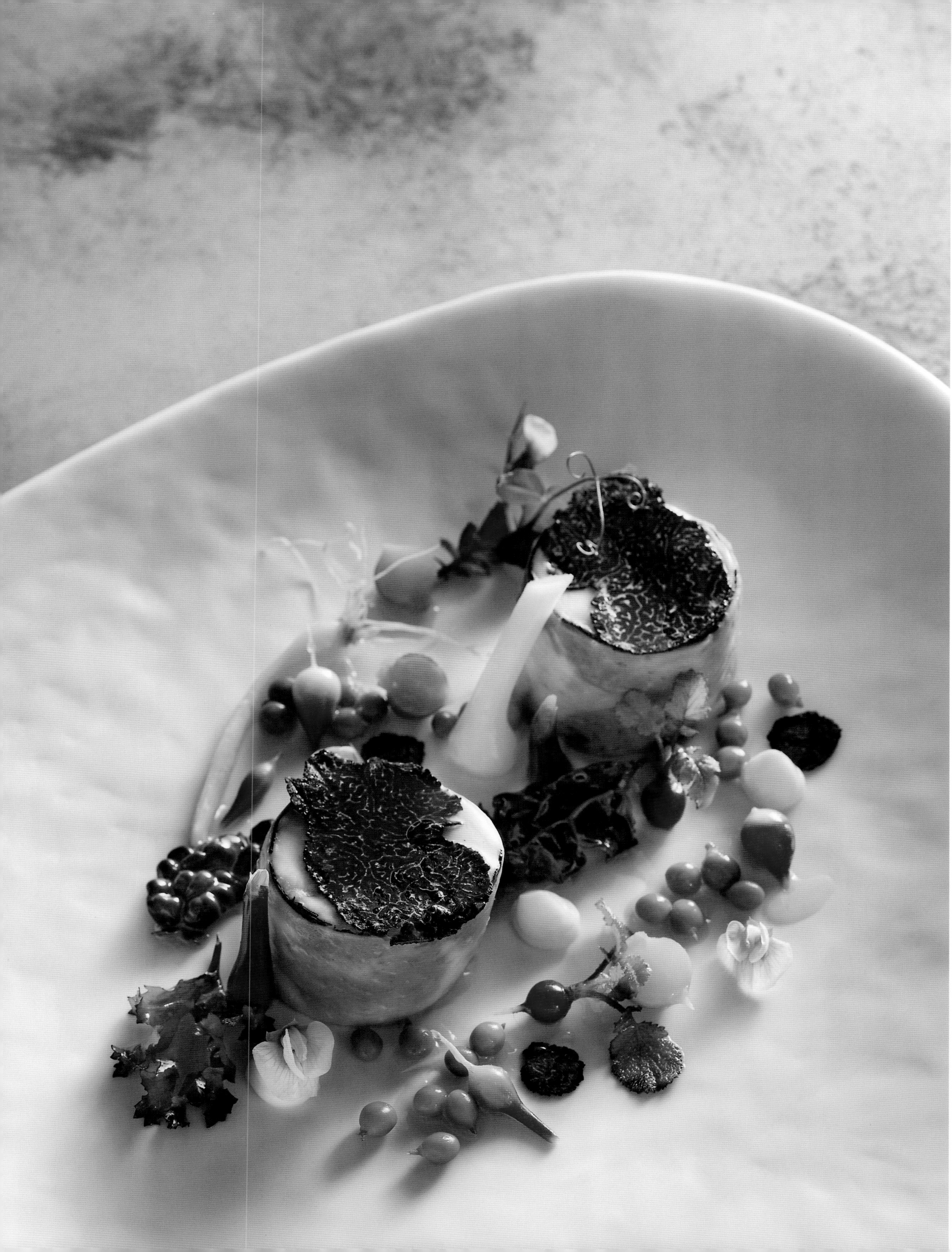

SERVES 8

confit of suffolk lamb loin with sheep's milk curd and spring vegetables

The cooking of the lamb for this recipe I refer to as confit because it is cooked in its own rendered fat, sous-vide style. The result is a very flavoursome and tender piece of lamb. It's served with spring vegetables, including Egyptian walking onions, which are an unusual variety of onion. They form bulbs on the top of the onion greens, the weight of the bulb forces the onion to bend and eventually replant itself, hence its unusual name. The white broad beans are produced by placing a small black plastic bag around each bean pod for the last 10 days of growing. This is something that I have experimented with in my own garden. It is quite a labour-intensive process and you won't find them available commercially, so you will need to grow your own or just use green broad beans instead. I like to use the blanched white broad beans in this dish for their rarity and because they are extremely tender.

ingredients

JUICE OF ½ LEMON
100 ML (3½ FL OZ) WHITE WINE
120 ML (4 FL OZ) EXTRA VIRGIN OLIVE OIL
½ ONION, FINELY CHOPPED
½ CARROT, FINELY CHOPPED
2 BAY LEAVES
2 SPRIGS THYME
5 GLOBE ARTICHOKES
4 FRENCH SHALLOTS, FINELY DICED
1 WHITE CELERY STALK (INNER STALK),
    FINELY DICED
1 GARLIC CLOVE, FINELY DICED
500 ML (17 FL OZ/2 CUPS) CHICKEN STOCK
    (BASIC RECIPES, PAGE 262)
100 G (3½ OZ) UNSALTED BUTTER
FINE SEA SALT
4 X 8-BONE SUFFOLK LAMB RACKS, WITH CAP ON
24 ASPARAGUS SPEARS

4 PODS BLANCHED BROAD (FAVA) BEANS
16 EGYPTIAN WALKING ONIONS
8 BULB SPRING ONIONS (SCALLIONS)
16 BABY LEEKS
24 BABY WHITE TURNIPS
8 CELERY FLOWER HEADS
8 PARSLEY FLOWER HEADS
200 ML (7 FL OZ) REDUCED LAMB STOCK (GLAZE)
    (BASIC RECIPES, PAGE 263)
16 HAZELNUTS, ROASTED
50 G (1¾ OZ) PINE NUTS, ROASTED
50 G (1¾ OZ) SUNFLOWER SEEDS, ROASTED
10 G (¼ OZ) PUFFED QUINOA
50 ML (1¾ FL OZ) CLARIFIED BROWN BUTTER
    (BASIC RECIPES, PAGE 264)
100 ML (3½ FL OZ) CREAM (35% FAT)
8 NASTURTIUM LEAVES
8 FLOWERING PEA SHOOTS

method

To cook the artichokes, first prepare the cooking liquid. Place the lemon juice, white wine, 100 ml (3½ fl oz) of olive oil and 1 litre (35 fl oz/4 cups) of water in a saucepan. Add the onion, carrot, bay leaves and thyme and bring the liquid to the boil. There are two ways you can cook the artichokes. You can peel the artichokes and strip back the outside leaves to expose the heart, then poach them in the liquid for 10–15 minutes (you will need to cover them with silicone paper). Alternatively, you can prepare this cooking liquid using only 250 ml (9 fl oz/1 cup) of water and place it in a vacuum bag with the peeled artichokes. Seal in a vacuum sealer and steam in a temperature-controlled combi oven at 90°C (195°F) for 10–12 minutes. Once the artichokes are tender, split them in half and remove the choke.

Sweat the shallots, celery and garlic in a pan with the remaining 20 ml (½ fl oz) of olive oil, being careful not to brown the vegetables. Add the cooked artichokes and chicken stock. Simmer for 15 minutes until almost all the liquid has evaporated. Place the contents of the saucepan into a blender and add 50 g (1¾ oz) of butter. Blend on high until smooth, then pass the purée through a drum sieve. Season to taste with sea salt and put aside.

To prepare the lamb, remove the fat cap with a sharp knife. Remove the meat from the bone and completely remove the sinew from the meat. Cut each piece of meat in half to yield eight equal

sheep's milk curd

**400 ML (14 FL OZ) SHEEP'S MILK (OR USE
HOMOGENISED JERSEY COW'S MILK)
FINE SEA SALT
2 ML (¹⁄₁₆ FL OZ) VEGETARIAN RENNET
10 ML (¼ FL OZ) STILL MINERAL WATER**

To make the sheep's milk curd, you will need eight
small round-bottomed ceramic ramekins of at least
50 ml (1¾ fl oz) capacity. Warm the milk to 40°C
(105°F) and season with sea salt to taste. Mix the
rennet and the mineral water together. Stir the milk
with a spoon to create a whirlpool effect, then add
the rennet and water to the swirling milk. This will
ensure an even distribution of rennet. Immediately
ladle the milk into the ramekins. The milk will only
take 1 or 2 minutes to completely set and it should
be stable and remain warm for a good 5–10 minutes
in the ramekins. Keep the ramekins in a warm part of
the kitchen.

to finish and plate

portions. Place the meat in the refrigerator. Render
down all the fat from the cap of the lamb rack in
a small saucepan over low heat. When the fat is
completely melted, pass it through a fine sieve and
allow the fat to cool slightly. Remove the lamb from
the refrigerator and coat each piece of meat with the
rendered lamb fat. The lamb fat should solidify on
the cold meat. Place the meat in one large vacuum
bag and seal. Refrigerate the lamb until required.

Peel the asparagus and cut the tips off at about
4–5 cm (1½–2 inches) in length. Reserve the rest
of the asparagus for another use. Pod the broad
beans, blanch them in boiling water for 30 seconds,
then refresh in iced water. Remove the outer shell
to expose the tender inner beans. Trim the walking
onions, leaving the green shoots on. Trim and peel
the spring onions and baby leeks. Remove the green
leaves from the baby turnips, leaving 5 mm (¼ inch)
of stem, and rub the skin with the edge of a sharp
knife. Put the vegetables aside until required.

Prepare the celery and parsley flower heads by
removing the flowers and immature seeds from the
stalks. Discard the stalks.

Using a temperature-controlled water bath set
at 65°C (149°F), submerge the lamb in the water and,
depending on the thickness of the loins, cook them
for 20–25 minutes to produce an even medium-rare.

Prepare a pan of boiling salted water. Blanch all the vegetables, starting with the onions, then the turnips,
asparagus and leeks. The vegetables will need about 2 minutes; add the double shelled broad beans in the
last 5 seconds, then drain. Melt the remaining 50 g (1¾ oz) of butter and brush it over the vegetables, then
season with sea salt and keep warm.

Preheat the oven to 180°C (350°F/Gas 4). Remove the lamb from the water bath. Cut open the vacuum
bags and place the loins on a baking tray lined with silicone paper. Season with sea salt. Coat the lamb loins
with the lamb glaze and flash in the oven for 1 minute. Warm the roasted hazelnuts, pine nuts, sunflower
seeds and puffed quinoa in a small saucepan with the brown butter.

To finish the artichoke cream, whip the cream until soft peaks form. Reheat the artichoke purée, then
fold through the whipped cream. Place a small amount of artichoke cream in the centre of each plate and
place a lamb loin in the centre of the cream. Garnish with the seasoned vegetables and nut mixture. With a
round soup spoon, scoop out each individual sheep's milk curd and place it on top of the lamb. Sprinkle each
curd with the celery and parsley flowers. Garnish with nasturtium leaves and flowering pea shoots, and serve.

SERVES 8

slow-cooked quail breasts with truffle custard, black pudding, pink turnips and milk skin

This is a complex first course. The quail breasts go through two cooking methods: they are poached in a salted stock to tenderise and season, and then finished in butter to impart flavour. The addition of the truffle, morels and black pudding give the dish a distinctive earthy tone. The sweetness of the marble onions and pink turnips balances the dish.

ingredients

BITTERSWEET CHOCOLATE BLACK PUDDING
    (BASIC RECIPES, PAGE 268)
TRUFFLE CUSTARDS (BASIC RECIPES, PAGE 268)
8 LARGE QUAILS
50 G (1¾ OZ) FINE SEA SALT
1.5 LITRES (52 FL OZ/6 CUPS) CHICKEN STOCK
    (BASIC RECIPES, PAGE 262)
1 LITRE (35 FL OZ/4 CUPS) HOMOGENISED
    JERSEY MILK
32 PINK TURNIPS
48 RED MARBLE ONIONS
1 LITRE (35 FL OZ/4 CUPS) CLARIFIED BUTTER
    (BASIC RECIPES, PAGE 264)
20 ML (½ FL OZ) GRAPESEED OIL
20 G (¾ OZ) UNSALTED BUTTER
FINE SEA SALT
24 RADISH FLOWERS

method

Prepare the bittersweet chocolate black pudding. When completely cool, carefully remove from the bag and cut into eight 3 cm (1¼ inch) squares and put aside. You will have some black pudding leftover, which you can use elsewhere. Prepare the truffle custards and refrigerate until needed.

To prepare the quails, remove the legs, wings and necks, leaving the breasts on the bone. You can use the legs, wings and necks for the quail glaze.

Add the sea salt to the chicken stock. This will make a type of brine to cook the quail in, which has the dual effect of tenderising and seasoning the breast meat. Heat the salted stock to 70°C (155°F) and maintain this temperature. Submerge the quail breasts in the stock and cook for 10 minutes, then remove and allow to cool at room temperature for 10 minutes. Refrigerate the quail. You can freeze the salted stock to use again within a month or discard the stock. The quail breasts will be medium-rare at this stage and will finish cooking in clarified butter. This is a two-stage cooking method.

To make the milk skin, put 500 ml (17 fl oz/2 cups) of milk in a large saucepan. Heat the milk until it just reaches boiling point, then remove the pan from the heat and allow to sit for 15 minutes. The milk will form a natural skin on top. Release the milk skin from around the edge of the pan with a sharp knife. Carefully grab the edge of the skin with your fingers and peel it away, lifting it from the surface. Place the milk skin flat on a baking tray lined with lightly oiled silicone paper. Reheat the milk to repeat the process once more, then discard the milk. Heat the remaining 500 ml (17 fl oz/2 cups) of milk and repeat the process

twice more. Dry the milk skins in a very low oven, 50°C (120°F/Gas ¼), for 1–2 hours until the milk skins curl and are crisp. Remove from the oven and cool at room temperature, then store in an airtight container with moisture-absorbing beads.

Peel the pink turnips and cut eight of them in half. Slice another eight of them into 3 mm (⅛ inch) slices and leave the rest of them whole. Peel one layer from the red marble onions and trim the stalk so there is only 5 mm (¼ inch) above the bulb, then remove the root of the onion.

quail and sherry glaze

500 G (1 LB 2 OZ) QUAIL BONES (CARCASSES
    AND LEGS)
15 ML (½ FL OZ) GRAPESEED OIL
70 G (1¾ OZ) UNSALTED BUTTER
1 CARROT, CHOPPED
1 WHITE CELERY STALK (INNER STALK), CHOPPED
½ BROWN ONION, DICED
1 GARLIC CLOVE, DICED
300 ML (10½ FL OZ) DRY OLOROSO SHERRY
2 LITRES (70 FL OZ/8 CUPS) CHICKEN STOCK
    (BASIC RECIPES, PAGE 262)

Sauté the quail bones in a heavy-based pan in the grapeseed oil and 50 g (1¾ oz) of butter until golden brown. Add the carrot, celery, onion and garlic and continue to sauté for 2 minutes. Deglaze with the sherry and continue to cook until almost all the sherry has evaporated. Add the chicken stock and simmer over low heat for 2 hours.

Pour the stock through a fine sieve and remove any fat from the surface with a ladle. Reserve 300 ml (10½ fl oz) of the quail stock (to use for the morel and white lentils). Return the rest of the stock to a clean saucepan and reduce the liquid until a thick glaze is formed. Whisk in the remaining 20 g (¾ oz) of butter towards the end of the reducing process. Refrigerate the quail and sherry glaze until required.

morels and white lentils

20 DRIED MORELS
40 G (1½ OZ) UNSALTED BUTTER, SOFTENED
2 FRENCH SHALLOTS, FINELY CHOPPED
½ GARLIC CLOVE, FINELY CHOPPED
100 G (3½ OZ) WHITE LENTILS (URID DAHL), RINSED
    AND DRAINED
FINE SEA SALT

Soak the morels in 250 ml (9 fl oz/1 cup) of warm water for at least 1 hour. Strain the morel soaking liquid through a sieve lined with a double layer of muslin cloth, reserving the liquid. Transfer the strained liquid to a small saucepan and reduce over high heat until you have 10 ml (¼ fl oz) of liquid remaining. Reserve the reduced liquid. This liquid contains the majority of the flavour of the morels.

Thoroughly wash the morels in five or six changes of cold water. Mix the morels vigorously with your hands each time, as the morels contain lots of fine dirt. Cut the morels in half and remove and discard the stems. Resoak the morels one last time, then drain and squeeze out as much water as possible. Finely chop the morels and place in a bowl. Add the reduced morel liquid and mix thoroughly. Refrigerate the morels until required.

Heat 20 g (¾ oz) of butter in a small saucepan over low–medium heat. Add the shallots and garlic and sauté until translucent, then add the lentils and stir thoroughly. Add the 300 ml (10½ fl oz) of reserved quail stock to the lentils, then cover the lentils with a piece of silicone paper. Cook over low heat for 10–15 minutes, or until all the liquid has absorbed. Stir the lentils and add the chopped morels and the remaining 20 g (¾ oz) of butter. Season to taste with sea salt and reserve the lentils until required.

to finish and plate

Remove the quail breasts from the bone using a sharp knife, leaving the skin attached. Heat the clarified butter in a saucepan until it reaches 68°C (154°F), and maintain this temperature. Add the quail breasts to the pan and poach for about 6 minutes. In the meantime, place the truffle custards in a steamer for 8–10 minutes, or until just set. Reheat the lentil and morel mixture. Reheat the quail and sherry glaze. Seal the black pudding squares in a hot non-stick frying pan with the grapeseed oil for 30 seconds on each side.

Blanch the turnips and red marble onions in a saucepan of boiling salted water for 2 minutes, then drain. Melt the butter and brush it over the turnips and onions, season with sea salt and keep warm. Remove the quail breasts from the butter, peel away the skin and spoon the quail and sherry glaze over the breasts. Unwrap the truffle custards and, using a round soup spoon, scoop the custard from the moulds and place in the centre of each warmed serving bowl. Top the custard with two quail breasts and place a spoonful of the morel and lentil mixture to the side. Divide the turnips and onions among the bowls and arrange them on top of the lentils. Place one square of black pudding on each dish and garnish with some curls of milk skin and radish flowers. Serve immediately.

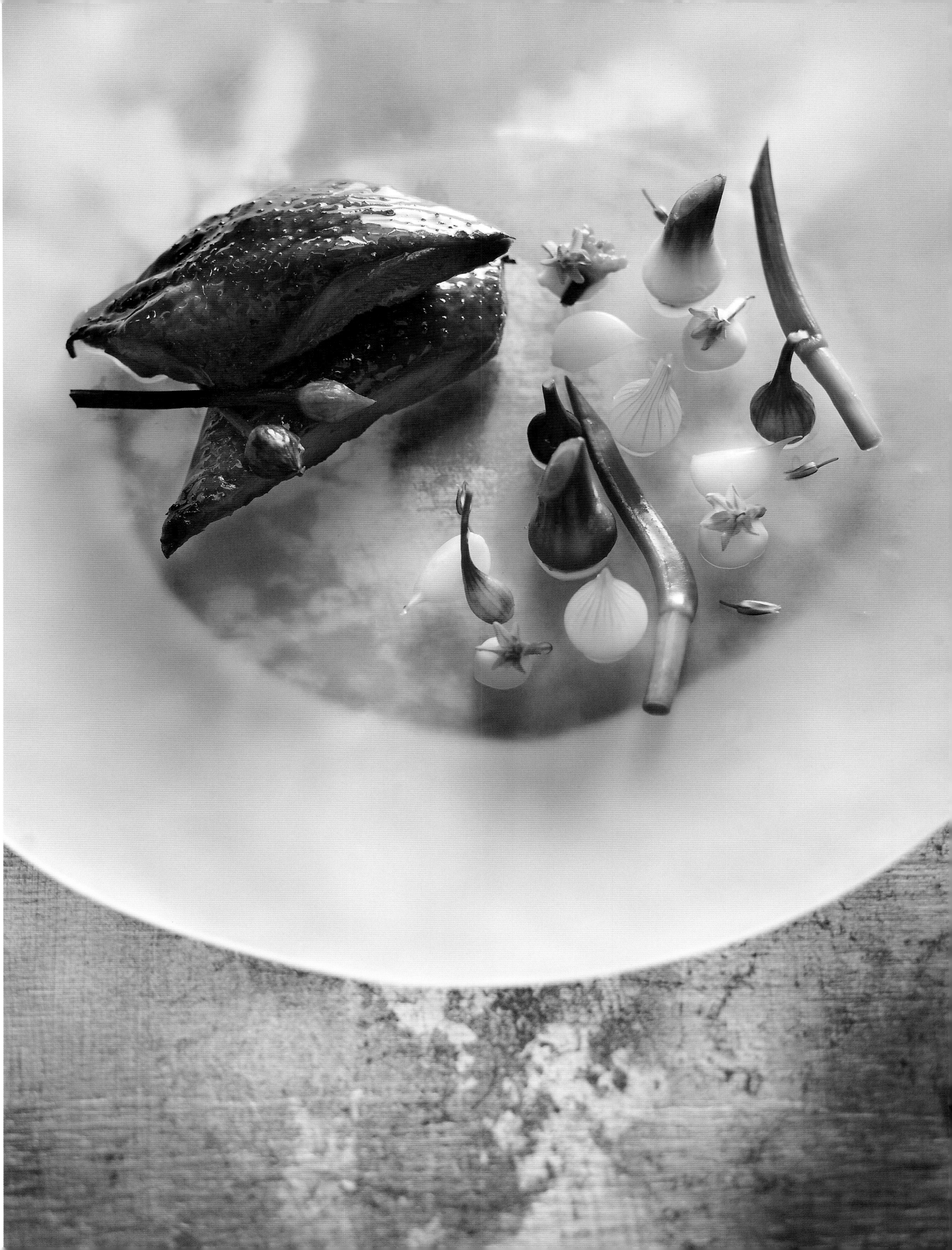

SERVES 8

chinese-style roast squab with onions and garlic

This dish is based on the classic Chinese technique used for Peking duck. The genius who came up with the technique will probably never be known, but the idea of steaming and imparting fragrance from the inside and roasting and caramelising the skin from the outside is simply brilliant. This recipe needs only simple accompaniments: here I've used different varieties of garlic and onions.

ingredients

8 X 500 G (1 LB 2 OZ) SQUABS, WITH NECKS AND
    HEADS ATTACHED
8 STAR ANISE, BROKEN
4 CINNAMON STICKS, HALVED
1 LARGE KNOB GINGER, PEELED AND SLICED
400 ML (14 FL OZ) CHICKEN STOCK (BASIC RECIPES,
    PAGE 262)
200 ML (7 FL OZ) LIQUID MALTOSE
100 ML (3½ FL OZ) SALT-REDUCED SOY SAUCE
100 ML (3½ FL OZ) MIRIN
GARLIC CREAM (BASIC RECIPES, PAGE 265)
16 PURPLETTE ONIONS
16 BULB SPRING ONIONS (SCALLIONS)
24 YOUNG GARLIC CLOVES
24 BABY RED GARLIC
16 GARLIC SCAPES
16 GARLIC CHIVE BUDS
8 ONION CHIVE BUDS, BUDS SEPARATED
80 G (2¾ OZ) UNSALTED BUTTER
FINE SEA SALT
32 SOCIETY GARLIC FLOWERS
32 SEPARATED FLOWERING ONION CHIVE BUDS

method

To prepare and cook the squab, remove the wing tips and head from the top of the neck with a sharp knife. Tie a 15 cm (6 inch) piece of kitchen string around the middle of the neck. Place a broken star anise, half a cinnamon stick and two slices of ginger in the cavity of each squab. Add 50 ml (1¾ fl oz) of chicken stock to the cavity of each squab and close the cavity with a thin metal skewer. Hang the birds suspended from a wooden spoon propped up in a suitable location in your kitchen, with a large drip tray underneath.

In a small saucepan, gently heat the maltose, soy sauce and mirin together. Once the ingredients are combined, use a pastry brush to apply one coat of the maltose mixture to each squab. Allow the birds to dry. (A small portable fan is useful for this.) After 15 minutes, apply a second coat of the maltose mixture to the squabs. Allow another 15 minutes to pass, then apply a third coat of the mixture all over the birds. When the third coat has had time to dry, remove the top shelf of your oven and preheat your oven to the highest possible setting, 250°C–300°C (500°F–570°F/Gas 9). With the aid of another person, tie the squab to the top shelf of the oven. When the oven has reached its maximum temperature, place the top shelf back into the oven with the squabs suspended. Place a drip tray in the bottom of the

oven and fill the tray with a couple of inches of water so it can catch the drips and hopefully stop too much smoke forming. (This is a difficult dish to prepare in a domestic oven. You may find it easier to purchase roast squab from a Chinese specialist restaurant.)

Cook the squabs for 10 minutes, then remove from the oven and rest for at least 5 minutes. The squabs should be golden roasted with a crisp skin on the outside, while the stock and the aromatics will steam and perfume the flesh from the inside.

Meanwhile, make the garlic cream and put aside until needed. The garlic cream should be the consistency of mayonnaise when reheated. Peel and trim the onions, young garlic and garlic scapes.

to finish and plate

While the squabs are cooking, you will need to blanch the following ingredients in boiling salted water. The purplette onions, bulb spring onions and garlic will need 3–4 minutes, the garlic scapes 1 minute, and the garlic chive and onion chive buds will need only 30 seconds. Melt the butter and brush it over the drained vegetables, then season with sea salt. Reheat the garlic cream and place four small spoonfuls on the serving plates. Arrange the onions, garlic, scapes and buds on the plates. Garnish with society garlic flowers and flowering onion chive buds. Carve the breasts from each bird (the squab should be cooked to a nice medium), arrange next to the onions and garlic, and serve immediately. The roasted squab legs and frames can be used to make a fragrant squab broth that can be served with noodles at another time.

SERVES 8

masterstock braised quail, pig's trotter and shaved squid dumplings with bamboo fungi, black sesame tofu, tapioca and black lentils

This is an exotic combination of masterstock quail, pig's trotter and squid. I have taken my inspiration for this dish from the Chinese idea of mixing proteins to achieve textural complexity. Bamboo fungus is grown in bamboo forests and has a very interesting, sponge-like texture and a natural cavity that is ideal for stuffing. The lentils, tapioca and raw mushroom all add to the textural element of this dish.

ingredients

1.2 LITRES (44 FL OZ) MASTERSTOCK (BASIC RECIPES, PAGE 264)

4 QUAILS

1 FRESH PIG'S TROTTER

2 FRENCH SHALLOTS, FINELY DICED

1 GARLIC CLOVE, FINELY DICED

80 G (2¾ OZ) UNSALTED BUTTER

FINE SEA SALT

100 ML (3½ FL OZ) VIRGIN SESAME OIL

10 G (¼ OZ) PEELED GINGER, SLICED

20 G (¾ OZ) GREEN SPRING ONIONS (SCALLIONS), WHITE PART ONLY, SLICED

200 ML (7 FL OZ) SHAOXING RICE WINE

500 ML (17 FL OZ/2 CUPS) CHICKEN STOCK (BASIC RECIPES, PAGE 262)

1 STAR ANISE

10 ML (¼ FL OZ) DARK SOY SAUCE

4 G (⅛ OZ) XANTANA (FERMENTED CORN STARCH)

16 DRIED BAMBOO FUNGI

100 G (3½ OZ) SILKEN TOFU

30 G (1 OZ) BLACK SESAME POWDER

50 G (1¾ OZ) BLACK BELUGA LENTILS

50 G (1¾ OZ) TAPIOCA PEARLS

4 LARGE SOUTHERN SQUID

8 VERY FRESH WHITE BUTTON MUSHROOMS

32 SOCIETY GARLIC FLOWERS

method

Prepare the masterstock. Put 1 litre (35 fl oz/4 cups) of masterstock in a large saucepan and bring to 70°C (155°F). Remove the legs and backbones from the quails and reserve for later. Put the breasts on the bone into the masterstock and poach for 20 minutes, maintaining the temperature at 70°C (155°F). Remove the breasts from the stock and put in the refrigerator to cool completely. Place the pig's trotter in a vacuum bag with 200 ml (7 fl oz) of masterstock and seal in a vacuum sealer. Steam in a temperature-controlled combi oven at 85°C (185°F) for 8 hours. Alternatively, if cooking conventionally, place the pig's trotter in a casserole dish with a lid and enough masterstock to completely cover the pig's trotter. Braise in a 95°C (200°F/Gas ½) oven for 6 hours, being careful to top up the masterstock with water so the trotter remains covered at all times. Once the pig's trotter is cooked, remove all the bones and hard cartilage with your hands. Chop all the remaining flesh, fat and skin with a knife until you have a fine homogenised mix. Remove the quail breasts from the bone and peel away and discard the skin. The breast meat should still be slightly pink. Dice the quail flesh into 5 mm (¼ inch) cubes. Mix the quail and trotter meat together.

Sweat the shallots and garlic in a saucepan with 30 g (1 oz) of butter until transparent, then remove from the pan. When cool, add the shallot mixture to the meat mixture. Season with sea salt and put aside.

To make the thickened broth, sauté the reserved quail bones in a heavy-based pan with the remaining butter and 50 ml (1¾ fl oz) of virgin sesame oil. (If you can't find a virgin sesame oil, do not use roasted sesame oil as the flavour is too strong. I would suggest using 40 ml/1¼ fl oz of grapeseed oil and just 10 ml/ ¼ fl oz of roasted sesame oil as a substitute.) Add the ginger and spring onions and sweat for a further minute. Deglaze with the rice wine and reduce until the wine has evaporated. Add the chicken stock, star anise and dark soy sauce. Bring to simmering point and simmer for 1 hour, then strain and remove any fat on the surface with a ladle. Reheat the stock and whisk in the xantana to thicken it. Put the thickened broth aside.

Soak the dried bamboo fungi in cold water for 5 minutes, changing the water three times, then completely squeeze out all water from the fungi. Place on a clean kitchen cloth to drain. Trim each fungus so that it is no more than 4 cm (1½ inches) in length from the closed end. Cut the silken tofu into 5 mm (¼ inch) dice, then put in a bowl and add the black sesame powder and a couple of pinches of sea salt. Mix well, then add 20 ml (½ fl oz) of virgin sesame oil. Using a piping bag, pipe the tofu mixture into each piece of bamboo fungus. Using a sheet of plastic wrap, tie the bamboo fungus into a ball and tie a knot in the end of the plastic. Refrigerate the fungi until required.

to finish and plate

Blanch the beluga lentils in a small amount of water until they are tender. Cook the tapioca pearls in boiling salted water for about 10 minutes, or until they become transparent, with the smallest dot of undissolved starch remaining in the centre. Strain and put aside.

Remove the tentacles, head and intestines from the squid and discard them. Cut each squid tube in half lengthways and spread them out on the work bench. Use a clean kitchen cloth to rub off the skin, then use a sharp knife to cut each tube into two rectangles, about 9 x 7 cm (3½ x 2¾ inches). Using a sharp filleting knife, shave each squid rectangle horizontally; you should get four thin rectangles out of each squid. Repeat with the remaining tubes.

Place 2 teaspoons of quail and trotter mixture in the centre of each squid rectangle. Gather the edges of the squid together to form a wonton-shaped dumpling by pinching the squid in the centre and tying it with a piece of string. This should completely seal the quail and trotter mixture in the centre. Refrigerate the dumplings for a minimum of 2 hours before steaming.

Reheat the thickened broth, then add the beluga lentils and tapioca to the broth. Set a steamer up and bring the water to the boil. Place the squid dumplings and bamboo fungi in the steamer and steam for 2 minutes. Remove the dumplings from the steamer and unwrap the bamboo fungi. Cut the strings off the squid dumplings. Brush the dumplings and fungi with the remaining 30 ml (1 fl oz) of virgin sesame oil and lightly season. Place two bamboo fungi and two squid dumplings in each serving bowl. Spoon over the thickened broth with the tapioca and lentils, then finely shave the button mushrooms and place the shavings in the middle of the dish. Garnish with society garlic flowers and serve immediately.

SERVES 8

roasted squab with cherries, beetroot purée, chocolate ganache and pastilla

I love serving squab with ingredients such as cherries, sherry, chocolate, beetroot, black pudding and truffle. The flavours are rich and earthy and really complement the rare meaty flesh of the squab. The Moorish spices in the pastilla accentuate the exotic nature of the dish.

ingredients

BITTERSWEET CHOCOLATE BLACK PUDDING
    (BASIC RECIPES, PAGE 268)
150 G (5 OZ) ALMOND CREAM (BASIC RECIPES,
    PAGE 265)
2 BEETROOTS, TRIMMED
ROCK SALT
5 FRENCH SHALLOTS
250 G (9 OZ) UNSALTED BUTTER
40 ML (1¼ FL OZ) PEDRO XIMÉNEZ NOBLE SOUR
    VINEGAR
70 G (2½ OZ) CASTER (SUPERFINE) SUGAR
1 LITRE (35 FL OZ/4 CUPS) CHICKEN STOCK
    (BASIC RECIPES, PAGE 262)
FINE SEA SALT
4 X 500 G (1 LB 2 OZ) SQUABS
1 CARROT, DICED
1 WHITE CELERY STALK (INNER STALK), DICED
½ BROWN ONION, DICED
½ TEASPOON CORIANDER SEEDS
¼ TEASPOON CUMIN SEEDS
⅛ TEASPOON BROKEN CINNAMON QUILL
20 G (¾ OZ) WHOLE BLANCHED ALMONDS, ROASTED
1 TEASPOON HONEY
1 GARLIC CLOVE, FINELY DICED
2 SHEETS TUNISIAN BRIK PASTRY
16 PINK TURNIPS
8 RED MARBLE ONIONS
8 WHOLE LARGE RED CHERRIES
20 ML (½ FL OZ) PEDRO XIMÉNEZ SHERRY
70 ML (2½ FL OZ) GRAPESEED OIL
20 G (¾ OZ) FINELY DICED BLACK WINTER TRUFFLE
50 ML (1¾ FL OZ) REDUCED VEAL STOCK (GLAZE)
    (BASIC RECIPES, PAGE 263)
1 HEAD FRESH ELDERFLOWERS
PURE ICING (CONFECTIONERS') SUGAR, FOR DUSTING
32 BUTTER BEAN FLOWERS
16 OKRA SHOOTS

method

Prepare the bittersweet chocolate black pudding. When completely cool, carefully remove from the bag and roughly cut into 1 cm (½ inch) cubes. You will need only 150 g (5½ oz) for this recipe; you can use the leftover black pudding elsewhere. Make the almond cream and refrigerate until needed.

Preheat the oven to 180°C (350°F/Gas 4). Wrap the beetroots in foil, place on a bed of rock salt and roast in the oven for 25 minutes, or until tender. While the beetroot is warm, peel away the skin wearing gloves, and dice the beetroot into 2 cm (¾ inch) cubes. Finely dice three of the shallots and sauté in a small saucepan with 50 g (1¾ oz) of butter. Add the diced beetroot, 20 ml (½ fl oz) of vinegar and 50 g (1¾ oz) of sugar. Reduce the mixture for a couple of minutes, then add 200 ml (7 fl oz) of chicken stock and reduce until there is virtually no liquid remaining in the saucepan. Place the contents of the pan into a blender, add 30 g (1 oz) of butter and blend on high until smooth. Pass through a drum sieve and season to taste with sea salt. Put the purée aside.

To make the pastilla, remove the legs and backbone from the squabs. (Refrigerate the breasts on the bone until needed.) Heat 20 g (¾ oz) of butter in a saucepan and sauté the carrot, celery and onion. Add the legs and backbones and sauté for a further minute. Add the remaining 800 ml (28 fl oz) of chicken stock, cover the pan with a lid and continue to cook on a very slow simmer for 1½ hours. Be careful not to reduce the chicken stock too much, as the legs need to be covered by stock at all times. Once cooked, carefully remove the legs from the stock and put aside. Strain the stock through a fine sieve, then transfer the strained liquid to a small saucepan and reduce it to 30 ml (1 fl oz). Remove the meat from the legs of the squab, being careful to remove any fine bones.

Chop the meat finely, then add the reduced stock and put the mixture aside.

Lightly roast the coriander seeds, cumin seeds and cinnamon in a small frying pan, then chop them very finely with a sharp knife or spice grinder. Finely chop the roasted almonds and combine the almonds and spices with the honey. Put aside.

Finely dice the remaining two shallots. Sweat the shallots and garlic in a saucepan with 30 g (1 oz) of butter. Add the spices, almonds and honey and, while warm, add the squab leg and stock mixture and stir to combine.

To finish the pastillas, cut the pastry into 24 strips, 15 cm (6 inches) long and 2 cm (¾ inch) wide. Melt 40 g (1½ oz) of butter and brush it over the pastry strips. Place ½ teaspoon of squab leg mixture on the first 2 cm (¾ inch) of the pastry strip. Roll the strip of pastry on itself and then twist the strip so it covers the exposed sides, and continue to roll until you have a covered 2 cm (¾ inch) square parcel. Repeat until all the pastillas are finished. Brush the finished squares with melted butter and place them on a baking tray lined with silicone paper. Place in the refrigerator until required.

Peel the pink turnips. Leave eight whole and cut eight in half. Peel the red marble onions. Put the turnips and onions aside.

chocolate ganache

200 G (7 OZ) VALRHONA MANJARI CHOCOLATE (64%)
50 G (1¾ OZ) UNSALTED BUTTER, SOFTENED
200 ML (7 FL OZ) CREAM (35% FAT)

Put the chocolate and butter in a small stainless-steel bowl over a pan of barely simmering water. When the chocolate starts to melt a little, place the cream into a separate pan and warm to 90°C (195°F), just before boiling point. Pour the cream onto the chocolate and butter, mix well and allow the chocolate and butter to dissolve completely in the cream. Once the mixture is homogenised, remove from the heat and store the ganache at room temperature. Make the ganache 1 hour before serving.

to finish and plate

Preheat the oven to 200°C (400°F/Gas 6). Cut the cherries in half and remove the stones. In a small saucepan, put the sherry, the remaining 20 ml (½ fl oz) of vinegar and 20 g (¾ oz) of sugar. Bring to the boil, add the cherries and then remove the pan from the heat. Stir the cherries around the sauce to warm them through, then put aside.

Heat 40 ml (1¼ fl oz) of grapeseed oil in a heavy-based ovenproof frying pan. When the pan is hot, add the squab breasts on the bone and seal them on all sides. Add 50 g (1¾ oz) of butter, allow the butter to melt completely, then place the squabs on their ends and spoon the melted butter and oil into the cavities (you may need to add extra butter to fill all the cavities). This will help cook the squab from the inside as well as the outside. Place the squabs in the oven and cook for 4 minutes. Halfway through cooking time, spoon the melted butter back into the cavities. Remove the squabs from the oven and rest for 10 minutes in a warm place in the kitchen.

Meanwhile, reheat the beetroot purée and warm the almond cream. Bring a saucepan of salted water to the boil and blanch the pink turnips for 2 minutes and the marble onions for 1 minute, then drain. Melt the remaining 30 g (1 oz) of butter and brush it over the vegetables, then season with sea salt. Fry the black pudding cubes in a non-stick frying pan with the remaining 30 ml (1 fl oz) of grapeseed oil. Once the pudding is well sealed, remove from the pan, allow to cool slightly and crumble the pudding with the back of a spoon. Add the diced truffle and stir to combine. Bake the pastillas in the oven for 5 minutes until golden brown.

To assemble, carve the squab breasts from the bone. Remove the skin and cut each breast in half lengthways. Warm the veal glaze and brush it over the breasts, then season with sea salt. Reheat the breasts in the oven for 30 seconds. Place two slices of breast on each serving plate and smear 2 teaspoons of beetroot purée near each quail breast. Top the purée with the black pudding and truffle crumbs and garnish with a few elderflowers. Divide the turnips and marble onions among the plates and add a couple of dots of the almond cream. Dust the pastillas with icing sugar (this is traditional in Morocco when making pastilla), and place three pastillas on each plate. Place 2 teaspoons of warm chocolate ganache and two warmed cherry halves on each plate. Garnish the plates with bean flowers and okra shoots. Serve immediately.

SERVES 8

poached fillet of rose veal and slow-braised veal tail with morels, lentils, quinoa and parsley root cream

This dish combines two cuts of veal and two cooking methods — poaching and slow braising. The contrast of the different cuts of meat and styles of cooking makes an interesting combination. Accompanying the veal is a rustic mixture of nuts and grains with parsley root cream and shaved winter truffle.

ingredients

2 X 700 G (1 LB 9 OZ) ROSE VEAL FILLETS
2 CARROTS, CUT INTO 2 CM (¾ INCH) DICE
1 ONION, CUT INTO 2 CM (¾ INCH) DICE
2 WHITE CELERY STALKS (INNER STALKS), CUT INTO
    2 CM (¾ INCH) DICE
50 ML (1¾ FL OZ) OLIVE OIL
1 GARLIC CLOVE, FINELY CHOPPED
2 SPRIGS THYME
1 BAY LEAF
8 X 12 CM (4½ INCH) LONG STRIPS OF VEAL TAIL
2 LITRES (70 FL OZ/8 CUPS) REDUCED VEAL STOCK
    (DEMI-GLAZE) (BASIC RECIPES, PAGE 263)
FINE SEA SALT
40 GARLIC CHIVE BUDS
1 X 50 G (¾ OZ) BLACK WINTER TRUFFLE

method

Trim both ends of the rose veal fillets until you have a 20 cm (8 inch) uniform middle cut section. Reserve the trimmings for another use. Cut each fillet into two 10 cm (4 inch) long sections. Wrap tightly in plastic wrap to form a nice cylinder shape and refrigerate.

Preheat the oven to 100°C (200°F/Gas ½). Take a large roasting tin with sides high enough to hold the volume of liquid required. Add the carrot, onion and celery and sauté over medium heat in the olive oil until lightly brown, then add the garlic, thyme and bay leaf. Place the veal tails on top of the mirepoix and pour in the veal demi-glaze. The stock should submerge the veal tails completely. Cover the tin in foil, cutting a few holes to allow the steam to escape. Place in the oven and cook for 6–8 hours, until the meat is very soft and easily comes off the bone. Check from time to time to make sure the glaze is still covering the veal tails, topping up with more stock if necessary. While the tails are still warm, remove from the glaze. With a small knife, carefully remove the meat from the bones, keeping the meat intact as much as possible.

Strain the remaining glaze through a fine sieve into a saucepan and reduce to one-third of its original volume and until it forms a thicker glaze. Skim regularly with a ladle during this process. When you have achieved a thick glaze, remove the pan from the heat. Coat the boned tails with a few teaspoons of the glaze. Season with sea salt. Place each veal tail on a 30 cm (12 inch) square of plastic wrap. Roll the veal tails tightly in the plastic wrap to form a bon bon. Twist tightly at both ends and tie a small knot to form a watertight cylinder. Place in the refrigerator until required. Keep the remaining reduced glaze for poaching the veal fillets.

parsley root cream

250 G (9 OZ) PARSLEY ROOT
100 G (3½ OZ) CELERIAC
1 WHITE CELERY STALK (INNER STALK)
2 FRENCH SHALLOTS, FINELY CHOPPED
½ GARLIC CLOVE, FINELY CHOPPED
100 G (3½ OZ) UNSALTED BUTTER
500 ML (17 FL OZ/2 CUPS) CHICKEN STOCK
    (BASIC RECIPES, PAGE 262)
100 ML (3½ FL OZ) CREAM (35% FAT)

Peel and chop the parsley root, celeriac and celery. Sweat the shallots and garlic in a saucepan with 50 g (1¾ oz) of the butter, being careful not to add colour. Add the parsley root, celeriac, celery and chicken stock and simmer rapidly over high heat until almost all the stock has evaporated and the vegetables are soft. Place the contents of the pan into a blender, add the remaining 50 g (1¾ oz) of butter and blend on high until smooth. Pass the purée through a drum sieve. Place the purée in a clean container and refrigerate until required.

nut, lentil and mushroom mixture

100 G (3½ OZ) WHITE LENTILS (URID DAHL)
100 G (3½ OZ) RED QUINOA
100 G (3½ OZ) WALNUT KERNELS
20 G (¾ OZ) DRIED MORELS
50 G (1¾ OZ) UNSALTED BUTTER
2 FRENCH SHALLOTS, FINELY DICED
1 GARLIC CLOVE, FINELY DICED
100 ML (3½ FL OZ) CHICKEN STOCK (BASIC RECIPES,
PAGE 262)
20 G (¾ OZ) BLACK WINTER TRUFFLE, CUT INTO
JULIENNE
50 ML (1¾ FL OZ) REDUCED VEAL STOCK (GLAZE)
(BASIC RECIPES, PAGE 263)
FINE SEA SALT

To make the nut, lentil and mushroom mixture, soak the lentils and quinoa separately in water overnight. Boil the lentils in fresh water for 6–8 minutes, or until just tender to the bite. Boil the quinoa in fresh water for about 8 minutes, or until just tender to the bite. Drain the lentils and quinoa well.

Preheat the oven to 180°C (350°F/Gas 4). Place the walnuts on a baking tray and roast in the oven for 5–6 minutes, or until lightly brown. Remove the walnuts from the oven and rub them in a kitchen cloth to remove as much skin as possible. Use the point of a sharp knife to scrape away the skin, as the skin can be a little bitter. Finely dice the walnuts.

Soak the dried morels in 200 ml (7 fl oz) of warm water for 2 hours. Strain the morel soaking liquid through a double layer of muslin cloth to remove any dirt, reserving the liquid. Transfer the strained liquid into a small saucepan and reduce it to 30 ml (1 fl oz) over high heat. Reserve the reduced liquid. Cut the morels in half lengthways and remove and discard the stems. Rinse thoroughly under cold running water, then soak in at least three changes of cold water to remove all the grit. Finely dice the morels and return them to the reduced liquid and allow them to soak until needed.

In a large saucepan, melt the butter and gently sauté the shallots and garlic without colouring. Add the cooked lentils, quinoa and chicken stock and heat until almost all the stock has evaporated. Add the morels, walnuts and truffle, then add the veal glaze and heat until the mixture is hot. Taste and season with sea salt as required. Keep this mixture warm while you are finishing the rest of the dish.

to finish and plate

Just before you heat and assemble the dish, you will need to poach the veal fillets and reheat the veal tails. To poach the veal fillets, reheat the reserved reduced glaze until it reaches 70°C (155°F). Unwrap the veal fillets and submerge them in the stock — maintain the temperature by using a thermometer and adjusting the heat. Alternatively, the veal fillets can be cooked in a vacuum bag with 200 ml (7 fl oz) of the reduced glaze in a temperature-controlled water bath set at 70°C (155°F). They will take 15–20 minutes to cook, depending on how you like your meat. When the veal is cooked, slice each fillet in half lengthways, trim the sides and season. This will give you eight portions of veal. While you are cooking the veal, reheat the veal tails. Poach the veal tails sealed in a vacuum bag in a temperature-controlled water bath set at 90°C (195°F) for 10–15 minutes. Unwrap the veal tails when they are ready. You can flash both the veal tail and fillets in a hot oven for a minute or so just before serving.

To finish the parsley root cream, whip the cream until soft peaks form. Reheat the parsley root purée, fold through the whipped cream and season to taste with sea salt. Place five small mounds of the warm lentil, walnut and mushroom mixture on each warmed serving plate. Fill the gaps with the parsley root cream. Place one veal fillet and one veal tail next to each other on top of the lentil mixture and parsley root cream. Briefly blanch the garlic chive buds in boiling water for 20 seconds, then place them on top of the veal fillet and veal tail. Finish the dish by shaving fresh winter truffle over the meat. Serve immediately.

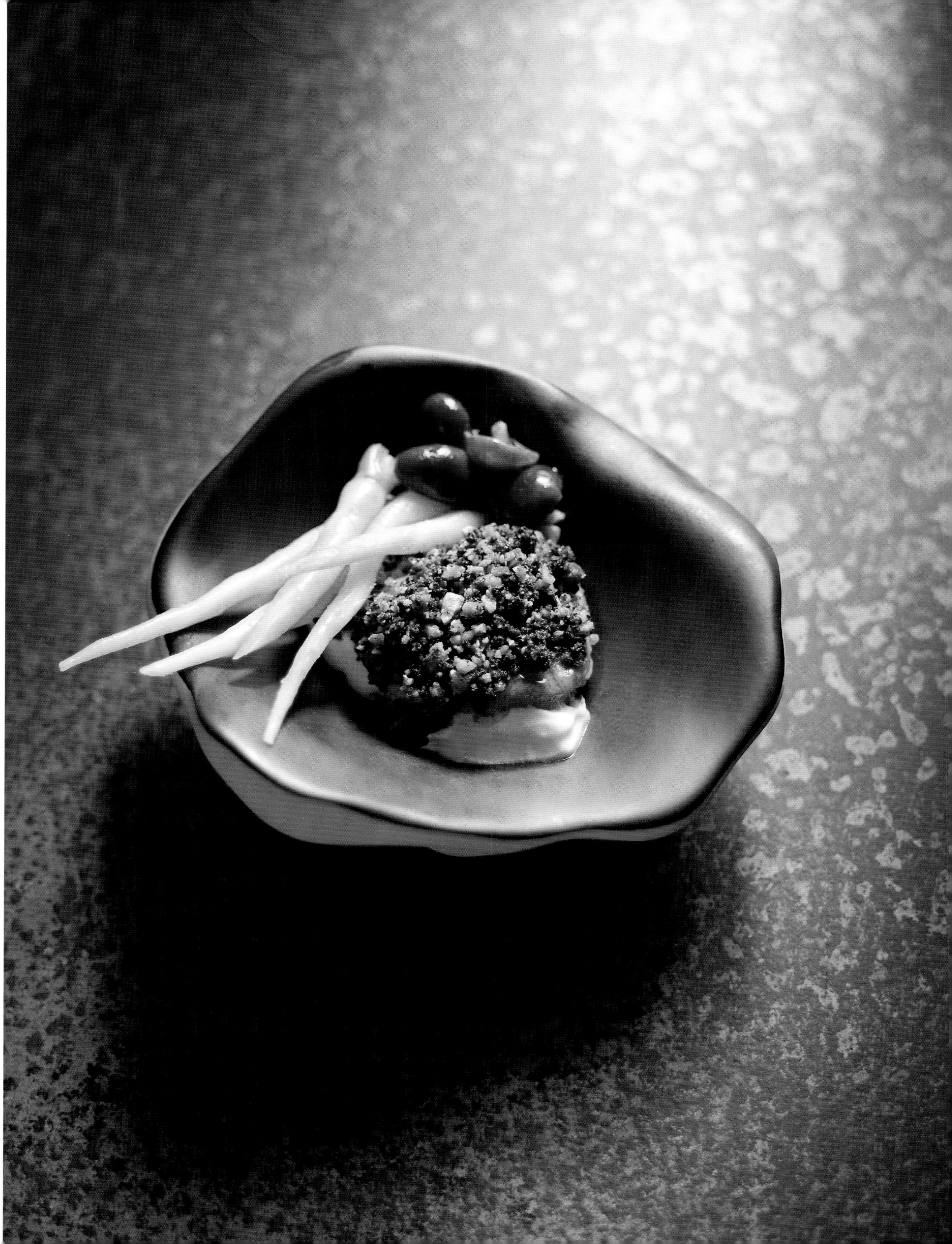

SERVES 8

roasted veal sweetbreads with walnut and black pudding crumbs

Carrots and sweetbreads are a classic flavour marriage, and the combination of black pudding and walnut crumbs adds an earthy textural component to the sweetbreads. This makes a lovely first course for an autumnal meal.

ingredients

8 X 120 G (4¼ OZ) VEAL SWEETBREADS
400 ML (14 FL OZ) MILK
BITTERSWEET CHOCOLATE BLACK PUDDING
    (BASIC RECIPES, PAGE 268)
100 G (3½ OZ) GOOD QUALITY BRIOCHE CRUMBS
200 G (7 OZ) WALNUT KERNELS
40 BABY WHITE CARROTS
150 G (5½ OZ) UNSALTED BUTTER
FINE SEA SALT
40 ML (1¼ FL OZ) GRAPESEED OIL
200 ML (7 FL OZ) REDUCED VEAL STOCK (GLAZE)
    (BASIC RECIPES, PAGE 263)
200 G (7 OZ) CHESTNUT MUSHROOMS, TRIMMED

WHITE CARROT CREAM
½ ONION, FINELY DICED
2 WHITE CELERY STALKS (INNER STALKS), FINELY DICED
1 GARLIC CLOVE, FINELY DICED
150 G (5½ OZ) UNSALTED BUTTER
6 LARGE WHITE CARROTS, DICED
750 ML (26 FL OZ/3 CUPS) CHICKEN STOCK
    (BASIC RECIPES, PAGE 262)
150 ML (5 FL OZ) CREAM (35% FAT)

method

Trim the sweetbreads with a sharp knife, removing as many sinews as possible. Soak the sweetbreads in the milk in the refrigerator overnight.

Bring a large saucepan of salted water to a slow simmer. Remove the sweetbreads from the milk, add to the simmering water and cook for 1 minute. Remove the sweetbreads and plunge into iced water to stop the cooking process. When the sweetbreads are cold, use a knife to peel away any remaining sinews. Place the sweetbreads between two baking trays lined with silicone paper. Weight the top tray with a few heavy plates, then refrigerate the sweetbreads for a minimum of 2 hours. This will give the sweetbreads a good shape.

To make the white carrot cream, sweat the onion, celery and garlic in a saucepan with 75 g (2½ oz) of butter. Add the carrots and chicken stock and bring to a rapid simmer until all the stock has just about evaporated. Transfer the contents of the pan to a blender and blend on high. Dice the remaining 75 g (2½ oz) of butter, add to the blender

and blend until smooth. Pass the purée through a drum sieve. Cover and refrigerate the carrot purée until needed.

Prepare the bittersweet chocolate black pudding. When completely cool, remove from the bag and roughly dice 100 g (3½ oz) for this recipe. You can use the leftover black pudding elsewhere. Combine with the brioche crumbs. You can rub the crumbs through your fingers with the black pudding to form a slightly drier, crumbly mixture. Put aside.

Preheat the oven to 180°C (350°F/Gas 4). Place the walnuts on a baking tray and roast in the oven for 5–6 minutes, or until lightly brown. Remove the walnuts from the oven and rub them in a clean kitchen cloth to remove as much skin as possible. Use the point of a sharp knife to scrape away the skin, as the skin can be a little bitter. Break the walnuts into small pieces and put aside. Peel the baby carrots and put aside.

to finish and plate

To finish the white carrot cream, whip the cream until soft peaks form. Reheat the carrot purée, then fold through the whipped cream. Bring a pan of salted water to the boil and blanch the carrots for 2 minutes, then drain. Melt 50 g (1¾ oz) of butter and brush it over the carrots, then season with sea salt and keep warm.

Heat a large, heavy-based cast-iron pan, then add 20 ml (½ fl oz) of grapeseed oil and 20 g (¾ oz) of butter. When hot, sauté the sweetbreads on each side for 1–2 minutes. Add another 50 g (1¾ oz) of butter to the pan, allow the butter to foam, then baste the sweetbreads with the foaming butter for 1 minute. Drain the butter completely, then add 150 ml (5 fl oz) of veal glaze. Allow the glaze to simmer and coat the sweetbreads. When sufficiently glazed, remove the sweetbreads and keep them warm.

In a separate pan, add the remaining 30 g (1 oz) of butter and briefly sauté the chestnut mushrooms. After a minute or so, add the remaining 50 ml (1¾ fl oz) of veal glaze and glaze the mushrooms. Keep the mushrooms warm. Heat the remaining grapeseed oil in a non-stick frying pan. When the pan is hot, add the black pudding and brioche crumb mixture, stir well and sauté for 1 minute. Remove the pan from the heat and add the walnut pieces. Fold the walnuts through the black pudding crumb mixture, put aside and keep warm.

In the centre of each serving bowl, place 2 tablespoons of white carrot cream. Top each sweetbread with the walnut and black pudding crumbs and carefully place it on the white carrot cream. Garnish each bowl with five baby white carrots and a spoonful of chestnut mushrooms. Serve immediately.

SERVES 8

slow-braised berkshire pig jowl, maltose crackling, prunes, soubise cream perfumed with prune kernel oil

The Berkshire pig has an amazing amount of intermuscular fat, which makes it incredibly tender and flavoursome. I use the jowl, which is a cut taken from the jaw of the pig. The jowl is surrounded by a good layer of pure white fat, which has a very fine flavour, and cooking the jowl very slowly makes for an incredibly tender piece of meat. To make a crackling from the pig skin would mean leaving an inch of fat on the meat, so I have made a crackling from maltose instead. The maltose is a great alternative, giving you the sensation of crackling. Maltose is a unique sugar, it's not as sweet as regular cane sugar, and it makes a toffee that doesn't stick to your teeth; it tends to shatter and then dissolve. The dish is finished with prune kernel oil, which comes from France, and has the wonderful aroma of marzipan. The aroma and perfume of food can be such a powerful component to a truly great dish.

ingredients

2 WHOLE BERKSHIRE PIG JOWLS, ABOUT 600 G
(1 LB 5 OZ) EACH
10 G (¼ OZ) FINE SEA SALT
200 ML (7 FL OZ) CHICKEN STOCK (BASIC RECIPES,
PAGE 262)
250 ML (9 FL OZ/1 CUP) LIQUID MALTOSE
50 ML (1¾ FL OZ) BANYULS VINEGAR
50 G (1¾ OZ) CASTER (SUPERFINE) SUGAR
32 RED MARBLE ONIONS
32 BABY WHITE TURNIPS
50 G (1¾ OZ) UNSALTED BUTTER
16 ML (½ FL OZ) PRUNE KERNEL OIL

method

Place each pig jowl in a vacuum bag. Add the sea salt to the chicken stock. Put 100 ml (3½ fl oz) of the salted chicken stock in each bag with the jowls and seal in a vacuum sealer. Steam in a temperature-controlled combi oven at 85°C (185°F) for 12 hours.

Remove the bags from the steamer and plunge into iced water for 30 minutes. Remove from the iced water, open the bags and remove the jowls. Place the jowls on a chopping board and use a sharp knife to remove the skin and most of the fat around the meat (leave 5 mm/¼ inch of fat attached to the meat). Cut each jowl into four equal portions. Cover the jowls and refrigerate until required.

Preheat the oven to 220°C (425°F/Gas 7) and line a large baking tray with a silicone mat. To make the maltose crackling, pour the maltose onto the silicone mat and bake in the oven until the maltose is bubbling and sufficiently caramelised (a deep golden colour). Remove the maltose from the oven and allow to cool completely. Once the maltose is cold and hard, put it in a food processor and process to form a fine powder. Make a template from an acetate sheet by cutting out a 10 x 15 cm (4 x 6 inch)

rectangle from the centre of the sheet. Place the template on a large tray lined with a silicone mat. Put the maltose powder into a sieve and shake the sieve over the template, to cover with maltose powder to a depth of about 1 mm (1/16 inch). Remove the template, leaving behind a perfect maltose rectangle. You will need at least eight rectangles on your tray. Reduce the oven temperature to 180°C (350°F/Gas 4), place the tray in the oven and bake the maltose until it melts and bubbles. Remove the tray from the oven and allow the maltose to cool. Once cool, store the maltose crackling in an airtight container, layered between silicone paper.

Heat the Banyuls vinegar in a small saucepan with the sugar and 50 ml (1¾ fl oz) of water. Bring to the boil, then remove the syrup from the heat. Peel the first layer from the red marble onions. Coat the onions in the syrup, wrap into a silicone paper parcel and bake in a 180°C (350°F/Gas 4) oven for 10 minutes. Allow to cool and put aside.

Remove the greens from the turnips, leaving 5 mm (¼ inch) of stems attached. Carefully peel the turnips and leave in water until required.

sherry prunes

32 UNPITTED PRUNES
100 ML (3½ FL OZ) PEDRO XIMÉNEZ NOBLE SOUR
   VINEGAR
100 ML (3½ FL OZ) PEDRO XIMÉNEZ SHERRY

Place the prunes in a ceramic bowl and pour over 300 ml (10½ fl oz) of cold water. Leave to soften overnight in the refrigerator. Place the prunes in a single layer in a large saucepan. Add the vinegar and sherry and any remaining soaking juices and cook the prunes over low heat for 10–15 minutes, then remove the pan from the heat and set aside to cool. Using a sharp knife, make a slit on the side of each prune and remove the stone, trying to keep the prunes as whole as possible. Return the prunes to the pan, cover and refrigerate until required.

soubise cream

10 BULB SPRING ONIONS (SCALLIONS),
   ROUGHLY DICED
2 WHITE CELERY STALKS (INNER STALKS),
   ROUGHLY DICED
1 SMALL GARLIC CLOVE, ROUGHLY DICED
50 G (1¾ OZ) UNSALTED BUTTER
500 ML (17 FL OZ/2 CUPS) CHICKEN STOCK
   (BASIC RECIPES, PAGE 262)
100 ML (3½ FL OZ) CREAM (35% FAT)

Sweat the spring onion, celery and garlic in a pan with 25 g (1 oz) of butter, being careful not to add any colour. Add the chicken stock and simmer rapidly until all the stock has just about evaporated and the vegetables are very soft. Transfer the contents of the saucepan to a blender, add the remaining 25 g (1 oz) of butter and blend on high until smooth. Pass the purée through a drum sieve and put aside.

to finish and plate

Preheat the oven to 180°C (350°F/Gas 4). Wrap the eight portions of pig jowl in two silicone paper parcels, place the parcels on a baking tray and place in the oven for 10 minutes. Bring a small saucepan of water to the boil and blanch the baby turnips for 1 minute, then drain. Melt 25 g (1 oz) of butter and brush it over the turnips, then season with sea salt. Place the red marble onions in a small saucepan with 25 g (1 oz) of butter and reheat gently. Gently reheat the prunes. To finish the soubise cream, whip the cream until soft peaks form. Reheat the soubise purée in a small saucepan, then fold through the whipped cream.

Remove the pig jowls from the oven. Unwrap the parcels and place each jowl 15 cm (6 inches) apart on a large baking tray lined with a silicone mat. Place an oblong of maltose crackling on each jowl, return the tray to the oven and allow the crackling to melt over the jowls. Leave in the oven for 1–2 minutes until the maltose starts to bubble. Remove the tray from the oven.

Place four sherry prunes in the centre of each serving dish. Add four red marble onions and four baby turnips to each dish and then place 3–4 teaspoons of soubise cream on top. Using a palette knife, carefully lift the jowls off the tray and place on top of the prunes, onions and turnips. Drizzle each jowl with 2 ml (1/16 fl oz) of prune kernel oil and serve.

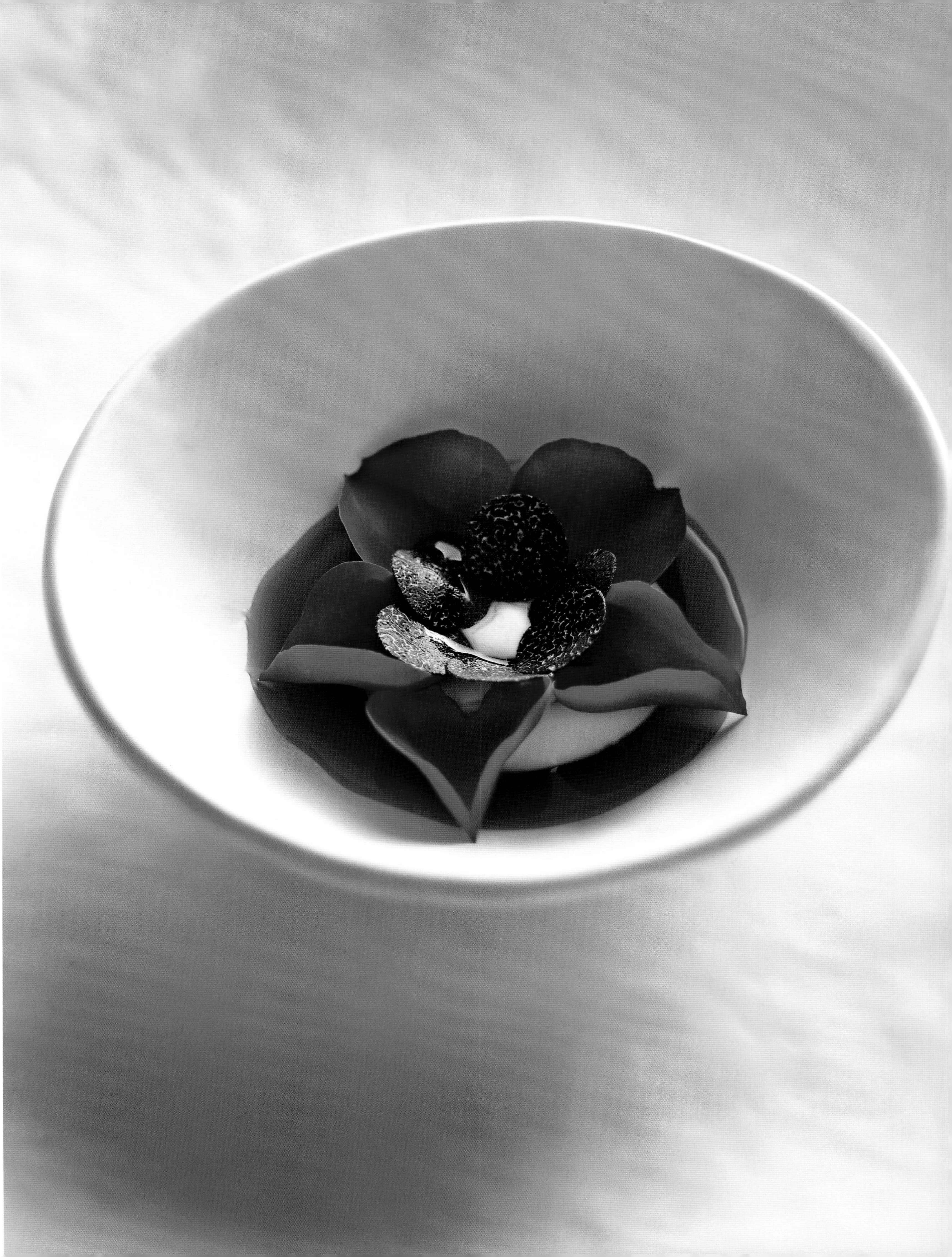

SERVES 8

fresh milk curd with venison consommé scented with rose and truffle

I like to serve this dish as an indulgent middle course in a degustation-style menu to take diners from lighter seafood and vegetable dishes towards the meat courses. The venison consommé scented with rose and truffle is very elegant and the fresh milk curd completely dissolves in the mouth, creating a very sensual texture.

ingredients

2 KG (4 LB 8 OZ) AGED RED VENISON NECK, CHOPPED THROUGH THE BONE INTO 2 CM (¾ INCH) THICK STRIPS (ASK YOUR BUTCHER TO DO THIS FOR YOU)

2 KG (4 LB 8 OZ) OXTAIL, CHOPPED THROUGH THE BONE INTO 2 CM (¾ INCH) THICK PIECES (ASK YOUR BUTCHER TO DO THIS FOR YOU)

100 ML (3½ FL OZ) GRAPESEED OIL

250 G (9 OZ) UNSALTED BUTTER

1 ONION, DICED

2 CARROTS, DICED

2 WHITE CELERY STALKS (INNER STALKS), DICED

2 SMALL GARLIC CLOVES, HALVED

400 ML (14 FL OZ) OLOROSO SHERRY

6 LITRES (210 FL OZ) CHICKEN STOCK (BASIC RECIPES, PAGE 262)

3 SPRIGS THYME

2 BAY LEAVES

15 BLACK PEPPERCORNS, CRUSHED

500 G (1 LB 2 OZ) MINCED (GROUND) LEAN VENISON MEAT

10 EGG WHITES

15 ML (½ FL OZ) GOOD QUALITY ROSE WATER

20 G (¾ OZ) FINELY GRATED TRUFFLE PEELINGS

80 G (2¾ OZ) PEELED BLACK WINTER TRUFFLE

40 ORGANIC ROSE PETALS

JERSEY MILK CURDS

400 ML (14 FL OZ) HOMOGENISED JERSEY MILK

FINE SEA SALT

2 ML (¹⁄₁₆ FL OZ) VEGETARIAN RENNET

method

Sauté the venison neck and oxtail together in a heavy-based pot with the grapeseed oil. Make sure you get good colour and caramelisation on the meat. Add the butter, half the onion, half the carrot, half the celery and the garlic cloves. Sauté until the butter and vegetables are golden brown in colour. Deglaze with the sherry and reduce until most of the sherry has evaporated. Add the chicken stock, thyme, bay leaves and peppercorns. Bring the stock up to simmering point, being careful not to let the stock boil; you want the gentlest movement possible on the surface. Simmer for 5 hours and only skim the stock at the end of the cooking period, as you want the flavour of the brown butter to permeate the stock. Carefully strain the stock through a fine sieve, then remove any surface fat with a ladle. Allow the stock to set overnight in the refrigerator. In the morning, remove any additional fat that has set on the surface. Gently reheat the stock so that it becomes liquid. Do not allow the stock to get too hot or boil.

To make a raft for the consommé, put the remaining onion, carrot and celery in a food processor. Process, then add the venison mince and process again briefly. Transfer the contents to a stainless-steel bowl. In a separate bowl, lightly whisk the egg whites by hand until you have very soft peaks, then fold the egg whites through the processed vegetables and meat. Add the rose water and grated truffle peelings and mix well. Vigorously whisk the raft into the venison stock until well incorporated, stirring occasionally to make sure the raft is not sticking to the bottom of the pan. Allow the stock to come close to boiling point, then turn the heat down to the lowest possible setting; you want the stock to be barely simmering under the raft. Do not stir the raft again at this point. Cook on very low heat for 30 minutes. Make a hole in the raft to check that it is fully cooked and that the stock is clear, then cook for a further 10 minutes. The raft will clarify and enrich your stock.

Remove the pot from the heat and set aside for 20 minutes. Carefully ladle the consommé into a sieve lined with a double layer of muslin cloth, making sure you don't break up the raft too much. Return to a clean pan and bring the consommé up to simmering point, then strain through a fresh double layer of muslin cloth to ensure a crystal clear consommé. Season to taste. Reserve the consommé until required.

to finish and plate

Slice the truffle into 1 mm (¹⁄₁₆ inch) thin slices and use a 2 cm (¾ inch) round pastry cutter to cut out 48 circles of truffle. Prepare 40 small rose petals.

To prepare the Jersey milk curds, you will need 8 small round-bottomed ceramic ramekins of at least 50 ml (1¾ fl oz) capacity. Warm the milk to 40°C (105°F) and season with sea salt to taste. Stir the milk with a spoon to create a whirlpool effect. This will ensure an even distribution of rennet. While the milk is swirling, use an eye dropper to drop the rennet into the milk. Immediately ladle the milk into the ramekins; the rennet will set the milk very quickly. Place the ramekins in a warm part of the kitchen and the curd should set within 1 or 2 minutes. Use a round soup spoon to scoop each curd into the centre of a warmed serving bowl. Reheat the consommé to simmering point. Arrange five rose petals and six slices of truffle on top of the milk curds. Pour the consommé into serving jugs. Present the curds to your guests and pour the consommé at the table.

heaven

Desserts are an area where texture, as well as harmony and balance of flavour, are essential. The level of sweetness has also got to be just right so as not to overpower a diner's palate. Desserts also need to look beautiful, as people really do eat with their eyes.

SERVES 8

raspberries with vanilla, almond and violet

This is one of my most complex but beautiful desserts. It combines a vanilla mousse with fresh raspberries and violets, violet jelly, raspberry jelly, white chocolate-coated caramelised almonds and raspberry sorbet. It really is a feast for the eyes as well as the palate.

vanilla mousse

330 ML (11¼ FL OZ) MILK
1 VANILLA BEAN, SPLIT AND SCRAPED
230 G (8 OZ) CASTER (SUPERFINE) SUGAR
2 SHEETS TITANIUM GELATINE
220 ML (7¾ FL OZ) CREAM (35% FAT)
100 G (3½ OZ) DOUBLE CREAM (45–50% FAT)
90 G (3¼ OZ) EGG WHITE

Put the milk in a small saucepan with the vanilla bean and 70 g (2½ oz) of sugar. When the milk reaches about 90°C (195°F), remove the pan from the heat. Meanwhile, soak the gelatine sheets in cold water until softened. Squeeze the excess water from the gelatine and add to the hot milk. Stir to dissolve the gelatine, then strain the milk into a clean bowl, discarding the vanilla bean. Place the bowl over ice and allow to cool but not completely set. Meanwhile whip the two creams together until they form soft peaks. Refrigerate until needed.

Next, make an Italian meringue by dissolving the remaining 160 g (5½ oz) of sugar with 100 ml (3½ fl oz) of water in a small heavy-based saucepan. Place the pan over high heat and heat the sugar to 117°C (243°F), soft ball stage. When the sugar reaches the desired temperature, remove the pan from the heat. Quickly whisk the egg whites in an electric mixer, and as soon as they start to form soft peaks, slowly pour in the syrup. Continue to mix the meringue for a minimum of 8 minutes on medium speed, or until the meringue is cool.

Combine all three mixtures (the milk gelatine mixture, whipped cream and Italian meringue) in a bowl and fold together gently. You will need to ensure that the milk gelatine mixture has not set but is just cool, and the Italian meringue has cooled down sufficiently. Place the mousse in the refrigerator for 4–5 hours to fully set.

sugar tuile

10 G (¼ OZ) LIQUID GLUCOSE
1 SHEET TITANIUM GELATINE
250 G (9 OZ) PURE ICING (CONFECTIONERS') SUGAR
CORNFLOUR (CORNSTARCH), FOR DUSTING

Put the glucose and 20 ml (½ fl oz) of boiling water in a bowl and stir to dissolve. Soak the gelatine sheet in cold water until softened. Squeeze the excess water from the gelatine, add to the hot water and stir to dissolve the gelatine.

Sieve the icing sugar thoroughly into a bowl and add the gelatine mixture. Knead to form a soft paste and put aside to rest for 30 minutes. Dust the work surface and rolling pin with cornflour and, working in small batches, roll out the paste to a 2 mm (¹⁄₁₆ inch) thickness. Using a 10 cm (4 inch) round cutter, cut the paste into rounds. Then, using a small teardrop cutter, cut out several pieces of the circle to make an attractive pattern. Carefully lift the cut-out discs onto a rolling pin and allow to dry for a minimum of 2–3 hours.

raspberry and milk jellies

RASPBERRY JELLY

165 G (5¾ OZ) FRESH RASPBERRIES
100 G (3½ OZ) CASTER (SUPERFINE) SUGAR
2 SHEETS TITANIUM GELATINE
8 FRESH RASPBERRIES, EXTRA

MILK JELLY

40 G (1½ OZ) CASTER (SUPERFINE) SUGAR
200 ML (7 FL OZ) MILK
2 SHEETS TITANIUM GELATINE

To make the raspberry jelly, place the raspberries in a bowl. Combine the sugar and 165 ml (5¾ fl oz) of water in a saucepan and bring to the boil. Pour the liquid onto the raspberries and soak for 5 minutes. Squeeze the mixture firmly through a muslin cloth back into the pan, discarding the seeds. Bring the syrup back to the boil, then remove the pan from the heat. Meanwhile, soak the gelatine sheets in cold water until softened. Squeeze the excess water from the gelatine and add to the syrup. Stir to dissolve the gelatine. Allow to cool but not set.

To make the milk jelly, combine the sugar and milk in a saucepan and heat to about 90°C (195°F). Remove from the heat. Meanwhile, soak the gelatine sheets in cold water until softened. Squeeze the excess water from the gelatine and add to the milk. Stir to dissolve the gelatine. Allow to cool but not set.

You will need eight thimble-sized moulds. First pour in the cold but not set raspberry jelly syrup to a depth of 1.5 cm (⅝ inch), then place 1 fresh raspberry in each mould. Put in the refrigerator to set. Then pour on the cold but not set milk jelly to a further depth of 1.5 cm (⅝ inch). Put in the refrigerator to set.

vanilla cream

100 G (3½ OZ) VANILLA CUSTARD BASE
(BASIC RECIPES, PAGE 269)
100 G (3½ OZ) DOUBLE CREAM (45–50% FAT)

In a small bowl, whisk together the vanilla custard base and cream until firm peaks form. Refrigerate until needed.

raspberry sorbet

150 G (5½ OZ) CASTER (SUPERFINE) SUGAR
1 VANILLA BEAN, SPLIT AND SCRAPED
350 G (12 OZ) RASPBERRIES

To make a sugar syrup, put 200 ml (7 fl oz) of water in a saucepan and add the sugar and vanilla bean. Bring to the boil, then immediately take the pan off the heat. When the syrup is cool, remove the vanilla bean and pour the syrup on to the raspberries. Blend the mixture and pass through a fine chinois sieve to remove the raspberry seeds. Transfer the mixture into an ice-cream machine and churn until frozen. Place the sorbet in a container in the freezer for at least 1 hour.

violet jelly

50 ML (1¾ FL OZ) VIOLET SYRUP
50 G (1¾ OZ) CASTER (SUPERFINE) SUGAR
1 SHEET TITANIUM GELATINE

Combine the violet syrup, sugar and 200 ml (7 fl oz) of water in a small saucepan and bring to the boil. Meanwhile, soak the gelatine sheet in cold water until softened. Remove the pan from the heat, squeeze the excess water from the gelatine and add to the syrup. Stir to dissolve the gelatine. Pour the syrup into a shallow tray with sides, to a depth of 1 cm (½ inch). Place in the refrigerator to set.

isomalt baskets

200 G (7 FL OZ) ISOMALT

Preheat the oven to 120°C (230°F/Gas ½). Put the isomalt in a small saucepan on the stovetop and heat to 150°C (300°F). Pour the liquid onto a large baking tray lined with silicone paper and use a spatula to spread it out as thinly as possible. Cover with another sheet of paper, then roll out to a 1 mm (¹⁄₁₆ inch) thickness. While the isomalt is still slightly warm, use a pair of scissors to cut it into eight 4 cm (1½ inch) squares. Cool, peel off the paper and place on a silicone mat. Warm the squares in the oven or under a heat light. Allow the isomalt squares to slightly soften and become pliable, then mould them around a small metal thimble-sized mould. Cool and place the isomalt baskets in an airtight container until needed. You will have some isomalt leftover.

white chocolate caramelised almonds

40 BLANCHED WHOLE ALMONDS
200 G (7 OZ) CASTER (SUPERFINE) SUGAR
200 G (7 OZ) GOOD QUALITY WHITE CHOCOLATE

Preheat the oven to 150°C (300°F/Gas 2). Place the almonds on a baking tray and roast in the oven until the almonds are lightly coloured. Remove and set aside. Combine the sugar and 50 ml (1¾ fl oz) of water in a small saucepan, stirring to dissolve the sugar, and heat over high heat until you have a caramel. Remove the pan from the heat and, working quickly, add the almonds to the caramel. Use two forks to coat each almond in the caramel. Remove the almonds from the pan and place on a silicone mat to set, spacing them so they don't touch each other.

Meanwhile, to melt the white chocolate, bring a saucepan of water to the boil, then remove from the heat. Finely chop the chocolate and place in a heatproof bowl. Put the bowl over the pan of hot water, making sure the base of the bowl isn't touching the water. Stir occasionally until melted. When cool, dip the almonds into the melted white chocolate to coat completely. Place the white chocolate almonds on a silicone mat to set.

to finish and plate

1 TABLESPOON GOOD QUALITY RASPBERRY JAM
80 FRESH RASPBERRIES
16 SWEET VIOLETS
24 NATIVE VIOLETS

Finely dice the violet jelly in the tray. Using a large tablespoon that has been gently heated in hot water, shape the vanilla mousse into eight quenelles and place one in the centre of each serving plate. Fill the isomalt baskets with ½ teaspoon of raspberry jam, add one fresh raspberry to each basket and top with a tiny quenelle of the vanilla cream and one sweet violet. Place a basket next to each quenelle on the serving plates. Remove the raspberry and milk jellies from their moulds by either dipping them in hot water or using a blow torch to heat the metal. Place a jelly on each plate. Arrange six raspberries around the base of each vanilla mousse quenelle, then arrange five small vanilla cream quenelles. Next place five white chocolate-coated almonds randomly over each mousse, then place small spoonfuls of diced jelly randomly around the dessert. Top the desserts with the remaining violets and raspberries. Finally add one small raspberry sorbet quenelle to the top of the dessert, then slide in the sugar tuile. Serve immediately.

SERVES 8

guava snow egg

This is my favourite dessert. It is an original creation that I first made about three years ago. The flavours change with the seasons; sometimes I make a white peach or a mulberry version, but this guava version is my favourite. Strawberry guavas have a deep pink flesh and an exotic intoxicating scent. The combination of the fool, granita and ice-cream filled poached meringue is a textural treat. Coating the snow egg in a maltose biscuit adds another dimension — as you crack through the toffee biscuit it gives way to the soft meringue filled with the custard apple ice cream. This dessert is incredibly refreshing and, for me, everything a dessert should be.

guava granita

600 G (1 LB 5 OZ) STRAWBERRY GUAVAS
100 G (3½ OZ) FRESH STRAWBERRIES
100 G (3½ OZ) CASTER (SUPERFINE) SUGAR

Cut the guavas in half, scoop out the seeds and flesh and discard the skin. Weigh out 400 g (14 oz) of flesh. Roughly dice the guava flesh and strawberries.

Combine the sugar and 500 ml (17 fl oz/2 cups) of water in a large saucepan, bring to the boil, then lower the heat to a slow simmer. Add the diced fruit and gently simmer for 10 minutes. Remove the pan from the heat and allow to infuse at room temperature for 2 hours. Pass the liquid through a sieve lined with muslin cloth and discard the solids. Pour the guava syrup into a ceramic or stainless-steel container to a depth of 5 cm (2 inches). Place the container in the freezer for a period of no less than 12 hours. Every 2–3 hours, remove the container from the freezer and scrape with a fork to form the granita crystals.

guava fool

800 G (1 LB 12 OZ) STRAWBERRY GUAVAS
175 G (6 OZ) CASTER (SUPERFINE) SUGAR
½ VANILLA BEAN, SPLIT AND SCRAPED

VANILLA CREAM
**100 G (3½ OZ) VANILLA CUSTARD BASE
  (BASIC RECIPES, PAGE 269)**
100 G (3½ OZ) DOUBLE CREAM (45–50% FAT)

Cut the guavas in half and scoop out the seeds and discard them, then scoop out the flesh from the skin. Weigh out 375 g (13 oz) of flesh.

Put 250 ml (9 fl oz/1 cup) of water in a saucepan and add the sugar and vanilla bean. Bring to the boil, then lower the heat to a gentle simmer, add the guava flesh and simmer for 10 minutes. Remove the pan from the heat and remove the vanilla bean. Drain the guava flesh from the liquid and place the flesh in a blender. Add just enough of the cooking liquid to process into a thick guava purée. Pass the purée through a fine sieve and set aside in the refrigerator.

To make the vanilla cream, whisk together the vanilla custard base and cream in a small bowl to form soft peaks. Place 400 g (14 oz) of guava purée in a small bowl and gently fold through the vanilla cream to form a rippled effect. Do this just before you are ready to assemble the dessert.

custard apple ice cream

200 ML (7 FL OZ) MILK
6 EGG YOLKS
200 G (7 OZ) CASTER (SUPERFINE) SUGAR
1–2 LARGE, EXTREMELY RIPE CUSTARD APPLES
100 ML (3½ FL OZ) CREAM (35% FAT)

Put the milk in a saucepan and bring to the boil. Whisk the egg yolks and sugar together, then, while whisking, pour the boiled milk onto the egg yolk and sugar mixture. Pour the mixture into a stainless-steel bowl, place over a pan of simmering water, without letting the base of the bowl touch the water, and continually whisk for 10 minutes. Place the bowl of sabayon over ice to cool.

Meanwhile, scoop out the flesh from one custard apple into a fine sieve lined with a double layer of muslin cloth. Gather the muslin at the top and squeeze the ripe custard apple flesh tightly to obtain a clear juice. You will need 300 ml (10½ fl oz) of clear juice (you may need to use the second custard apple). Whisk the juice into the sabayon, along with the cream. Transfer the mixture into an ice-cream machine and churn until frozen. Place the ice cream in a container in the freezer for at least 1 hour.

poached meringue

300 G (10½ OZ) EGG WHITE
300 G (10½ OZ) CASTER (SUPERFINE) SUGAR
PURE ICING (CONFECTIONERS') SUGAR, TO DUST

Preheat the oven to 120°C (230°F/Gas ½). For this recipe you will need a 6 cm (2½ inch) diameter half-hemisphere silicone mould sheet. Whisk the egg whites in an electric mixer until they form soft peaks, then slowly add the sugar. Once the meringue forms firm peaks and the sugar has dissolved, place the meringue into 16 half-hemisphere moulds. Place the meringues in a bain-marie large enough to hold the silicone mould sheet and cook in the oven for about 15 minutes. Allow to cool for 5 minutes, then remove from the water bath to cool completely. Unmould the meringues and store in the refrigerator on a tray lined with silicone paper.

maltose tuiles

200 G (7 OZ) LIQUID MALTOSE
100 G (3½ OZ) CASTER (SUPERFINE) SUGAR
20 G (¾ OZ) FLAKED ALMONDS

Heat the maltose and sugar in a medium-sized pan until it reaches 140°C (285°F). Add the flaked almonds and immediately pour the mixture onto a silicone mat. Put aside to cool completely.

Preheat the oven to 180°C (350°F/Gas 4). Line a baking tray with a silicone mat. Process the hard praline in a food processor to form a fine powder. Transfer the praline mixture into a course sieve and sift the praline onto the silicone mat in a fine layer, about 1 mm (¹⁄₁₆ inch) thick. You may have to work in batches, depending on the size of your tray. Place in the oven and melt the praline until it forms a clear liquid paste. Remove from the oven and before the praline becomes too hard, cut it into eight 15 cm (6 inch) circles using a metal circle cutter. When each circle is hard, store in an airtight container, placing a sheet of silicone paper between each one.

to finish and plate

Take eight of the poached half-hemisphere meringues. Using a teaspoon, remove a small scoop from the centre of each meringue, being careful not to break through the outer edge. Place a small scoop of custard apple ice cream inside the hole you have just made. Scoop a small hole in the remaining eight meringues and invert them over the ice-cream filled half-hemispheres to form a complete sphere. Place a maltose tuile on top of each sphere and, using a gentle kitchen blow torch, melt the tuile over the sphere. Dust all the spheres with icing sugar. Next, place a generous spoonful of the guava fool in the bottom of each serving glass. Top the fool with the guava granita, then place the ice-cream filled meringue spheres on top of the granita and serve.

eight-texture chocolate cake

I have been making a version of this chocolate cake for about 15 years now. It started as a simple four-layer cake containing a chocolate base, mousse, ice cream and dark chocolate cocoa. At De Beers it became a five-texture cake and a signature dessert. This year I celebrated my eighth anniversary at Quay, so I decided to make the cake an eight-textured experience. The combination is now more complex, with a fantastic interplay of temperatures and textures. The flavour components of the cake are essentially dark chocolate, hazelnuts, caramel, vanilla and milk chocolate. I like to use a combination of Amedei Chuao (70 per cent) dark chocolate and Valrhona milk chocolate, as I consider these chocolates to be the best examples available, but feel free to use any good quality chocolate available to you. My favourite part of this cake is the sense of theatre and anticipation when we serve it in the restaurant — the hot chocolate sauce appears to melt through the centre of the cake. It is this small moment of theatre that I hope creates a lasting memory and adds to the pleasure of eating the dessert.

chocolate mousse

325 G (11½ OZ) DARK CHOCOLATE (70%)
500 ML (17 FL OZ/2 CUPS) CREAM (35%)
4 EGG YOLKS
50 G (1¾ OZ) CASTER (SUPERFINE) SUGAR
½ VANILLA BEAN, SPLIT AND SCRAPED
3 EGG WHITES

Finely chop the chocolate and melt it over a double boiler and keep warm. Whip the cream until soft peaks form. Make a sabayon by combining the egg yolks, sugar and vanilla bean. Cook over a double boiler, whisking continuously until the egg yolks become thick and glossy, then remove the sabayon from the heat. Have the whipped cream nearby. Pour all of the melted chocolate into the warm sabayon and, with a large hand whisk, beat as fast as you can to incorporate all the chocolate into the sabayon. The chocolate will begin to seize; at that point you will need to add 1 large kitchen spoon of whipped cream. Continue to whisk; the cream will begin to soften the mixture. Add another large spoonful of cream and whisk vigorously for a further 1 minute. The chocolate, egg and cream mixture will now be more workable and relatively stable. You should have half the whipped cream left.

Immediately whisk the egg whites until soft peaks form. Place the whisked egg whites and the remaining cream on top of the chocolate mixture and gently fold through until well incorporated. Place the chocolate mousse in the refrigerator for a minimum of 6 hours before assembling the dessert.

caramel, vanilla and chocolate ganache

120 G (4¼ OZ) UNSALTED BUTTER
60 G (2¼ OZ) DARK CHOCOLATE (70%)
40 G (1½ OZ) MILK CHOCOLATE (40%)
40 G (1½ OZ) CASTER (SUPERFINE) SUGAR
125 ML (4 FL OZ/½ CUP) CREAM (35% FAT)
½ VANILLA BEAN, SPLIT AND SCRAPED
PINCH OF FINE SEA SALT

Cut the butter into small cubes and soften to room temperature. Finely chop the two chocolates and place in a medium stainless-steel or ceramic bowl.

Put the sugar in a small heavy-based saucepan and add enough water to just wet the sugar. Place the saucepan over high heat and turn the sugar into caramel. When the caramel turns a medium golden brown, slowly and carefully add the cream. This will cause a strong reaction and you will see the caramel and cream bubble dramatically. Using a wooden spoon, stir until the reaction settles down and the caramel has dissolved in the cream. Add the vanilla bean and whisk. While hot, pour the mixture onto the chocolate in the bowl and slowly stir. When the chocolate and cream mixture are fully incorporated, add the sea salt and softened butter. Mix well with a wooden spoon until fully incorporated. It is crucial that the butter is soft before adding it. Allow the ganache to cool completely, then refrigerate for at least 1 hour. Remove from the refrigerator 2 hours before assembly to allow the ganache to return to room temperature.

chocolate and hazelnut dacquoise

35 G (1¼ OZ) GROUND ALMONDS
90 G (3¼ OZ) HAZELNUTS, ROASTED, SKINNED AND FINELY CHOPPED
8 G (¼ OZ) FINEST DARK COCOA POWDER
4 EGG WHITES
110 G (3¾ OZ) CASTER (SUPERFINE) SUGAR

Preheat the oven to 160°C (315°F/Gas 2–3). Mix the ground almonds, hazelnuts and sifted cocoa powder together. In a separate bowl, whisk the egg whites until soft peaks form, then slowly add the sugar and whisk until the egg whites form stiff peaks. Fold the dry ingredients through the egg whites.

You will need a flat baking tray lined with a silicone mat. Using a palette knife, spread the mixture out to a thickness of about 3 mm (⅛ inch). Place the tray in the oven and bake for 6–8 minutes, or until crisp. Remove from the oven. While still warm, use a 6 cm (2½ inch) round cutter to cut out eight discs. Allow the discs to cool completely, then store the discs in an airtight container until needed, placing a sheet of silicone paper between each disc.

cake base

240 G (8½ OZ) DARK CHOCOLATE (70%)
250 G (9 OZ) UNSALTED BUTTER
200 G (7 OZ) CASTER (SUPERFINE) SUGAR
4 WHOLE EGGS
65 G (2½ OZ) PLAIN (ALL-PURPOSE) FLOUR

Preheat the oven to 180°C (350°F/Gas 4). Finely chop the chocolate and melt it over a double boiler, then remove from the heat and allow the chocolate to cool. Meanwhile, cream the butter and sugar in an electric mixer until they are well emulsified. Add the eggs, one at a time, mixing until all the eggs are incorporated. When the chocolate is cool but not set, pour it into the butter mixture and beat well. Sift over the flour and fold through the mixture.

You will need two flat baking trays lined with silicone mats. Using a palette knife, spread the chocolate mixture out to a thickness of 1 cm (½ inch). Place the trays in the oven and bake for 4–5 minutes, or until set. Remove from the oven and leave the cakes on the trays to cool completely. When cool, use a 10 cm (4 inch) round cutter to cut out eight circles from the cakes. Store the cake circles in an airtight container until needed, placing a sheet of silicone paper between each cake.

milk chocolate praline discs

40 G (1½ OZ) CASTER (SUPERFINE) SUGAR
20 G (¾ OZ) HAZELNUTS, ROASTED, SKINNED AND
   FINELY CHOPPED
200 G (7 OZ) MILK CHOCOLATE (40%)

Put the sugar in a small heavy-based saucepan and add enough water to just wet the sugar. Place the saucepan over high heat and turn the sugar into caramel. When the caramel turns a medium golden brown, add the hazelnuts and then pour the caramel onto a baking tray lined with a silicone mat. Allow the praline to cool and harden completely. Finely chop the praline with either a sharp heavy knife or use a food processor.

Finely chop the chocolate and melt it over a double boiler, then add the chopped praline and stir to combine. Spread the chocolate and praline mixture onto a silicone mat to a 2 mm (¹⁄₁₆ inch) thickness. Before the chocolate sets completely, use a 6 cm (2½ inch) round cutter to cut out eight discs. When the chocolate has set completely, remove the discs and store in an airtight container, placing a sheet of silicone paper between each disc.

chocolate caramel cream

60 G (2¼ OZ) MILK CHOCOLATE (40%)
60 G (2¼ OZ) CASTER (SUPERFINE) SUGAR
250 ML (9 FL OZ/1 CUP) CREAM (35% FAT)
250 G (9 OZ) DOUBLE CREAM (45–50% FAT)

Finely chop the chocolate and place in a stainless-steel bowl. Put the sugar in a small heavy-based saucepan and add enough water to just wet the sugar. Place the saucepan over high heat and turn the sugar into caramel. When the caramel turns a medium golden brown, slowly and carefully add the cream. This will cause a strong reaction and you will see the caramel and cream bubble dramatically. Using a wooden spoon, stir until the reaction settles down and the caramel has dissolved in the cream. Remove from the heat and allow to cool slightly.

Pour the warm caramel cream mixture onto the chocolate and stir until the chocolate has dissolved. Place the mixture into the refrigerator and allow to chill completely. When the mixture is cold, transfer it into a large stainless-steel bowl. Add the double cream and whisk until soft peaks form. Refrigerate the chocolate caramel cream until required.

hot chocolate sauce

250 G (9 OZ) DARK CHOCOLATE (70%)
150 ML (5 FL OZ) MILK

Finely chop the chocolate and melt it over a double boiler. Put the milk in a saucepan and heat to about 80°C (175°F). Stir the milk into the melted chocolate and keep the sauce warm. If the chocolate sauce becomes too thick, add more hot milk.

dark chocolate top disc

200 G (7 OZ) DARK CHOCOLATE (70%)

For the best results you will need to temper the chocolate for these discs. You will need a chocolate thermometer and a double boiler or a chocolate temperer. Firstly line a flat baking tray with a sheet of silicone paper. Cover the tray and silicone paper with plastic wrap. The plastic needs to be wrapped completely around the tray to form a tight taut surface. The tray needs to be perfectly flat.

To temper the chocolate, finely chop the chocolate and gently heat it in a double boiler until it reaches 48°C (118°F). Allow the chocolate to cool to 29°C (84°F). You can do this by working the chocolate on a marble slab or by turning the double boiler off and carefully stirring the chocolate with a spoon. The chocolate will now need to be heated back up to 34°C (93°F). Next, spread the tempered chocolate onto the prepared tray using a palette knife. Create a smooth thin layer of chocolate about 1–2 mm (1⁄16 inch) thick. Before the chocolate sets completely, use a 10 cm (4 inch) round cutter to cut out eight discs. When the chocolate has completely set, carefully remove the discs from the tray and transfer to an airtight container, placing a sheet of silicone paper between each disc. Store at a cool temperature until required.

to finish and plate

To assemble the chocolate cake, you will need eight stainless-steel rings, 10 cm (4 inches) in diameter and 2.5 cm (1 inch) high. We have had these custom-made for us at Quay. If you can find a similar ring, you can adjust the quantities and measurements to suit. You will also need a metal tray and a kitchen blow torch.

To begin, place the cake bases on a metal tray, leaving a good space between each base. Place a cake ring on top of each base, fitting the base into the ring. Next, add 1 large tablespoon of chocolate mousse mixture onto each base. Using a teaspoon, spread the mousse out and up the sides of the cake rings to an even thickness of about 1 cm (½ inch). Place the milk chocolate praline discs in the rings, on top of the mousse, and press down gently. Take 2 teaspoons of caramel, vanilla and chocolate ganache and spread this out over the milk chocolate praline disc. Next, place the chocolate and hazelnut dacquoise disc on the ganache and press down gently. Take the chocolate caramel cream and whisk until stiff peaks form. Place 1 large tablespoon of the chocolate caramel cream on top of the dacquoise and use a palette knife to spread the cream out to form a flush layer against the top of the ring. Carefully remove a 3 cm (1¼ inch) diameter circle of caramel cream from the centre of each cake; you can use a teaspoon to do this. You need to ensure that you have removed at least 1 cm (½ inch) of depth from the surface of the cake. (Essentially this is a small hole in the top of the cake for the hot chocolate sauce to melt through the thin chocolate disc, giving the effect of hot chocolate sauce melting through the cake.)

Use a kitchen blow torch to briefly heat the outside metal edge of the cake rings. Do this one at a time. Wait a couple of seconds and slide the metal ring up from the cake. Now top each cake with the dark chocolate top disc; this disc should sit flush with the edge of the cake. Flash the top of the chocolate to ensure an even sheen. Carefully move each cake from the tray to the centre of a serving plate, using a wide, bent palette knife. Place the hot chocolate sauce into a small copper saucepan, ensuring the sauce is at a reasonably hot temperature. Serve the cake and then serve a small spoonful of the hot chocolate sauce directly to the middle of each cake. Do this in front of your guests and they will see the chocolate sauce melt through the chocolate disc into the hole you previously made, adding a little theatre to the whole experience.

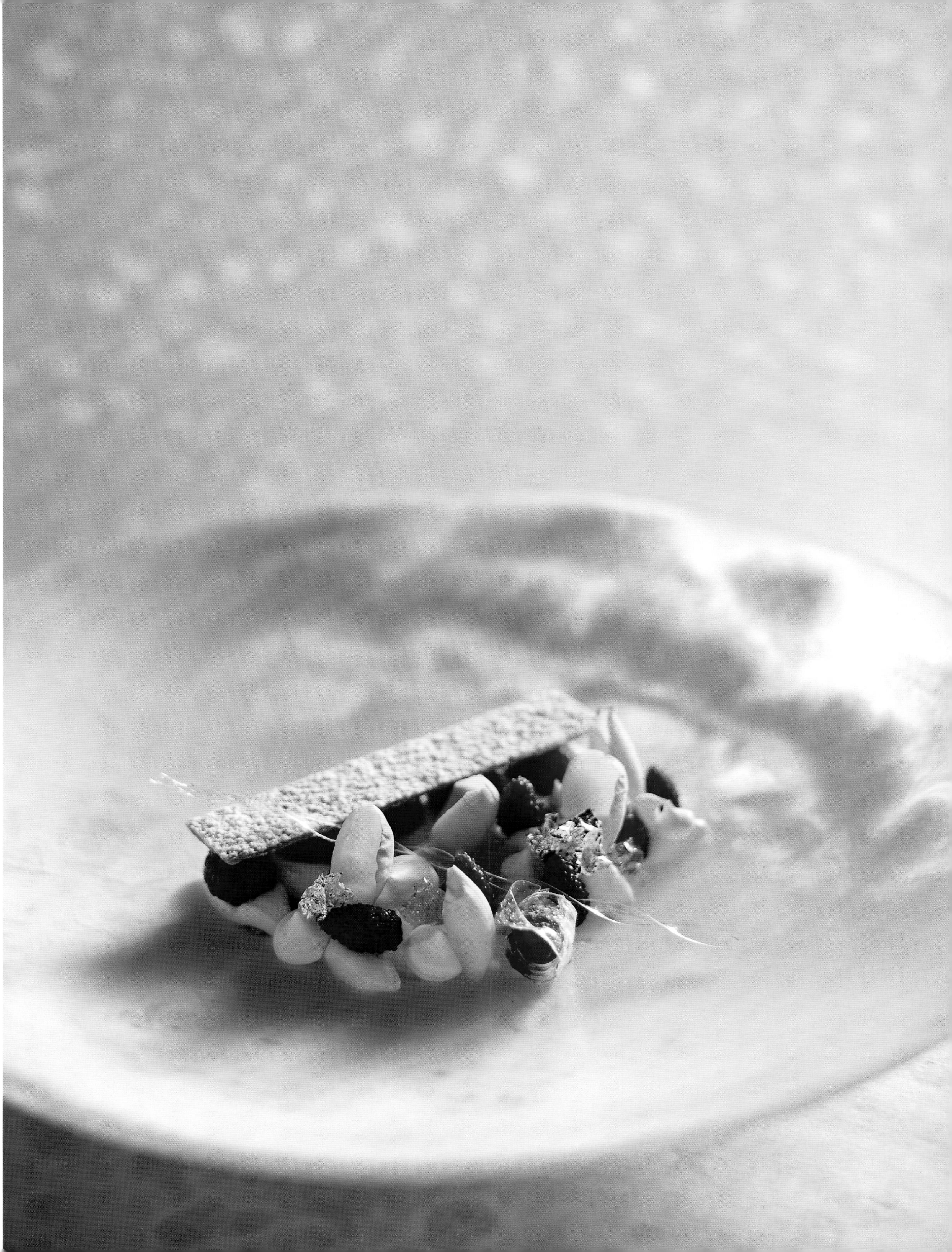

SERVES 8

puff pastry mille feuille with raspberries and fraise de bois

This is a whimsical free-style mille feuille with fresh raspberries and fraise de bois. Fraise de bois are not grown commercially in Australia, so we have these small wild strawberries grown for us in the Blue Mountains. Fraise de bois have a wonderful strawberry perfume and in this dessert I have matched them with rose-scented cream and jelly.

ingredients

150 G (5½ OZ) PURE ICING (CONFECTIONERS') SUGAR, SIFTED, FOR ROLLING AND DUSTING

1 QUANTITY PUFF PASTRY (BASIC RECIPES, PAGE 269)

200 ML (7 FL OZ) EGG WHITE

200 G (7 OZ) CASTER (SUPERFINE) SUGAR

200 G (7 OZ) PURE ICING (CONFECTIONERS') SUGAR, EXTRA, SIFTED

400 G (14 OZ) ROSE CREAM (BASIC RECIPES, PAGE 269)

200 ML (7 FL OZ) NATURAL ROSE JELLY (RECIPE, PAGE 256)

300 G (10½ OZ) ISOMALT

48 RASPBERRIES

48 FRAISE DE BOIS

40 ORGANIC ROSE PETALS

2 X 10 CM (4 INCH) SQUARE SHEETS PURE SILVER LEAF

VANILLA CREAM

200 G (7 OZ) VANILLA CUSTARD BASE (BASIC RECIPES, PAGE 269)

200 G (7 OZ) DOUBLE CREAM (45–50% FAT)

method

Preheat the oven to 160°C (315°F/Gas 2–3). Line a heavy-based baking tray with silicone paper. Dust the work surface liberally with icing sugar. Put the pastry on the icing sugar and liberally dust the pastry with more icing sugar. Roll the pastry out to a 2 mm (¹⁄₁₆ inch) thickness and place on the tray, cover with another sheet of paper and put two flat heavy-based trays on top. Bake the pastry for 10–15 minutes, checking after 10 minutes, until the pastry is golden brown. Cut a 2 x 10 cm (¾ x 4 inch) template from cardboard or plastic. Once the pastry has cooled a little, use a serrated bread knife to cut it to the shape of the template; you will need 16 oblongs of pastry. When completely cool, store in an airtight container.

Reduce the oven to 70°C (155°F/Gas ¼). To make the meringues, whisk the egg whites in an electric mixer on high, then gradually add the caster sugar; continue whisking on high for 5–6 minutes until very stiff peaks form. Using a hand whisk, fold in the extra sifted icing sugar. Place the meringue in a piping bag fitted with a 5 mm (¼ inch) round nozzle and pipe 64 small meringues onto a baking tray lined with a silicone mat. Dry the meringues out in the oven for 4–5 hours. When cool, store in an airtight container.

Meanwhile, to make the vanilla cream, whisk together the vanilla custard base and cream until firm peaks form. Refrigerate until needed. Make the rose cream and natural rose jelly, setting the jelly to a depth of 5 mm (¼ inch) in a shallow tray.

Increase the oven to 120°C (230°F/Gas ½). To make the isomalt twists and wraps, put the isomalt in a heavy-based pan and heat to 150°C (300°F). Pour half the liquid onto a baking tray lined with silicone paper and use a spatula to spread it out as thinly as possible in one motion. Cover with another sheet of silicone paper and put aside. Bring the remaining isomalt back to 150°C (300°F) and repeat. Bake the sheets of isomalt, one at a time, for 1–2 minutes, or until the isomalt becomes soft and pliable. Working quickly, remove the sheet, along with the silicone paper, from the oven and roll a rolling pin over the paper to make an even flatter sheet of isomalt, about 1 mm (¹⁄₁₆ inch) thick. Put aside and repeat for the other sheet. Heat one sheet briefly in the oven so it becomes pliable again, then use a pair of scissors to cut it into eight strips, 10 cm (4 inches) long and 5 mm (¼ inch) wide. Repeat the heating process and cut eight strips, 7 cm (2¾ inches) long and 1.5 cm (⅝ inch) wide.

When you have cut all your strips, you will need to reheat them one at a time. Reheat the longer strips in the oven until soft and pliable, then peel away the paper and quickly twist the isomalt strip to form a spiral. Place on a new sheet of silicone paper. Repeat this process until you have eight spirals. (If you have a heat lamp, you can work under this.) Similarly, reheat the shorter strips one at a time, peel away the paper and wrap it around a raspberry. Put aside to cool on silicone paper. The spiral strips can be stored in an airtight container with moisture-absorbing beads and can be made hours in advance. The wrapped raspberries need to be made just moments before you serve the dessert.

to finish and plate

Dice the rose jelly into 5 mm (¼ inch) squares. Whip the vanilla and rose creams separately to form firm peaks. In the centre of each serving plate, dot some vanilla cream to help stick down the first layer of puff pastry. Using a warm teaspoon, make five vanilla cream quenelles and place them along the pastry. Place five raspberries on top of the quenelles. Dust the top sheet of pastry with icing sugar and place it on the raspberries. Next to the mille feuille, place five quenelles of rose cream. Scatter eight meringues, six fraise de bois, 3 teaspoons of jelly, five rose petals and two torn pieces of silver leaf. Arrange an isomalt raspberry and spiral on the plate and serve.

SERVES 8

white nectarines, raspberries and cherries set in their juices with vanilla panna cotta

This dessert has been with me in one form or another since I started at Quay. There is a fair amount of preparation but it's a great dessert for a dinner party as all the work is done beforehand. The white raspberries, cherries and nectarines are in season at the same time for only a few weeks each year.

ingredients

1.3 KG (3 LB) CASTER (SUPERFINE) SUGAR
1 VANILLA BEAN, SPLIT AND SCRAPED
12 WHITE NECTARINES
24 WHITE CHERRIES
11 SHEETS TITANIUM GELATINE
4 X 10 CM (4 INCH) SQUARE SHEETS PURE GOLD LEAF
56 WHITE RASPBERRIES

VANILLA PANNA COTTA
800 ML (28 FL OZ) CREAM (35% FAT)
180 G (6½ OZ) CASTER (SUPERFINE) SUGAR
1 VANILLA BEAN, SPLIT AND SCRAPED
4 SHEETS TITANIUM GELATINE

method

To make the vanilla panna cotta, put the cream, sugar and vanilla bean in a saucepan. Bring the cream close to boiling point, then pass the cream through a fine sieve and discard the vanilla bean. Meanwhile, soak the gelatine sheets in cold water until softened. Squeeze the excess water from the gelatine, add to the hot cream and stir to dissolve the gelatine. Allow to cool but not set. Place eight rectangle moulds (see Note), 12 cm (4½ inches) long, 2.5 cm (1 inch) wide and 3 cm (1¼ inches) deep, on a flat tray lined with silicone paper. Pour in the cold liquid panna cotta to a depth of 1 cm (½ inch) in each mould and refrigerate for at least 4 hours to set before proceeding to the next step.

To make a white nectarine syrup, combine the sugar, vanilla bean and 2 litres (70 fl oz/8 cups) of water in a large pan. Bring to the boil, then reduce the heat to the barest simmer. Cut the nectarines in half and place them in the syrup. Cover them with a cartouche made from silicone paper and place two small plates on top of the cartouche to help submerge the nectarines. Gently poach the nectarines for 4 minutes, then remove the pan from the heat and leave the nectarines in the syrup for another 4 minutes. Remove the plates and cartouche and test the nectarines with the point of a sharp knife. If they are tender, remove them from the pan; if they are still firm, leave them in the syrup for another 5 minutes or so. Peel the skins from the nectarines and refrigerate to cool. Pour the syrup through a fine sieve, but not so fine that it catches the

vanilla seeds. Discard the vanilla bean. Measure out 1.6 litres (55½ fl oz) of syrup and put aside.

Slice the cheeks from the nectarines. Using a 2 cm (¾ inch) round pastry cutter, cut out circles from the nectarines; you will need five circles for each dessert. Trim the circles to a thickness of 1 cm (½ inch). Reserve the rest of the nectarine flesh for another use. Halve and stone the white cherries.

Bring the reserved syrup up to simmering point, then remove from the heat. Meanwhile, soak the gelatine sheets in cold water until softened. Squeeze the excess water from the gelatine, add to the hot syrup and stir to dissolve the gelatine. Add the cherry halves and allow the syrup to cool, but don't let it set.

Place five nectarine discs and six cherry halves on each panna cotta. Pour in enough of the poaching syrup to fill a further 1 cm (½ inch). Return to the refrigerator to set for 1 hour. Cut each piece of gold leaf into eight pieces. Once the jelly has set, place seven white raspberries and four small pieces of gold leaf on top. Fill the moulds with more jelly, leaving 3 mm (⅛ inch) unfilled; you may need to rewarm the rest of the jelly if it has set. If you do, make sure it has cooled completely before you pour the last layer. Return the desserts to the refrigerator and set fully. Once set, top up the final 3 mm (⅛ inch) with cold liquid jelly. This way you will finish with a smooth surface and the fruit will be suspended at different levels throughout the jelly. Refrigerate for a minimum of 3 hours before serving.

to finish and plate

Lift the moulds from the tray and wipe away any jelly or panna cotta that is clinging to the outside of the mould. Place each mould in the centre of the serving plate. With a kitchen blow torch, gently heat each side of the metal mould with the flame. Cool for a couple of seconds and then lift the mould away carefully. Serve.

Note: We have these moulds custom-made for this dessert. The moulds have no bottom, so you must make sure the panna cotta is almost set when you pour the first layer. You could use a regular metal dariole mould but you would need to set the fruit jelly first and the panna cotta last. When set, simply invert the mould onto a plate, flash it with a blow torch and lift off the mould.

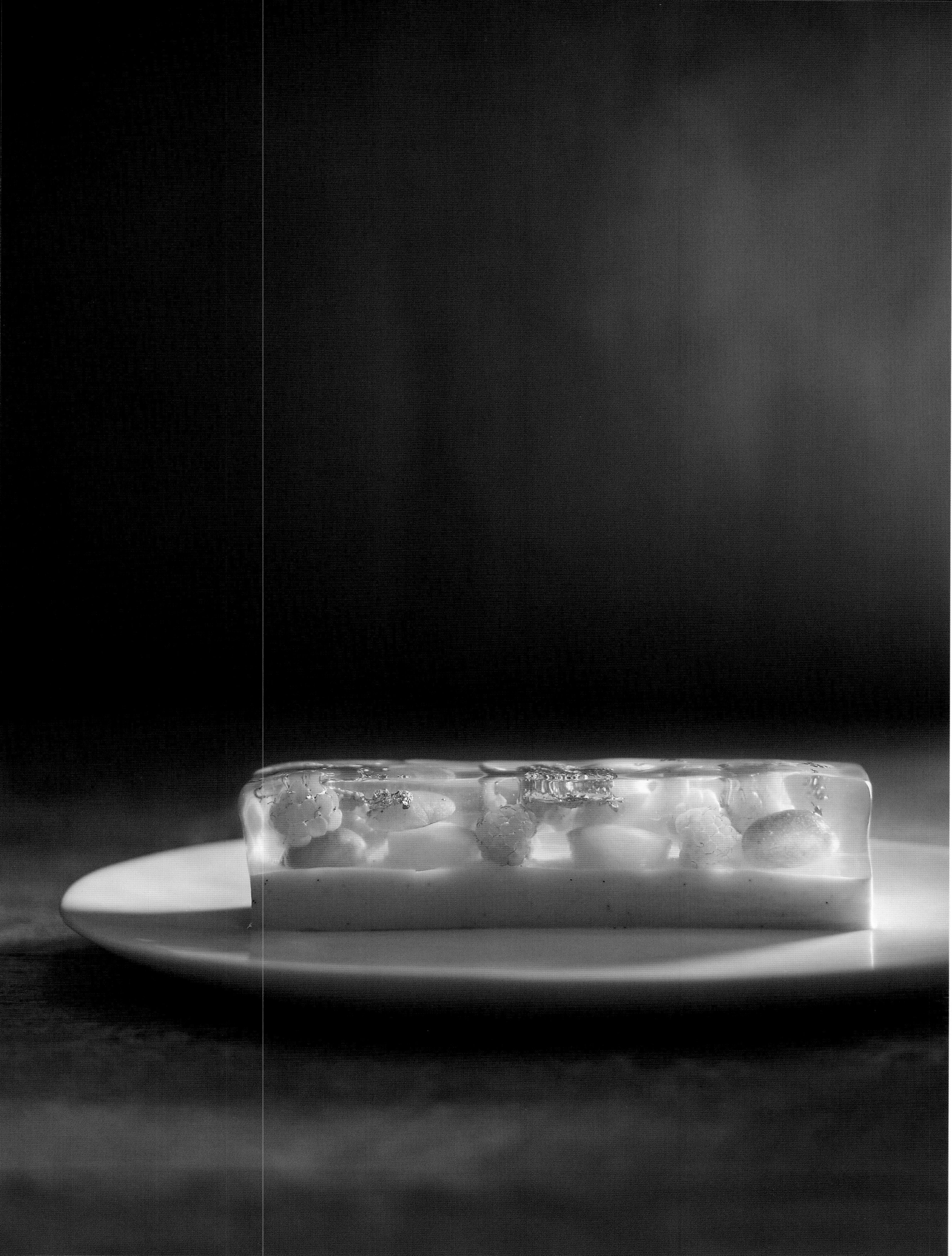

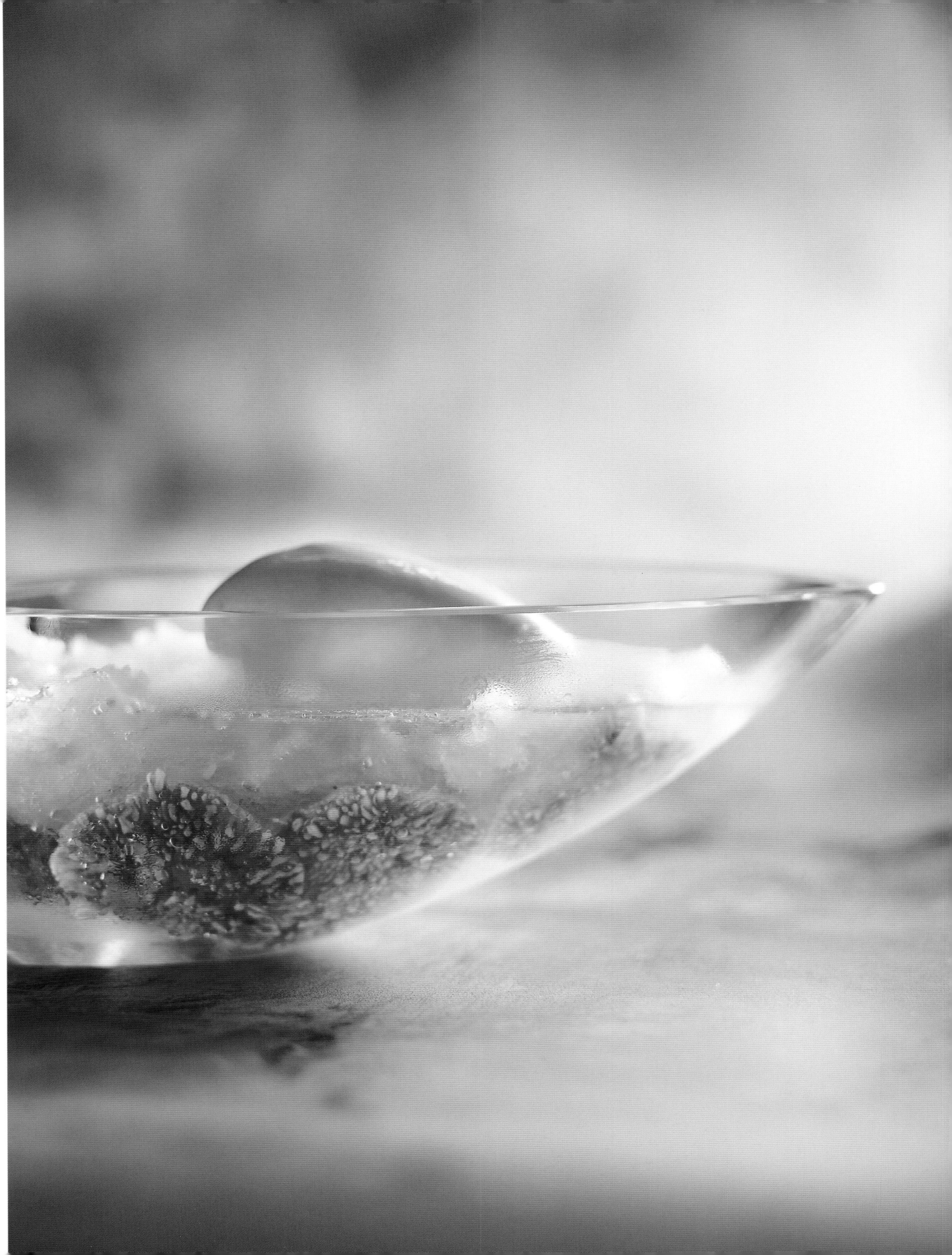

SERVES 8

fresh figs with fig leaf ice cream, granita and syrup

This is a very refreshing dessert to serve in summer when figs are at the height of their season. I recently discovered that fresh leaves from the fig tree contain just as much flavour and probably more perfume than the figs themselves when infused into a liquid. The advantage of using fig leaves is that you can obtain a pure fig flavour without the coarseness of using the fig flesh, and they give the ice cream the most amazing flavour and perfume.

fig leaf granita

450 G (1 LB) CASTER (SUPERFINE) SUGAR
8 FRESH FIG LEAVES

Put 1 litre (35 fl oz/4 cups) of water and the sugar in a saucepan and bring to the boil. Pour the boiling syrup over the fig leaves and infuse for 30 minutes at room temperature. Place the syrup and fig leaves into a container and allow to macerate in the refrigerator overnight. Remove the fig leaves and pour the syrup into a shallow tray with sides, to a depth of 5 cm (2 inches), then place the tray in the freezer. Remove from the freezer once every hour and break up the ice crystals with a fork. Do this four or five times to form the granita.

fig leaf ice cream

800 ML (28 FL OZ) MILK
500 G (1 LB 2 OZ) CASTER (SUPERFINE) SUGAR
10 FRESH FIG LEAVES
10 EGG YOLKS

Combine the milk, 200 ml (7 fl oz) of water and 250 g (9 oz) of sugar in a saucepan. Bring to the boil, then pour the mixture onto the fig leaves and allow to infuse for 30 minutes.

Whisk the egg yolks and remaining 250 g (9 oz) of sugar together in a large stainless-steel bowl to make a sabayon. Place the bowl over a saucepan of simmering water and cook the mixture, whisking continuously, for 8–10 minutes. Strain the milk and fig leaves and discard the fig leaves. Whisk the milk and sabayon together. Place the mixture into a blender and blend on high for 2 minutes. Cool the mixture over an ice bath. When completely cold, transfer the mixture into an ice-cream machine and churn until frozen. Place the ice cream in a container in the freezer for at least 1 hour. This ice cream is best served within 12 hours of making.

fig leaf syrup

325 G (11½ OZ) CASTER (SUPERFINE) SUGAR
½ VANILLA BEAN, SPLIT AND SCRAPED
4 FRESH FIG LEAVES

Put 500 ml (17 fl oz/2 cups) of water, the sugar and vanilla bean in a saucepan. Bring to the boil, then pour the syrup over the fig leaves and allow to infuse for 30 minutes at room temperature. Place the syrup and fig leaves in a container and allow to macerate in the refrigerator overnight. Remove the vanilla bean and fig leaves. Whisk well and pass the syrup through a sieve that allows the vanilla seeds to come through.

to finish and plate

16 FRESH GREEN FIGS (OR USE BLACK FIGS)

This dessert is best served in glass bowls or martini glasses. Peel the green figs with a sharp knife, removing the skin and white pith, and cut into 2 cm (¾ inch) thick slices. Line the bowls or glasses with the fig slices. Spoon in the fig leaf granita and pour over a couple of tablespoons of fig leaf syrup. Using a tablespoon, shape a quenelle of fig leaf ice cream and place it on top of the granita. Serve immediately.

SERVES 8

florentine

This is a dessert I've been making for several years now. Originally I made a terrine of almond milk and muscatel raisin semifreddo, chocolate sorbet, amaretto cream and topped it with a florentine biscuit, but here I've made a more free-formed version, and have incorporated shards of dried vanilla-flavoured milk skin. The classic flavour marriage of almond, chocolate and raisin work beautifully in this dessert.

milk skins

8 LITRES (280 FL OZ) HOMOGENISED JERSEY MILK
4 VANILLA BEANS, SPLIT AND SCRAPED

Preheat the oven to 50°C (125°F/Gas ¼). Put the milk and vanilla beans into a large bowl and gently whisk. Pour 500 ml (17 fl oz/2 cups) of the vanilla-infused milk into a large saucepan and carefully bring the milk to a simmer. Remove the pan from the heat and cool for 15 minutes. A skin will form on top of the milk. Using a palette knife, release the milk skin from around the edge of the pan. Then, with your fingers, carefully remove the skin from the surface of the milk and lay it flat on a baking tray lined with a sheet of lightly oiled silicone paper. (You will need 3 or 4 trays lined with lightly oiled silicone paper.) Reheat the milk to repeat the process again, then discard the milk. Repeat the process until all the milk is used. You will need a minimum of 4 curled milk skins for each dessert. Place the milk skins in the oven for 1–2 hours, or until crisp. The skins will dry out and naturally curl. Cool at room temperature, then store in an airtight container with moisture-absorbing beads.

almond ice cream

100 G (3½ OZ) WHOLE BLANCHED ALMONDS
450 ML (16 FL OZ) MILK
6 EGG YOLKS
175 G (6 OZ) CASTER (SUPERFINE) SUGAR
200 ML (7 FL OZ) CREAM (35% FAT)

Preheat the oven to 150°C (300°F/Gas 2). Place the almonds on a baking tray and roast in the oven until golden brown. Finely chop the almonds and add to the milk in a pan. Warm the milk and almonds on the stove until just before boiling point, then remove the pan from the heat and allow to infuse for 30 minutes. Strain the milk through a sieve lined with a double layer of muslin cloth.

Whisk the egg yolks and sugar together in a large stainless-steel bowl. Place the bowl over a pan of simmering water and cook the mixture, whisking continuously, for 8–10 minutes, to form a light sabayon. Remove from the heat, place the bowl over ice and continue to whisk until cool. Whisk through the cream, then transfer the mixture to an ice-cream machine and churn until frozen. Place the ice cream in a container in the freezer for at least 1 hour.

florentine biscuit

150 G (5½ OZ) FLAKED ALMONDS
250 G (9 OZ) CASTER (SUPERFINE) SUGAR
150 G (5½ OZ) AMADEI CHUAO CHOCOLATE (70%)

Preheat the oven to 150°C (300°F/Gas 2). Place the almonds on a baking tray and roast in the oven until golden brown. Remove and set aside. Put the sugar in a small heavy-based saucepan and add enough water to just wet the sugar. Place the saucepan over high heat and turn the sugar into a golden caramel. Remove the pan from the heat, add the almonds and quickly fold through the caramel. Spread the almond praline out on a baking tray lined with silicone paper and allow to cool completely.

Line a flat heavy-based baking tray with a silicone mat. Process the almond praline in a food processor to form a fine powder. Transfer the praline to a sieve and sift the praline onto the silicone mat in a fine layer, about 2 mm (1/16 inch) thick. Bake in the oven for 4–5 minutes, or until golden brown, then remove and put aside. When the praline has cooled slightly, use the point of a sharp knife to gently score 8 cm (3¼ inch) squares into the praline. Once set, remove the squares with a palette knife and allow the praline biscuits to cool.

Finely chop the chocolate and melt it over a double boiler. Using a palette knife, spread the chocolate over the top surface of each biscuit. Allow the chocolate to cool and set.

chocolate sorbet

300 G (10½ OZ) CASTER (SUPERFINE) SUGAR
40 G (1½ OZ) FINEST DARK COCOA POWDER
25 G (1 OZ) DARK CHOCOLATE (70%)

Put the sugar and 500 ml (17 fl oz/2 cups) of water in a saucepan and bring to the boil. Remove the pan from the heat and add the sifted cocoa powder, whisking until smooth. Return the pan to the stovetop over low heat and simmer for 3 minutes. Remove from the heat and allow to cool slightly. Chop the chocolate, add to the pan and whisk well. Pass the mixture through a sieve lined with muslin cloth, then refrigerate until cool. Whisk the mixture again, then transfer to an ice-cream machine and churn until frozen. Place the sorbet in a container in the freezer for at least 1 hour.

amaretto cream

200 G (7 OZ) VANILLA CUSTARD BASE
  (BASIC RECIPES, PAGE 269)
200 G (7 OZ) DOUBLE CREAM (45–50% FAT)
50 ML (1¾ FL OZ) AMARETTO

In a small bowl, whisk together the vanilla custard base, cream and amaretto until it forms soft peaks. Refrigerate until needed.

almond marzipan crumble

100 G (3½ OZ) WHOLE BLANCHED ALMONDS
65 G (2¼ OZ) GOOD QUALITY MARZIPAN

Preheat the oven to 150°C (300°F/Gas 2). Place the almonds on a baking tray and roast in the oven until golden. Remove and set aside. When the almonds are cool, place them in a food processor with the marzipan and process for a few seconds until a loose crumble is formed. Put aside.

chocolate-coated raisins

25 ML (1 FL OZ) AMARETTO
25 G (1 OZ) CASTER (SUPERFINE) SUGAR
16 LARGE MUSCATEL RAISINS, SEEDS REMOVED
100 G (3½ OZ) AMADEI CHUAO CHOCOLATE (70%)

Put the amaretto, sugar and 50 ml (1¾ fl oz) of water in a saucepan and bring to the boil. Remove the pan from the heat and add the raisins, then put aside to macerate for 1 hour. Drain the raisins well on kitchen paper. Finely chop the chocolate and melt it over a double boiler. Carefully dip the raisins in the chocolate, then place the chocolate-coated raisins on a sheet of silicone paper to set.

to finish and plate

Using a warmed tablespoon, form two quenelles of amaretto cream and place them in the centre of each serving bowl. Cut the florentine biscuits into rough shards and sprinkle on top of the quenelles. Place two chocolate-coated raisins on top and sprinkle with the almond marzipan crumble. Using a tablespoon, form one quenelle of almond ice cream and one quenelle of chocolate sorbet and place each quenelle on top of the cream and crumble mixture. Place shards of the curled milk skin around the ice cream to form a teepee-like structure. Serve immediately.

SERVES 8

warm cherry cake with cherry confit, milk biscuits and white cherry ice cream

This dessert of warm cherry cake with a water-based chocolate ganache, fresh cherries, confit of wild cherries, coconut cream and a special white cherry ice cream is a particularly luscious combination of flavours, textures and temperatures. The white cherry ice cream took several weeks to perfect, as it was difficult to harness all the flavour from the cherries, while preventing them from oxidising.

milk biscuits

100 ML (3½ FL OZ) LIQUID GLUCOSE
1 LITRE (35 FL OZ/4 CUPS) HOMOGENISED JERSEY MILK

Preheat the oven to 65°C (150°F/Gas ¼). Combine the liquid glucose and milk in a saucepan and heat to 80°C (175°F), then froth the mixture with a hand-held blender. Scoop the froth off onto a baking tray lined with a silicone mat. Repeat the frothing process until you have obtained all the available froth from the milk. Place the froth into the oven for 2 hours to dry out. When the milk froth is dry, allow it to cool completely and then store in an airtight container with moisture-absorbing beads.

cherry juice syrup

1.5 KG (3 LB 5 OZ) DARK CHERRIES SUCH AS BING

Pit the cherries and put them through an electric juicer. Pass the cherry juice through a sieve lined with muslin cloth. Place the juice in a saucepan and reduce over high heat by three-quarters. You should have about 200 ml (7 fl oz) of reduced cherry juice syrup.

sugar crystals

300 G (10½ OZ) CASTER (SUPERFINE) SUGAR
90 ML (3 FL OZ) LIQUID GLUCOSE

Preheat the oven to 200°C (400°F/Gas 6). Combine the sugar, liquid glucose and 90 ml (3 fl oz) of water in a saucepan over medium heat, stirring to dissolve the sugar and glucose. Increase the heat to high and heat to 155°C (310°F). Use a sugar thermometer to get an accurate temperature. Pour the hot liquid onto a large baking tray lined with a silicone mat and spread the liquid thinly with a palette knife. Allow the liquid to cool completely and harden, then break the sugar crystal into small shards. Place the shards into a food processor and process to a fine powder. Using a sieve with a medium-fine hole, sift a fine layer of sugar crystal powder onto a baking tray lined with a clean silicone mat. Place in the oven for a few minutes. When you see the sugar crystals melting and coming together to form small balls, remove the tray from the oven. Cool for a couple of minutes, then use a palette knife to scrape the crystals off the mat. Some of the crystals will stick together; you can either break them apart into fine crystals or leave them linked together. When the crystals are completely cool, store in an airtight container with moisture-absorbing beads.

wild cherry confit

100 G (3½ OZ) PRESERVED WILD ITALIAN CHERRIES
100 G (3½ OZ) GOOD QUALITY CHERRY JAM

Pit the wild cherries and place them in a small pan over low heat. Add the cherry jam and simmer gently for 5 minutes. Add a little water if necessary. Allow the confit to cool, then put aside.

white cherry ice cream

275 G (9¾ OZ) CASTER (SUPERFINE) SUGAR
1.1 KG (2 LB 7 OZ) WHITE CHERRIES, PITTED
6 EGG YOLKS
65 G (2¼ OZ) CASTER (SUPERFINE) SUGAR
175 ML (5½ FL OZ) CREAM (35% FAT)

Make a sugar syrup by combining the sugar with 330 ml (11 ¼ fl oz) of water in a saucepan. Bring to the boil, then pour directly onto the pitted white cherries. Allow the cherries to infuse for 10 minutes, then, wearing a pair of clean rubber gloves, squeeze the cherries in the syrup. Allow to infuse for a further 10 minutes. Strain the cherry syrup into a bowl and chill over ice.

Whisk the egg yolks and sugar together in a large stainless-steel bowl. Place the bowl over a pan of simmering water and cook the mixture, whisking continuously, for 5 minutes to make a sabayon. Warm the cream, add it to the sabayon and continue to cook for a further 5 minutes, whisking. Strain and chill the mixture over ice.

Combine the chilled sabayon and chilled cherry syrup together, transfer to a blender and blend for 2 minutes. Pass the mixture through a fine sieve, then transfer into an ice-cream machine and churn until frozen. Place the ice cream in a container in the freezer for at least 1 hour. This ice cream is best served within 12 hours of making.

chocolate ganache

400 G (14 OZ) AMADEI CHUAO CHOCOLATE (70%)

Put 350 ml (12 fl oz) of water in a saucepan and bring to the boil. Finely chop the chocolate and place in a heatproof bowl. Pour the boiling water over the chocolate and allow it to melt, stirring occasionally. When the chocolate has completely melted, place it into a bowl over ice. Using a hand-held mixer, mix the chocolate on medium speed. You need to watch the chocolate carefully — as soon as it begins to set and form thick ribbons, stop the mixer. Spoon the water ganache into a bowl and place in the refrigerator to cool for a minimum of 30 minutes. (You will need to remove the ganache from the refrigerator 1 hour prior to serving.) This type of ganache is made without cream and butter, and relies on the cocoa butter to set it. It is very light on the palate and has a very pure chocolate taste. This method is based on a Heston Blumenthal recipe.

cake

100 G (3½ OZ) UNSALTED BUTTER, SOFTENED
200 G (7 OZ) CASTER (SUPERFINE) SUGAR
3 EGGS
200 G (7 OZ) PLAIN (ALL-PURPOSE) FLOUR
4 G (⅛ OZ) BICARBONATE OF SODA (BAKING SODA)
10 G (¼ OZ) BAKING POWDER
120 ML (4 FL OZ) MILK

Preheat the oven to 160°C (315°F/Gas 2–3). Grease a 20 x 9 x 7 cm (8 x 3½ x 2¾ inch) loaf tin.

Cream the butter and sugar together, then add the eggs, one at a time, while continuing to mix. Combine the flour, bicarbonate of soda and baking powder and sift onto the butter and egg mixture. Fold in the dry ingredients with a spatula, then fold in the milk. Place the cake batter into the tin and bake for about 40 minutes, or until cooked when tested with a skewer. Remove from the oven and place on a wire rack to cool.

coconut cream

100 ML (3½ FL OZ) MILK
100 ML (3½ FL OZ) CREAM (35% FAT)
50 G (1¾ OZ) CASTER (SUPERFINE) SUGAR
100 G (3½ OZ) COCONUT CREAM POWDER
80 G (2¾ OZ) DOUBLE CREAM (45–50% FAT)

Combine the milk, cream and sugar in a saucepan and bring to the boil. Put the coconut cream powder into a heatproof bowl and pour over the boiling milk and cream mixture, whisking well as you pour in the liquid. Place in the refrigerator to cool completely. Put the cooled coconut cream mixture into a bowl with the double cream and whisk together with a hand whisk until soft peaks form. Store in the refrigerator until required.

to finish and plate

24 DARK CHERRIES SUCH AS BING

Preheat the oven to 180°C (350°F/Gas 4). Cut the dark cherries in half and remove the stones. Coat the cherries in 40 ml (1¼ fl oz) of the reduced cherry juice syrup. Place the cherries on a large sheet of silicone paper and fold the paper up around the cherries to form an airtight parcel. Place the parcel on a baking tray and bake in the oven for 2 minutes to warm the cherries. Trim the edges of the cake, then cut into 16 small pieces, about 2 cm (¾ inch) square, and soak the cake well in the remaining cherry juice syrup. Place the cake pieces on a baking tray lined with silicone paper and bake for 3–4 minutes. The cake will have absorbed the syrup but should still hold together and be warm.

Divide the cake and cherries evenly among eight serving bowls. Add a couple of spoonfuls of the coconut cream and two quenelles of the chocolate ganache. Crumble some milk biscuits over the dessert and add a couple of small pieces of sugar crystals. Spoon some wild cherry confit on top, then finish with a quenelle of white cherry ice cream. Serve immediately.

SERVES 8

cherries and berries

This dessert is a celebration of summer when cherries and all types of berries are in season. A crumble is made using caramelised puff pastry and white chocolate caramelised almonds, which adds a great texture and crunch to the cherries, berries, cream and jelly. The addition of raspberry and cherry sorbet adds a nice temperature contrast to the dish.

raspberry sorbet

150 G (5½ OZ) CASTER (SUPERFINE) SUGAR
1 VANILLA BEAN, SPLIT AND SCRAPED
350 G (12 OZ) RASPBERRIES

To make a sugar syrup, put 200 ml (7 fl oz) of water in a saucepan and add the sugar and vanilla bean. Bring to the boil, then immediately take the pan off the heat. When the syrup is cool, remove the vanilla bean and pour the syrup on to the raspberries.

Blend the mixture and pass through a fine chinois to remove the raspberry seeds. Transfer the mixture into an ice-cream machine and churn until frozen. Place the sorbet in a container in the freezer for at least 1 hour.

cherry sorbet

1.1 KG (2 LB 7 OZ) DARK CHERRIES
250 G (9 OZ) CASTER (SUPERFINE) SUGAR

Pit the cherries and put them through an electric juicer. Pass the cherry juice through a chinois. Put the sugar and 250 ml (9 fl oz/1 cup) of water in a saucepan and bring to the boil. Remove from the heat and allow to cool, then add to the cherry juice. Transfer the mixture into an ice-cream machine and churn until frozen. Place the sorbet in a container in the freezer for at least 1 hour.

strawberry jelly balls

200 G (7 OZ) CASTER (SUPERFINE) SUGAR
1 VANILLA BEAN, SPLIT AND SCRAPED
500 G (1 LB 2 OZ) STRAWBERRIES, HULLED
7 SHEETS TITANIUM GELATINE

VANILLA CREAM
400 G (14 OZ) VANILLA CUSTARD BASE
 (BASIC RECIPES, PAGE 269)
100 ML (3½ FL OZ) CREAM (35% FAT)
200 G (7 OZ) DOUBLE CREAM (45–50% FAT)

Combine 500 ml (17 fl oz/2 cups) of water, the sugar and vanilla bean in a small pan and bring to the boil. Add the strawberries and simmer on the lowest possible heat for 10 minutes. Pass the liquid through a fine sieve and discard the vanilla bean and strawberries. Meanwhile, soak the gelatine sheets in cold water until softened. Squeeze the excess water from the gelatine, add to the warm syrup and stir to dissolve the gelatine. Pour the jelly into a shallow tray with sides, to a depth of 1 cm (½ inch). Place the jelly in the refrigerator to set.

Meanwhile, to make the vanilla cream, put the custard base and creams in a bowl. Whisk until firm peaks form and refrigerate until needed.

Dice the set jelly into 1 cm (½ inch) cubes using a sharp knife. Take eight 20 cm (8 inch) squares of plastic wrap and place them over eight coffee cups. Place a tablespoon of diced jelly in the centre of the plastic and then make a small indentation in the centre of the jelly. Place a teaspoon of vanilla cream into the indentation, then place another tablespoon of diced jelly on top. Carefully lift up the corners of the plastic and twist them together to form a ball. Tie a knot in the plastic. Place the jelly balls in the refrigerator to set for a minimum of 5 hours. Leftover vanilla cream will be used in plating the dessert.

caramelised puff pastry

100 G (3½ OZ) PURE ICING (CONFECTIONERS') SUGAR
200 G (7 OZ) PUFF PASTRY (BASIC RECIPES, PAGE 269)

Preheat the oven to 200°C (400°F/Gas 6). Line a heavy-based baking tray with silicone paper. Dust the work surface and rolling pin liberally with the icing sugar. Put the puff pastry on the icing sugar and liberally dust the top of the pastry with more icing sugar. Roll the pastry out to a 1 mm (1/16 inch) thickness and place on the tray. Cover with another sheet of silicone paper, then put two flat heavy-based trays on top. Bake the pastry for 10–15 minutes, checking after 10 minutes, until the pastry is caramelised and golden brown. Remove the puff pastry from the silicone paper and allow to cool completely.

white chocolate caramelised almonds

40 BLANCHED WHOLE ALMONDS
200 G (7 OZ) CASTER (SUPERFINE) SUGAR
200 G (7 OZ) GOOD QUALITY WHITE CHOCOLATE

Preheat the oven to 150°C (300°F/Gas 2). Place the almonds on a baking tray and roast in the oven until the almonds are lightly coloured. Remove and set aside. Combine the sugar and 50 ml (1¾ fl oz) of water in a small saucepan, stirring to dissolve the sugar, and heat over high heat until you have a caramel. Remove the pan from the heat and, working quickly, add the almonds to the caramel. Use two forks to coat each almond in the caramel. Remove the almonds from the pan and place on a silicone mat to set, spacing them so they don't touch each other.

Meanwhile, to melt the white chocolate, bring a saucepan of water to the boil, then remove from the heat. Finely chop the chocolate and place in a heatproof bowl. Put the bowl over the pan of hot water, making sure the base of the bowl isn't touching the water. Stir occasionally until melted. When cool, dip the almonds into the melted white chocolate to coat completely. Place the white chocolate almonds on a silicone mat to set.

to finish and plate

PURE ICING (CONFECTIONERS') SUGAR, FOR DUSTING
16 DARK CHERRIES
16 LIGHT RED CHERRIES
16 WHITE CHERRIES
16 BLACKBERRIES
16 RASPBERRIES
16 TAI BERRIES
16 BOYSENBERRIES
16 SMALL STRAWBERRIES
64 WILD STRAWBERRIES

Finely chop the caramelised puff pastry and white chocolate caramelised almonds. Mix them together and spread the mixture out in a long thin line across the middle of each serving plate. Carefully dust the mixture with icing sugar. Place a small dot of the vanilla cream in the centre of each plate. Use a small pair of scissors to cut the knot from the strawberry jelly balls and carefully peel away the plastic wrap. Place a jelly ball on the cream. Using a teaspoon, make three quenelles of vanilla cream and place them randomly on each plate. Cut the cherries in half around the seed with a small sharp knife. Twist the cherries to separate the halves and use a small sharp knife to remove the stones. Randomly place four halves of each type of cherry on the plates, then scatter with the berries. Place two quenelles of raspberry sorbet and one quenelle of cherry sorbet on top of the quenelles of vanilla cream. Serve immediately.

SERVES 8

crème caramel with sauternes jelly, pear ice cream and caramel cream

It's hard to beat the classic crème caramel as a dessert. Here I have just enhanced it with the addition of sauternes jelly and pear ice cream, which work harmoniously together.

sauternes jelly

250 G (9 OZ) CASTER (SUPERFINE) SUGAR
225 ML (7½ FL OZ) SAUTERNES
1 VANILLA BEAN, SPLIT AND SCRAPED
4 SHEETS TITANIUM GELATINE

Put 80 g (2¾ oz) of the sugar in a small heavy-based pan. Put aside for the moment. Put the remaining sugar, 450 ml (16 fl oz) of water, the sauternes and vanilla bean into a separate pan and bring to simmering point. Remove from the heat. Whisk well and remove the vanilla bean. You should have lots of fine specks of vanilla through your syrup.

Take the reserved saucepan of sugar and add enough water to just wet the sugar. Place the pan over high heat and turn the sugar into caramel. When the caramel turns a dark golden colour but is not burnt, add a small amount of the water, sugar and sauternes mixture, about 50 ml (1¾ fl oz) to start with. This will cause a violent reaction, so be careful. Continue to add small amounts of the sauternes mixture to the caramel until the caramel has completely dissolved. Then add the dissolved caramel to the main sauternes mixture. The reason for doing this is to add a deep colour to the sauternes jelly. Reheat the sauternes caramel liquid to simmering point. Meanwhile, soak the gelatine sheets in cold water until softened. Squeeze the excess water from the gelatine, add to the sauternes caramel liquid, and stir to dissolve the gelatine. Pour the jelly into a shallow tray with sides, to about 1 cm (½ inch) in depth. Refrigerate the jelly until set.

pear ice cream

3.75 KG (8 LB 4 OZ) PEARS
10 EGG YOLKS
300 G (10½ OZ) CASTER (SUPERFINE) SUGAR
250 ML (9 FL OZ/1 CUP) CREAM (35% FAT)

Place a large coffee filter in a chinois. Peel 2.5 kg (5 lb 8 oz) of the pears, then grate them over the filter and squeeze to extract the juice. You need to yield 800 ml (28 fl oz) of juice. Put the pear juice in a small saucepan and bring to the boil. Reduce the juice until you have 400 ml (14 fl oz) left.

Put the egg yolks and sugar in a stainless-steel bowl and whisk well. Pour the warm pear juice onto the eggs while whisking. Place the bowl over a pan of simmering water and cook the mixture, whisking continuously, for 6–8 minutes, to form a thin sabayon. Place the bowl over ice to cool while continuing to whisk.

Now peel and freshly grate and filter the remaining 1.25 kg (2 lb 12 oz) of pears until you have 400 ml (14 fl oz) of pear juice. Add this directly into the cooled sabayon along with the cream. Transfer the mixture into an ice-cream machine and churn until frozen. Place the ice cream in a container in the freezer for at least 1 hour. This ice cream is best served within 12 hours of making.

crème caramel

380 G (13½ OZ) CASTER (SUPERFINE) SUGAR
1 LITRE (35 FL OZ/4 CUPS) MILK
2 WHOLE EGGS
10 EGG YOLKS

Preheat the oven to 170°C (325°F/Gas 3). Have eight crème caramel moulds standing by. Put 200 g (7 oz) of sugar in a heavy-based saucepan and add enough water to just wet the sugar. Place the pan over low heat and stir to dissolve the sugar, brushing down the side of the saucepan with a wet pastry brush to ensure no crystallisation occurs. Increase the heat to high and turn the sugar into a golden caramel. As soon as the caramel is ready, pour a small amount into each mould to just cover the base.

Heat the milk in a saucepan until just simmering. Meanwhile, whisk the whole eggs and yolks together in a bowl with the remaining 180 g (6½ oz) of sugar, then slowly pour on the hot milk while whisking. Ladle the custard mixture into the caramel-lined moulds. Put the moulds into a deep baking tray and fill with enough warm water to come three-quarters of the way up the sides of the moulds. Place the tray in the oven and cook for about 40 minutes, or until set. Keep an eye on the crème caramels and test them by tapping on the outside rim to see if they are set. Remove from the oven, cool to room temperature, then refrigerate.

caramel syrup

300 G (10½ OZ) CASTER (SUPERFINE) SUGAR

Put the sugar in a small heavy-based saucepan and add enough water to just wet the sugar. Place the pan over high heat and turn the sugar into a medium-coloured caramel. Slowly add 75 ml (2½ fl oz) of water, being careful as you add the water as this will cause a violent reaction. Once all the water is added to the sugar and the caramel has come back to the boil, remove the pan from the heat and stir to make sure the caramel has completely dissolved into the water. Allow the caramel syrup to cool to room temperature.

caramel cream

125 G (4½ OZ) CASTER (SUPERFINE) SUGAR
500 ML (17 FL OZ/2 CUPS) CREAM (35% FAT)
100 G (3½ OZ) DOUBLE CREAM (45–50% FAT)

Put the sugar in a small heavy-based saucepan and add enough water to just wet the sugar. Place the pan over high heat and turn the sugar into a dark but not burnt caramel. Slowly add 50 ml (1¾ fl oz) of cream — again, this will cause a violent reaction, so be careful. Continue to slowly add the remaining cream. Allow the mixture to come back to the boil and stir well to make sure all the caramel is dissolved. Once it is, remove the pan from the heat and refrigerate for a few hours until the mixture is very cold. Place the caramel cream in a small stainless-steel bowl and add the double cream. Whisk the mixture together until soft peaks form. Your caramel cream is now ready to use.

to finish and plate

This dessert is best served in a tall glass or martini glass. To assemble the dessert, start by adding some caramel syrup to the base of the glass. Next, dice the sauternes jelly on the tray, using the point of a sharp knife. Scoop a spoonful of the jelly and place it on top of the caramel syrup. Next, pipe or spoon on some of the caramel cream. Invert the crème caramels onto the caramel cream, allowing the excess caramel to form a layer between the caramel cream and the crème caramel. Top this with some more diced jelly and finish with a scoop of pear ice cream. Serve immediately.

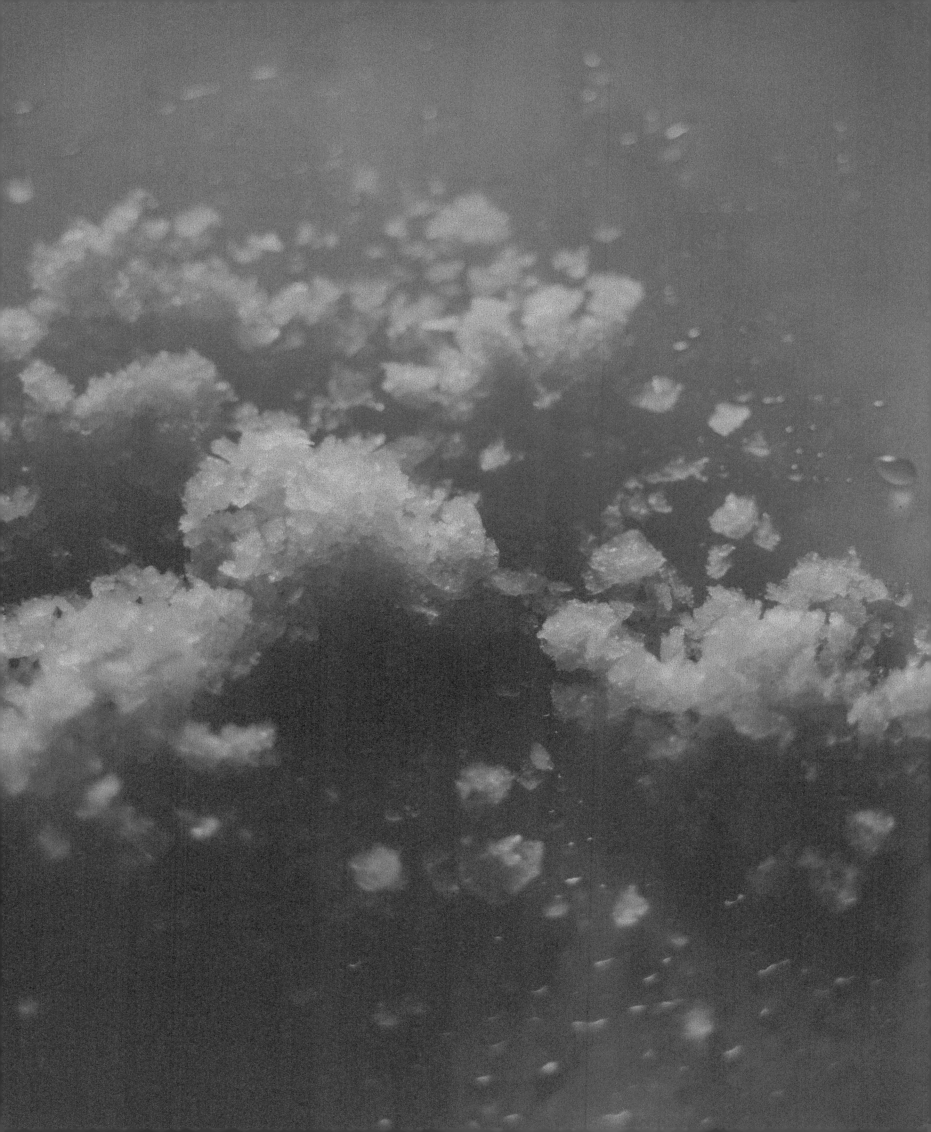

SERVES 8

rose, vanilla, pistachio and watermelon

This dessert is inspired by the Middle Eastern flavours of pistachio and rose. The rose and vanilla cream jelly sphere is an original idea of mine made by dicing the rose and vanilla jelly and reforming the jelly with vanilla cream inside, which has the effect of creating a translucent crystal. The shredded kataifi pastry adds great texture and ties in with the theme of this dessert, along with the candied watermelon rind and rose-scented milk ice cream.

rose jelly balls

300 G (10½ OZ) CASTER (SUPERFINE) SUGAR
1 VANILLA BEAN, SPLIT AND SCRAPED
5 ML (⅛ FL OZ) ROSE WATER
3 SHEETS TITANIUM GELATINE
15 FRESH RASPBERRIES

VANILLA CREAM
100 G (3½ OZ) DOUBLE CREAM (45–50% FAT)
100 ML (3½ FL OZ) CREAM (35% FAT)
¼ VANILLA BEAN, SPLIT AND SCRAPED
20 G (¾ OZ) PURE ICING (CONFECTIONERS')
    SUGAR, SIFTED

Combine 500 ml (17 fl oz/2 cups) of water, the sugar and vanilla bean in a small pan. Bring to the boil, then remove from the heat. Cool slightly, then strain through a fine sieve and add the rose water. Meanwhile, soak the gelatine sheets in cold water until softened. Squeeze the raspberries through a muslin cloth, allowing the juice to drip into the sugar syrup. This will give the syrup a light pink colouring. Squeeze the excess water from the gelatine, add to the warm syrup and stir to dissolve the gelatine. Pour the jelly into a shallow tray with sides, to a depth of 1 cm (½ inch). Place the jelly in the refrigerator to set.

Meanwhile, to make the vanilla cream, place the two creams in a small bowl. Place the vanilla bean seeds on top of the cream, discarding the bean. Add the icing sugar and whisk to form firm peaks.

Dice the set jelly into 5 mm (¼ inch) cubes. Take eight 20 cm (8 inch) squares of plastic wrap and place over eight coffee cups. Put a tablespoon of jelly in the centre of the plastic, then make a small indentation in the centre of the jelly. Place ½ teaspoon of the vanilla cream into the indentation, then place another tablespoon of diced jelly on top. Carefully lift up the corners of the plastic and twist them together to form a ball. Tie a knot in the plastic. Place the jelly balls in the refrigerator to set for a minimum of 4 hours.

rose-scented ice cream

400 ML (14 FL OZ) MILK
250 G (9 OZ) CASTER (SUPERFINE) SUGAR
5 EGG YOLKS
½ TEASPOON ROSE WATER

Combine 100 ml (3½ fl oz) of water, the milk and 125 g (4½ oz) of sugar in a small saucepan. Bring the mixture to just before boiling point, then remove the pan from the heat. Put the egg yolks and remaining 125 g (4½ oz) of sugar into a stainless-steel bowl and whisk well. Pour the hot milk onto the eggs while whisking. Place the bowl over a pan of simmering water and cook the mixture, whisking continuously, for 6–8 minutes, to form a very thin sabayon. Chill the mixture over ice. When completely cold, place the mixture into a blender and blend on high for 2–3 minutes. Add the rose water, then strain the mixture through a fine sieve lined with muslin cloth. Transfer the mixture into an ice-cream machine and churn until frozen. Place the ice cream in a container in the freezer for at least 1 hour.

pistachio pastries

150 G (5½ OZ) SHELLED PISTACHIO NUTS
50 G (1¾ OZ) HONEY
230 G (8 OZ) UNSALTED BUTTER, MELTED
375 G (13 OZ) PACKET KATAIFI SHREDDED PASTRY
PURE ICING (CONFECTIONERS') SUGAR, FOR DUSTING

Preheat the oven to 180°C (350°F/Gas 4). Place the pistachio nuts on a baking tray and roast for about 8 minutes. Place the nuts in a food processor, add the honey and 30 g (1 oz) of melted butter and process briefly to form a rough paste. Remove the pistachio mixture and use your hands to mould the mixture into eight marble-sized balls. Take some of the kataifi pastry and form it into a single layer, about 30 cm (12 inches) long and 4 cm (1½ inches) wide. Keep the rest of the pastry covered with a damp tea towel to prevent it drying out. Generously brush the pastry with some of the remaining melted butter. Place a small ball of pistachio at one end of the pastry and roll the pastry around the ball loosely until you get to the end of the strip. The aim is to make a small nest-like ball, about the size of a golf ball. Use your hands to help mould it into shape. Repeat the process until you have eight nests. Place the pastries on a tray lined with silicone paper and bake for 8–10 minutes until golden brown.

watermelon granita

1.7 KG (3 LB 12 OZ) WATERMELON
250 G (9 OZ) STRAWBERRIES
100 G (3½ OZ) CASTER (SUPERFINE) SUGAR

Remove the rind from the watermelon and juice
the flesh through an electric juicer until you have
500 ml (17 fl oz/2 cups) of juice. Hull the strawberries
and juice them to obtain 100 ml (3½ fl oz) of juice.
Combine the two juices and then strain the liquid
through a triple layer of muslin cloth. Put the juice
in a small saucepan, add the sugar and bring to the
boil. Strain the juice one more time through muslin
cloth, then pour into a shallow tray with sides, to a
depth of about 3 cm (1¼ inches). Place the tray in
the freezer. Remove the tray from the freezer every
30 minutes or so and break up the ice crystals using
a fork. Repeat this process several times until you
have a fine-grained granita.

candied watermelon rind

500 G (1 LB 2 OZ) WATERMELON RIND
500 G (1 LB 2 OZ) CASTER (SUPERFINE) SUGAR
2 G (¹⁄₁₆ OZ) CITRIC ACID

To prepare the candied rind, remove the hard green
skin from the watermelon and cut into 10 cm (4 inch)
thick slices. Remove all the pink flesh, except the
1 cm (½ inch) closest to the rind.
 Put 300 g (10½ oz) of sugar, the citric acid
and 100 ml (3½ fl oz) of water in a saucepan. Mix
well and bring to simmering point, then remove
from the heat. Place the trimmed watermelon rind
into vacuum bags and pour in the prepared syrup.
Seal the bags in a vacuum sealer and steam in a
temperature-controlled combi oven at 85°C (185°F)
for about 1½ hours, or until the rind is soft to the
touch. Cool in the bags, then remove the rind and
slice into 2 mm (¹⁄₁₆ inch) thin strips.
 Combine the remaining 200 g (7 oz) of sugar in
a small saucepan with 200 ml (7 fl oz) of water. Bring
to the boil, then reduce the heat to very low. Add
the sliced strips of watermelon rind to the sugar
syrup and very gently cook for 10 minutes, or until
well glazed. Remove the pan from the heat and leave
the rind strips to steep in the syrup until cool. Place
the strips and syrup in a container in the refrigerator
until required.

to finish and plate

For the photograph of this dessert, we carved a bowl shape out of a block of ice, but it works just as well if
you serve it in a small bowl. To start, dust the pastries liberally with icing sugar and place one in each bowl.
Use a small pair of scissors to cut the knot from the rose jelly balls and carefully peel away the plastic wrap.
Place a jelly ball next to the pastry and surround it with some candied strips of watermelon. Scoop out some
watermelon granita and place it between the jelly ball and pastry. Using a tablespoon, shape a quenelle of
rose ice cream and place it on top of the granita, resting against the jelly ball and pastry. Serve immediately.

SERVES 8

mangosteens with lychee granita ice-cream spheres and rose-scented ice cream

Mangosteens are the ultimate tropical fruit. They are native to Southeast Asia and the ones I use are grown in far North Queensland. They have a white pearlescent flesh, a tart sweet flavour and an incredible perfume. Here they are served with a lychee granita and ice cream sphere, which is the central element of this dessert, their flavour nicely complemented by the rose-scented ice cream. The fresh tropical fruit, coconut cream and textural elements of the tiny meringues and sugar crystals make this a beautiful and refreshing dessert.

rose-scented ice cream

800 ML (28 FL OZ) MILK
500 G (1 LB 2 OZ) CASTER (SUPERFINE) SUGAR
10 EGG YOLKS
5 ML (⅛ FL OZ) ROSE WATER

Make the ice cream first. Combine 200 ml (7 fl oz) of water, the milk and 250 g (9 oz) of sugar in a saucepan. Bring the mixture to just before boiling point, then remove the pan from the heat.

Put the egg yolks and remaining 250 g (9 oz) of sugar into a large stainless-steel bowl and whisk well. Add the milk mixture, then place the bowl over a pan of simmering water and cook the mixture, whisking continuously, for 8–10 minutes, to form a thin sabayon. Remove the mixture from the heat and add the rose water. Put the bowl over ice to chill while continuing to whisk. When completely cold, place the mixture into a blender and blend on high for 2 minutes. Transfer the mixture into an ice-cream machine and churn until frozen. Place the ice cream in a container in the freezer for at least 1 hour.

lychee ice cream and granita spheres

1 KG (2 LB 4 OZ) APPLES
400 G (14 OZ) CASTER (SUPERFINE) SUGAR
12 EGG YOLKS
2 KG (4 LB 8 OZ) FRESH LYCHEES
150 ML (5 FL OZ) CREAM (35% FAT)

Place a large coffee filter in a chinois. Peel the apples and grate them over the filter. Squeeze to extract the juice. You should yield 400 ml (14 fl oz) of clear juice. Combine the apple juice, 350 g (12 oz) of sugar and the egg yolks in a stainless-steel bowl and whisk well. Place the bowl over a saucepan of simmering water and cook the mixture, whisking continuously, for 8–10 minutes, to form a sabayon. Remove from the heat and continue to whisk over a bowl of ice for 6–7 minutes until the sabayon is cool.

Using 1 kg (2 lb 4 oz) of the lychees, peel them and remove the seeds. Juice the flesh through an electric juicer and then pass the juice through a fine sieve. Measure 400 ml (14 fl oz) of lychee juice and add it to the cooled sabayon mixture, then add the cream. Place the mixture into a blender and blend on high for 2 minutes. Transfer the mixture into an ice-cream machine and churn until frozen. Place the ice cream in a container in the freezer for at least 1 hour.

To make the lychee granita, peel and remove the seeds from the remaining 1 kg (2 lb 4 oz) of lychees. Juice the flesh through an electric juicer and then pass the juice through a fine sieve. You will need 500 ml (17 fl oz/2 cups) of juice.

Put 100 ml (3½ fl oz) of the lychee juice in a small saucepan with the remaining 50 g (1¾ oz) of sugar. Bring to the boil, then remove the pan from the heat and allow the syrup to cool completely. When cool, add it to the remaining 400 ml (14 fl oz) of lychee juice. Pour the lychee liquid into a shallow tray with sides, to a depth of 4 cm (1½ inches). Break up the ice crystals with a fork every hour for the next 4–5 hours until you have a fine granita.

To make the lychee ice cream and granita spheres, you will first need to line eight 5 cm (2 inch) diameter half-hemisphere silicone moulds with plastic wrap. Cut eight 15 cm (6 inch) squares of plastic wrap and line the moulds, ensuring the plastic overlaps the moulds. Take the lychee granita and place 2 tablespoons of granita into the moulds, pressing it so that it comes up the sides of the moulds, leaving a small space in the centre. Freeze the granita for about 1 hour, or until it sets in this shape. Next, place a round scoop of lychee ice cream in the centre and spoon on another 2 tablespoons of lychee granita to form a mound on top of the moulds. Using the excess plastic wrap, gather the plastic together at the top of the granita mound. Twist the plastic together to help shape and form a sphere of granita. Twist the plastic tightly at the top and return to the freezer to set for a further 2 hours.

natural rose jelly

250 G (9 OZ) CASTER (SUPERFINE) SUGAR
50 ORGANIC ROSE PETALS
10 FRESH RASPBERRIES
2½ SHEETS TITANIUM GELATINE

Combine the sugar and 500 ml (17 fl oz/2 cups) of water in a saucepan. Heat to 65°C (150°F), then add the rose petals and remove the pan from the heat. Stir well and allow the rose petals to macerate for 1 hour, then gently crush the raspberries and add them to the syrup. The raspberries will give the syrup a lovely natural pink colour. Place the syrup, raspberries and rose petals in a vacuum bag and seal in a vacuum sealer. Place the bag in a temperature-controlled combi oven at 65°C (150°F) and steam for 20 minutes. Refrigerate the syrup overnight. Alternatively, if you do not have a combi oven, simply macerate the rose petals and raspberries in the syrup in a small pan on the stove for 20 minutes, then refrigerate overnight.

Strain the syrup through a fine sieve, discarding the rose petals and raspberry flesh. Heat 100 ml (3½ fl oz) of rose syrup in a small pan to simmering point. Meanwhile, soak the gelatine sheets in cold water until softened. Squeeze the excess water from the gelatine, add to the warm syrup and stir to dissolve the gelatine. Return the gelatine mixture to the remaining rose syrup. Pour the rose syrup into a shallow tray with sides, to a depth of 5 mm (¼ inch). Set the jelly in the refrigerator for a couple of hours. When the jelly is completely set, use the point of a sharp knife to dice the jelly into 5 mm (¼ inch) cubes. Lift the cubes free from the tray and store in a plastic airtight container in the refrigerator.

coconut cream

100 ML (3½ FL OZ) MILK
100 ML (3½ FL OZ) CREAM (35% FAT)
50 G (1¾ OZ) CASTER (SUPERFINE) SUGAR
100 G (3½ OZ) COCONUT CREAM POWDER
80 G (2¾ OZ) DOUBLE CREAM (45–50% FAT)

Combine the milk, cream (35% fat) and sugar in a saucepan and bring to the boil. Put the coconut cream powder into a heatproof bowl and pour over the boiling milk and cream mixture, whisking well as you pour in the liquid. Place in the refrigerator to cool completely. Put the cooled coconut cream mixture in a bowl with the double cream and whisk together with a hand whisk until firm peaks form. Store in the refrigerator until required.

meringues

100 ML (3½ FL OZ) EGG WHITE
100 G (3½ OZ) CASTER (SUPERFINE) SUGAR
100 G (3½ OZ) PURE ICING (CONFECTIONERS') SUGAR

Preheat the oven to 75°C (165°F/Gas ¼). To make the small meringues, whisk the egg whites in an electric mixer on high. Gradually add the caster sugar until stiff peaks form, then fold through the sifted icing sugar. Place the meringue into a piping bag with a very small round nozzle and pipe tiny dots of meringue onto a baking tray lined with a silicone mat. Bake in the oven for 30–40 minutes until firm. Remove from the oven and allow to cool. Store the meringues in an airtight container.

sugar crystals

300 G (10½ OZ) CASTER (SUPERFINE) SUGAR
90 ML (3 FL OZ) LIQUID GLUCOSE

Preheat the oven to 200°C (400°F/Gas 6). Combine the sugar, liquid glucose and 90 ml (3 fl oz) of water in a saucepan over medium heat, stirring to dissolve the sugar and glucose. Increase the heat to high and heat to 155°C (310°F). Use a sugar thermometer to get an accurate temperature. Pour the hot liquid onto a large baking tray lined with a silicone mat and spread the liquid thinly with a palette knife. Allow the liquid to cool completely and harden, then break the sugar crystal into small shards. Place the shards into a food processor and process until you have a fine powder. Using a sieve with a medium-fine hole, sift a fine layer of sugar crystal powder onto a baking tray lined with a fresh silicone mat. Place in the oven for a few minutes. When you see the sugar crystals melting and coming together to form small balls, remove the tray from the oven. Cool for a couple of minutes, then use a palette knife to scrape the crystals off the mat. Some of the crystals will stick together; you can either break them apart into fine crystals or leave them linked together. When the crystals are completely cool, store in an airtight container with moisture-absorbing beads.

to finish and plate

32 FRESH LYCHEES
16 SMALL RIPE MANGOSTEENS

Peel the lychees, cut them in half and remove the seeds. Next, peel the mangosteens with a sharp knife, being careful to keep the fruit whole. The mangosteen is made up of many segments, one of which contains a small seed. You can either remove the segment with the seed (this is usually the largest segment) or leave the mangosteen whole and tell your guests there is a seed inside.

Unwrap the lychee ice cream and granita spheres. Place a small spoonful of coconut cream in the centre of each serving bowl and place a sphere on top of the cream. Place two mangosteens in each bowl, one on either side of the sphere, then add eight lychee halves to each dessert. Place four quenelles of coconut cream around the sphere. Top two of the quenelles with tiny meringues and sugar crystals and top the other two quenelles with small quenelles of rose-scented ice cream. Place 1 teaspoon of natural rose jelly in between each coconut cream quenelle and serve immediately.

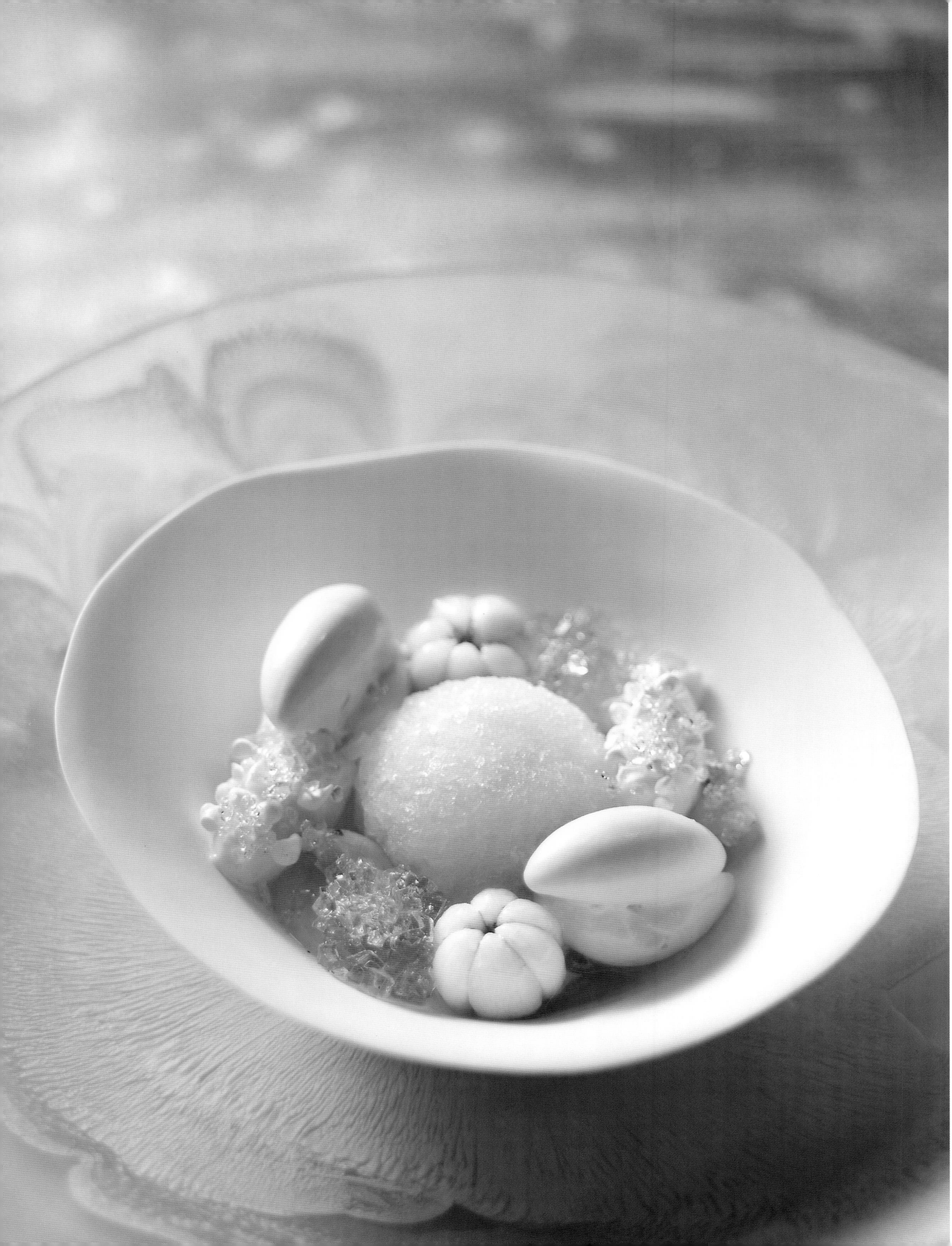

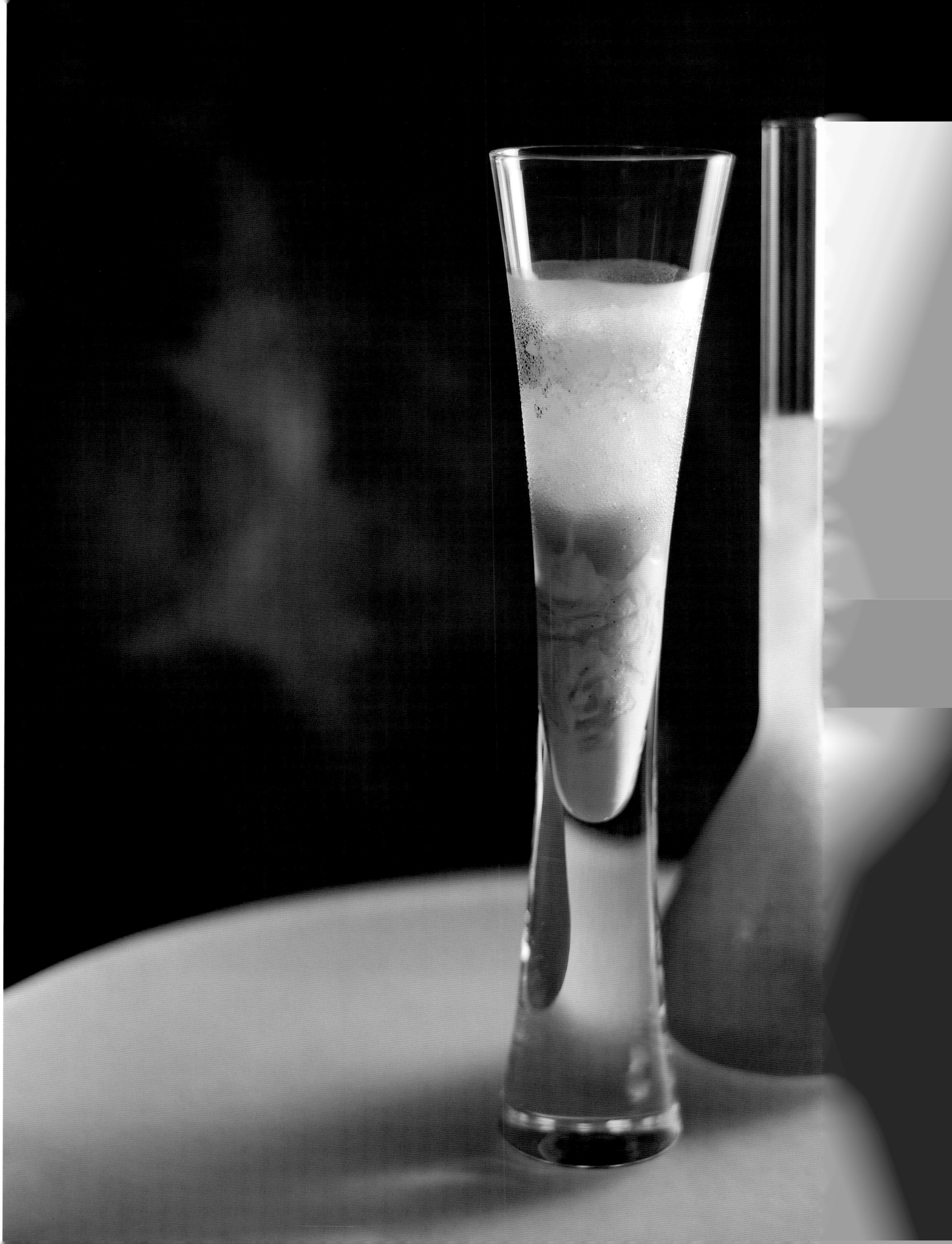

SERVES 8

quay's white peach bellini

This dessert was inspired by the bellini cocktail, first created at Harry's Bar in Venice. I have made a two-part dessert: one part being a white peach granita and fool, the other being a bellini frappé. The bellini frappé can also be served as a lovely cocktail or at a Christmas party. The dessert component could also be served with white peach ice cream on its own.

ingredients

WHITE PEACH GRANITA
150 G (5½ OZ) CASTER (SUPERFINE) SUGAR
350 ML (12 FL OZ) MOSCATO D'ASTI
8 RIPE WHITE PEACHES

WHITE PEACH PURÉE
700 G (1 LB 9 OZ) CASTER (SUPERFINE) SUGAR
2 VANILLA BEANS, SPLIT AND SCRAPED
12 LARGE RIPE WHITE PEACHES

VANILLA CREAM
300 G (10½ OZ) VANILLA CUSTARD BASE
   (BASIC RECIPES, PAGE 269)
100 ML (3½ FL OZ) CREAM (35% FAT)
200 G (7 OZ) DOUBLE CREAM (45–50% FAT)

method

To make the white peach granita, combine 600 ml (21 fl oz) of water, the sugar and Moscato d'Asti in a saucepan. Bring to the boil, then reduce the heat to a low simmer. Halve the peaches and place them in the simmering syrup. Simmer for 5 minutes, then remove the pan from the heat. Allow the syrup to cool a little, then put two pairs of clean rubber gloves on and squeeze and break up the peaches with your hands. Allow the peaches and the syrup to macerate and cool completely. Pass the cooled syrup through a sieve lined with muslin cloth, then pour the syrup into a shallow tray with sides, to a depth of 4 cm (1½ inches). Freeze the liquid and break up with a fork every hour for the next 4–5 hours until you have a fine granita.

   To make the white peach purée, combine 1 litre (35 fl oz/4 cups) of water, the sugar and vanilla beans in a saucepan. Bring to the boil, then reduce the heat to a low simmer. Peel the peaches with a sharp knife, cut in half and remove the stones. Add the peach

flesh to the simmering syrup and simmer gently for 5 minutes. Remove from the heat and allow to cool completely. Once cool, remove the peaches from the syrup. Place the peaches into a blender and blend on high for 2 minutes until smooth. Pass the purée through a drum sieve. You should have 1.1 litres (38 fl oz). Store the purée in the refrigerator until required.

   To make the vanilla cream, place the vanilla custard base, cream and double cream in a bowl and whisk until soft peaks form. Store in the refrigerator until required.

to finish and plate

1 LITRE (35 FL OZ) ICE CUBES
500 ML (17 FL OZ) PROSECCO
500 ML (17 FL OZ) MOSCATO D'ASTI

Make the white peach fool by combining the vanilla cream and 600 ml (21 fl oz) of the white peach purée. Fold them gently together, creating a ripple effect. Place 150 ml (5 fl oz) of white peach fool in the bottom of a tall glass, then top the fool with an equal quantity of white peach granita. Repeat for the remaining glasses.

   To make the bellini frappé, put the ice in a blender along with the prosecco, Moscato and the remaining 500 ml (17 fl oz) of the white peach purée. Depending on the size of your blender, you might need to do this in two batches. Blend on high for 30 seconds. Pour the bellini frappé into a beaker. Serve the glass and the beaker together to your guests, with a long spoon and straw. The idea is to eat the fool and granita, then fill your glass with the bellini frappé and drink.

basic recipes

vegetable stock

2 CARROTS, FINELY DICED
½ FENNEL BULB, FINELY DICED
1 BROWN ONION, FINELY DICED
1 LEEK, FINELY DICED
4 WHITE CELERY STALKS (INNER STALKS), FINELY DICED
1 GARLIC CLOVE, FINELY DICED
30 ML (1 FL OZ) GRAPESEED OIL
200 ML (7 FL OZ) AROMATIC WHITE WINE
5 SPRIGS THYME
10 PARSLEY STALKS
10 SPRIGS CHERVIL
1 BAY LEAF
5 CRUSHED BLACK PEPPERCORNS

Sweat the finely diced vegetables in a saucepan with the grapeseed oil, being careful not to add any colour. Deglaze with the white wine and continue to cook until almost all the wine has evaporated. Add 1.2 litres (44 fl oz) of cold water to the pan along with the herbs and peppercorns and simmer very gently for 30 minutes. Remove the pan from the heat and allow to infuse for a further 30 minutes. Strain the stock through a fine conical strainer lined with muslin cloth. Cool and refrigerate the vegetable stock until required. This recipe should yield 1 litre (35 fl oz/4 cups) of vegetable stock.

chicken stock

5 KG (11 LB) CHICKEN BONES (FRAMES AND WINGS)
2 LARGE BROWN ONIONS, CHOPPED
3 CARROTS, CHOPPED
3 WHITE CELERY STALKS (INNER STALKS), CHOPPED
100 ML (3½ FL OZ) GRAPESEED OIL

Wash the chicken bones under cold running water to remove any excess blood, then drain and put aside. Sweat the vegetables in a large stockpot in the grapeseed oil. Add the chicken bones and lightly sauté, being careful not to add too much colour. Add 8 litres (270 fl oz) of cold water and bring to the boil. As soon as it boils, turn down the heat to achieve a very gentle simmer (the stock should be just ticking over). Skim the stock with a ladle and continue to simmer for 4 hours. After 4 hours, skim the stock again with a ladle. Strain the stock carefully through a fine conical strainer. Allow the stock to cool completely and refrigerate until required. This recipe should yield 5 litres (170 fl oz) of chicken stock.

lamb stock

10 KG (22 LB) LAMB BONES
4 PIG'S TROTTERS, SPLIT IN HALF
5 BROWN ONIONS, CHOPPED
4 CARROTS, CHOPPED
50 ML (1¾ FL OZ) GRAPESEED OIL
10 RIPE TOMATOES, CUT IN HALF

Preheat the oven to 200°C (400°F/Gas 6). Wash the lamb bones and trotters under cold running water, then drain well. Place the bones and trotters in a heavy-based baking tray and roast in the oven until nicely browned. When the bones are browned, remove them from the tray and place into a large stockpot. Take the tray that the bones were browned in and place it on the stovetop. Remove any rendered fat, then heat the tray over medium heat and add 500 ml (17 fl oz/2 cups) of water. Use a wooden spoon to scrape the bottom of the tray to release any caramelisation left from the bones. Reduce the water until 200 ml (7 fl oz) remains, then pour the water into the pot with the bones.

In a large frying pan, sauté the onion and carrot in the grapeseed oil until they are well coloured. Deglaze the pan with 500 ml (17 fl oz/2 cups) of water, stir well and add the contents to the stockpot. Add another 14 litres (470 fl oz) of water to the pot, bring the stock close to boiling point, then turn the heat down so the stock is barely simmering. Add the tomato halves and slowly simmer for 8 hours, skimming the stock occasionally with a ladle to remove any excess fat. Strain the stock through a fine conical strainer, being careful not to disturb the bones too much. Do not remove the bones before straining as this will make the stock cloudy. Allow the stock to cool, then refrigerate until required. Any excess fat will solidify on top of the stock and is easily removed before use. This recipe should yield about 8 litres (270 fl oz) of lamb stock.

reduced lamb stock (glaze)

1 BROWN ONION, CHOPPED
1 CARROT, CHOPPED
50 ML (1¾ FL OZ) GRAPESEED OIL
500 G (1 LB 2 OZ) LAMB TRIMMINGS
4 GARLIC CLOVES, BRUISED WITH THE BACK
   OF A KNIFE
500 ML (17 FL OZ/2 CUPS) GOOD QUALITY
   WHITE WINE
8 LITRES (270 FL OZ) LAMB STOCK
6 RIPE TOMATOES, CUT IN HALF
2 SPRIGS THYME

In a large stockpot, sauté the onion and carrot in the grapeseed oil until lightly browned. Add the lamb trimmings and continue to sauté until the meat is well browned. Add the garlic and white wine. Reduce the wine until there is 100 ml (3½ fl oz) of liquid left, then add the stock, tomatoes and thyme. Reduce the stock on a medium simmer until the stock has halved in quantity. Strain through a fine conical strainer lined with muslin cloth. You should now have a demi-glaze (half reduced stock).

To make a glaze, return the demi-glaze to a clean pot and reduce over high heat until you have the required viscosity for glazing and saucing meats. Generally from 4 litres (140 fl oz) of demi-glaze you will need to reduce it to 500 ml (17 fl oz/2 cups) to achieve a glaze.

veal stock

10 KG (22 LB) VEAL BONES (KNUCKLES AND SHINS)
4 PIG'S TROTTERS, SPLIT IN HALF
750 ML (26 FL OZ) BOTTLE GOOD QUALITY RED WINE
5 BROWN ONIONS, CHOPPED
4 CARROTS, CHOPPED
50 ML (1¾ FL OZ) GRAPESEED OIL
10 RIPE TOMATOES, CUT IN HALF

Preheat the oven to 200°C (400°F/Gas 6). Wash the veal bones and trotters under cold running water, then drain well. Place the bones and trotters in a heavy-based baking tray and roast in the oven until nicely browned. When the bones are browned, remove them from the tray and place into a large stockpot. Take the tray that the bones were browned in and place it on the stovetop. Remove any rendered fat, then heat the tray over medium heat and add the red wine. Use a wooden spoon to scrape the bottom of the tray to release any caramelisation left from the bones. Reduce the wine until 200 ml (7 fl oz) remains, then pour the wine into the pot with the bones.

In a large frying pan, sauté the onion and carrot in the grapeseed oil until well coloured. Deglaze the pan with 500 ml (17 fl oz/2 cups) of water, stir well and add the contents to the stockpot. Add another 14.5 litres (490 fl oz) of water to the pot, bring the stock close to boiling point, then turn the heat down so the stock is barely simmering. Add the tomato halves and slowly simmer for 8 hours, skimming the stock occasionally with a ladle to remove any excess fat. Strain the stock through a fine conical strainer, being careful not to disturb the bones too much. Do not remove the bones before straining, as this will make the stock cloudy. Allow the stock to cool, then refrigerate until required. Any excess fat will solidify on top of the stock and is easily removed before use. This recipe should yield about 8 litres (270 fl oz) of veal stock.

reduced veal stock (demi-glaze and glaze)

1 BROWN ONION, CHOPPED
1 CARROT, CHOPPED
50 ML (1¾ FL OZ) GRAPESEED OIL
500 G (1 LB 2 OZ) VEAL OR BEEF TRIMMINGS
4 GARLIC CLOVES, BRUISED WITH THE BACK
   OF A KNIFE
500 ML (17 FL OZ/2 CUPS) GOOD QUALITY RED WINE
8 LITRES (270 FL OZ) VEAL STOCK
6 RIPE TOMATOES, CUT IN HALF
2 SPRIGS THYME

In a large stockpot, sauté the onion and carrot in the grapeseed oil until lightly browned. Add the veal or beef trimmings and continue to sauté until the meat is well browned. Add the garlic and red wine. Reduce the wine until there is only 100 ml (3½ fl oz) of liquid left, then add the stock, tomatoes and thyme. Reduce the stock on a medium simmer until the stock has halved in quantity. Strain through a fine conical strainer lined with muslin cloth. You should now have a demi-glaze (half reduced stock).

To make a glaze, return the demi-glaze to a clean pot and reduce over high heat until you have the required viscosity for glazing and saucing meats. Generally from 4 litres (140 fl oz) of demi-glaze, you will need to reduce it to somewhere between 800 ml (28 fl oz) and 500 ml (17 fl oz/2 cups) to achieve a glaze. The further you reduce, the heavier the glaze.

masterstock

2 LITRES (70 FL OZ/8 CUPS) CHICKEN STOCK
    (PAGE 262)
1 LITRE (35 FL OZ/4 CUPS) SHAOXING RICE WINE
200 G (7 OZ) YELLOW ROCK SUGAR
200 ML (7 FL OZ) DARK SOY SAUCE
100 G (3½ OZ) PEELED GINGER, SLICED
1 BUNCH GREEN SPRING ONIONS (SCALLIONS),
    WHITE PART ONLY, SLICED
5 STRIPS DRIED MANDARIN PEEL
5 STAR ANISE
3 GARLIC CLOVES
100 G (3½ OZ) CASSIA BARK

Combine all the ingredients and 3 litres (105 fl oz/
12 cups) of water in a medium pan. Bring to the boil,
skimming the surface if necessary, then reduce the
heat to very low and cook for 2 hours. Take the pan
off the heat and then strain the liquid through a
sieve lined with muslin cloth. Discard the solids. Your
masterstock is ready to use.

Traditionally in Chinese kitchens, masterstocks
are used every day for poaching. At the end of
the day they are strained and then refrigerated
overnight. The next day they are reboiled and more
ingredients are added as required, such as water and
aromatics. Some masterstocks can be in continuous
use for decades. They retain a little of their original
stock and develop in flavour over the years. You can
only use a masterstock this way if you use it every
day, as this keeps it fresh. Alternatively, you can
freeze the masterstock for up to 1 month.

clarified butter

2 KG (4 LB 8 OZ) UNSALTED BUTTER

Use a large stockpot with a capacity of 15 litres
(500 fl oz). A stockpot is needed, as the butter will
foam and you do not want it to spill over. Place
the butter in the pot over medium–high heat. As
the butter melts it will begin to foam. Allow this to
happen but monitor the heat, as you do not want the
butter to caramelise (as you would for brown butter).
The foaming and melting will take about 10 minutes.
Reduce the heat to low and when the foaming
subsides use a ladle to skim off any scum from the
surface. Heat on low for a further 5–10 minutes, then
turn the heat off and allow to sit for a few minutes.
Once the surface is completely clear of impurities,
ladle out the clear butter into a clean container. Be
careful not to disturb the milk solids that will remain
on the bottom of the pot. Once all the clear butter
is ladled out, you can discard the milky solids in the
base of the pot. You should now have at least 1 litre
(35 fl oz/4 cups) of clarified butter.

Clarified butter is good to use for sautéing
meat and vegetables. It will not burn as easily as
unclarified butter because the milk solids have
been removed.

clarified brown butter

250 G (9 OZ) UNSALTED BUTTER

Place the butter in a tall heavy-based saucepan.
A tall pan is needed, as the butter will foam and
you do not want it to spill over. Place the pan over
high heat and boil the butter until it begins to
caramelise. When the foam and butter begin to
turn a light brown colour, remove the saucepan
from the heat and pour the contents into a large
stainless-steel bowl. Use a ladle to skim off any scum
from the surface. Once the surface is completely
clear of impurities, ladle out the butter into a clean
container. Be careful not to disturb the milk solids
that will remain on the bottom of the pan. You
should now have at least 175 ml (5½ fl oz) of clarified
brown butter.

spring onion and ginger oil

1 LITRE (35 FL OZ/4 CUPS) GRAPESEED OIL
50 G (1¾ OZ) PEELED GINGER, SLICED
50 G (1¾ OZ) GREEN SPRING ONIONS (SCALLIONS),
    SLICED

Heat the grapeseed oil in a saucepan to 70°C (155°F).
Add the sliced ginger and spring onion and heat
for 10 minutes, maintaining the oil at 70°C (155°F).
Remove the pan from the heat and allow to infuse
for 2 hours. Strain the oil through a sieve lined with
muslin cloth, discarding the ginger and spring onion.
Put the infused grapeseed oil aside until needed.
Makes 1 litre (35 fl oz/4 cups).

cauliflower cream

2 FRENCH SHALLOTS, FINELY DICED
2 WHITE CELERY STALKS (INNER STALKS),
    FINELY DICED
1 GARLIC CLOVE, FINELY DICED
20 ML (½ FL OZ) OLIVE OIL
½ SMALL CAULIFLOWER HEAD, CUT INTO FLORETS
750 ML (26 FL OZ/3 CUPS) CHICKEN STOCK (PAGE 262)
50 G (1¾ OZ) UNSALTED BUTTER
100 ML (3½ FL OZ) CREAM (35% FAT)

Sweat the shallots, celery and garlic in a saucepan
with the olive oil until the vegetables are translucent.
Add the cauliflower florets to the pan and sweat for
a further 1 minute. Add the chicken stock and
simmer rapidly over high heat until almost all the
stock has evaporated. Place the contents of the pan
into a blender, add the butter and blend on high to
form a smooth purée. Pass the purée through a drum
sieve. Cover the cauliflower purée and refrigerate
until required. The cream is whipped and folded
through the warmed purée just before serving time.

almond cream

100 G (3½ OZ) BLANCHED ALMOND KERNELS
500 ML (17 FL OZ/2 CUPS) MILK
5 G (⅛ OZ) AGAR AGAR POWDER
FINE SEA SALT

Preheat the oven to 180°C (350°F/Gas 4). Place the almonds on a baking tray and roast in the oven for 8–10 minutes, or until golden brown. Transfer the almonds into a food processor and process lightly. Put the milk in a small saucepan and bring close to boiling point, then remove from the heat and add the almonds. Allow the almonds and milk to infuse for about 20 minutes on the lowest heat possible, without any surface movement to the milk. Remove from the heat and infuse for a further 20 minutes.

Pour the milk through a fine sieve lined with a double layer of muslin cloth into a clean pan, then whisk in the agar agar. Return the pan to the heat and reheat the milk to 90°C (195°F), while continuing to whisk to activate the agar agar. Remove the pan from the heat and allow the almond milk to set. Once set, place the almond cream into a blender and blend until smooth. Season to taste with sea salt. Refrigerate until needed and reheat just before you are ready to serve.

oyster cream

12 UNSHUCKED SYDNEY ROCK OYSTERS
10 G (¼ OZ) DICED FENNEL
10 G (¼ OZ) DICED WHITE CELERY (INNER STALK)
10 G (¼ OZ) DICED BULB SPRING ONION (SCALLION)
10 ML (¼ FL OZ) GRAPESEED OIL
500 ML (17 FL OZ/2 CUPS) MILK
5 G (⅛ OZ) AGAR AGAR

Shuck the oysters, reserving the meat and juice. Sweat the fennel, celery and spring onion in a small saucepan with the grapeseed oil, being careful not to add any colour to the vegetables. Add the milk and bring close to boiling point, then remove the pan from the heat and add the oyster meat. Allow everything to infuse for 20 minutes while cooling. Strain the milk and discard the solids.

Pour the milk through a fine sieve into a saucepan. Return the pan to the heat and, while whisking, add the agar agar. Reheat the milk to 90°C (195°F), continuing to whisk to activate the agar agar, and cook for 1 minute. Remove the pan from the heat and allow to cool. Add the oyster juice, stir well and pass the mixture through a sieve lined with a double layer of muslin cloth. Refrigerate the milk until fully set. To reheat, put the mixture in a small pan and reheat, while mixing well with a hand blender. For the caviar, scallop and pearl meat recipe, refrigerate again until needed.

garlic cream

20 G (¾ OZ) UNSALTED BUTTER
3 GARLIC CLOVES, PEELED
500 ML (17 FL OZ/2 CUPS) MILK
5 G (⅛ OZ) AGAR AGAR POWDER
FINE SEA SALT

Melt the butter in a saucepan, add the garlic cloves and gently sweat them in the butter, being careful not to add any colour. Add the milk and bring it close to boiling point. Remove the pan from the heat and allow the garlic to infuse in the milk for 20 minutes. Pour the milk through a fine strainer into a clean saucepan, and discard the solids. Return the pan to the heat and then whisk in the agar agar. Reheat the milk to 90°C (195°F), continuing to whisk to activate the agar agar. Taste and season with sea salt. Refrigerate the milk and allow to set. Once set, place into a blender and blend on high until a smooth paste is formed. The garlic cream should be the consistency of mayonnaise when reheated.

truffle custards

400 ML (14 FL OZ) MILK
20 G (¾ OZ) WINTER TRUFFLE, FINELY GRATED
FINE SEA SALT
3 EGG YOLKS
1 WHOLE EGG

Put the milk in a saucepan and bring to simmering point. Add the grated winter truffle and a pinch of salt. Remove the pan from the heat and set aside for 10 minutes for the milk and truffle to infuse.

Place the egg yolks and whole egg in a bowl and slowly whisk in the truffle and milk mixture. Allow to cool completely, then divide the truffle milk mixture evenly between eight small ceramic ramekins. Cover each mould well with plastic wrap so there is a watertight seal. Place the moulds in the refrigerator while you prepare the rest of the recipe. The custards will be steamed just before serving.

oyster custard

12 UNSHUCKED SYDNEY ROCK OYSTERS
450 ML (16 FL OZ) MILK
FINE SEA SALT
3 EGG YOLKS
1 WHOLE EGG

Shuck the oysters, reserving the meat and all the juice. Put the milk into a saucepan and bring to simmering point, then add the oysters and juice and continue to simmer very gently for 2 minutes. Remove the pan from the heat and allow the oysters and milk to infuse for 15 minutes. Strain the milk through a fine sieve lined with muslin cloth, and discard the meat. Taste the milk and season with sea salt. Allow the milk to cool. When cold, whisk the milk with the yolks and whole egg. Place the custard into a ceramic bowl to a depth of 4 cm (1½ inches), cover tightly with plastic wrap and refrigerate until required. The custard will be steamed before serving.

artichoke aïoli

4 LARGE GLOBE ARTICHOKES
100 ML (3½ FL OZ) EXTRA VIRGIN OLIVE OIL
JUICE OF ¼ LEMON
2 GARLIC CLOVES, PEELED AND SPLIT IN HALF
2 SPRIGS THYME
1 SPRIG ROSEMARY
2 EGG YOLKS
FINE SEA SALT

Prepare the artichokes, removing most of the outside leaves, and peel the stems. Split the artichokes in half and remove the choke. As you finish each artichoke, place it in a bowl of acidulated water to prevent it from browning. Place the artichoke hearts in a vacuum bag with the extra virgin olive oil, lemon juice, garlic, thyme and rosemary. Seal the bag in a vacuum sealer and steam the artichokes in a temperature-controlled combi oven at 90°C (195°F) for 30 minutes. The artichokes will be very well cooked. Refrigerate the artichokes in the bag.

When the contents are very cold, remove the artichokes and garlic from the bag and reserve all the juices. Put the artichokes and garlic aside. Strain the juices through a fine sieve, discarding the solids. Place the artichokes and garlic in a food processor and process on high to form a smooth paste. Add the egg yolks and blend briefly. With the motor running, slowly pour in the cooking juices as you would to make a mayonnaise. When all the oil is incorporated, pass the artichoke aïoli through a drum sieve. Season to taste with sea salt and refrigerate until required.

bittersweet chocolate black pudding

500 ML (17 FL OZ/2 CUPS) PIG'S BLOOD (FRESH
  OR POWDERED)
25 ML (1 FL OZ) SHERRY VINEGAR
50 ML (1¾ FL OZ) OLOROSO SHERRY
200 G (7 OZ) PORK BACK FAT, FINELY DICED
8 SMALL FRENCH SHALLOTS, FINELY DICED
1 GARLIC CLOVE, FINELY DICED
80 G (2¾ OZ) DOUBLE CREAM (45–50% FAT)
100 G (3½ OZ) SOURDOUGH CRUMBS
10 G (¼ OZ) FINE SEA SALT
100 G (3½ OZ) BITTERSWEET CHOCOLATE (72%),
  FINELY GRATED

Put the pig's blood in a bowl and add the vinegar and sherry, then put aside. Take half the diced pork back fat and render it by gently heating it in a saucepan. Strain and discard any solids. Put the rendered fat into a pan and sauté the shallots and garlic until translucent. Remove the pan from the heat and cool slightly, then add the remaining fat and double cream and mix well. Add this to the pig's blood mixture in the bowl, then add the sourdough crumbs, salt and chocolate.

You can make a traditional blood sausage by filling fresh pig or lamb intestine skins and poaching the sausages in water for about 25 minutes at 75°C (165°F) or, as we do in the restaurant, you could place the blood sausage mixture in a large vacuum bag to a thickness of 3 cm (1¼ inches) and steam in a temperature-controlled combi oven at 75°C (165°F) for 25 minutes, carefully turning the bag half way through the cooking process to ensure even cooking. Alternatively, you could cook it in the vacuum bag by creating a water bath using a large deep baking tray on the stovetop and using a thermometer, carefully turning half way through.

Allow the black pudding to cool, then carefully remove it from the bag and cut into pieces as directed in the recipe. You can store the black pudding in the refrigerator for up to 4 days.

lemon confit

2 LEMONS
100 G (3½ OZ) SUGAR

With a sharp knife, carefully remove the zest from the lemons, making sure you leave behind the bitter white pith. Finely dice the zest. Segment the lemon flesh and remove all of the seeds. Place the segments into a small bowl and squeeze out any remaining juice from the lemon over the segments.

Bring a small saucepan of water to the boil and blanch the zest for 1 minute. Strain the zest, discarding the water. Repeat this process three times, using fresh water each time, to remove the bitterness from the zest. Add the zest to the lemon segments, mix in the sugar and place the contents into a small saucepan. Place the pan over low heat and simmer for about 15 minutes, or until the lemon segments have broken down and the mixture is well reduced and concentrated. Keep an eye on the confit as it cooks, adding a little water if necessary. Remove the confit from the pan and place in a clean container and refrigerate until required.

vanilla custard base

400 ML (14 FL OZ) CREAM (35% FAT)
2 VANILLA BEANS, SPLIT AND SCRAPED
3 EGG YOLKS
1 WHOLE EGG
80 G (2¾ OZ) CASTER (SUPERFINE) SUGAR

Preheat the oven to 160°C (315°F/Gas 2–3). Put the cream and vanilla beans in a saucepan. Heat together until the cream just begins to boil, then remove the pan from the heat. Whisk the egg yolks, whole egg and sugar together in a stainless-steel bowl. While whisking the eggs, slowly pour on the hot vanilla cream. Mix well and then remove the vanilla beans.

Strain the mixture into four 175 ml (5½ fl oz) ceramic ramekins, then place the ramekins into a baking tray of water to form a water bath. Place the water bath into the oven and cook the custard as you would a crème brûlée, for about 30–35 minutes, or until the custard is just set. Remove the custards from the bain-marie and place in the refrigerator for 5–6 hours, or until they are fully chilled and set. Remove the skin from the top before using. This recipe makes 400 g (14 oz).

rose cream

400 G (14 OZ) CUSTARD BASE (MAKE THE VANILLA
  CUSTARD BASE, FROM ABOVE, OMITTING THE
  VANILLA BEANS)
400 G (14 OZ) DOUBLE CREAM (45–50% FAT)
10 ML (¼ FL OZ) ROSE WATER

In a small bowl, whisk together the custard base, cream and rose water until it forms soft peaks. Refrigerate the rose cream until needed.

puff pastry

250 G (9 OZ) PLAIN (ALL-PURPOSE) FLOUR
25 G (¾ OZ) UNSALTED BUTTER, MELTED
PINCH OF SALT
160 G (5½ OZ) UNSALTED BUTTER, EXTRA

Place the flour into a bowl and make a well in the centre. Pour in 110 ml (3¾ fl oz) of water and add the melted butter and salt. Mix well with your hands and crumble the flour through your fingers until all the ingredients are homogenised. Place the dough on the work surface and roll into a ball. Cut a cross into the ball with a blunt knife, then wrap the dough in plastic wrap and chill in the refrigerator for 2 hours.

Lightly flour your work surface and flour the rolling pin. Working from the centre, roll the dough out in four directions until the dough is about 5 mm (¼ inch) thick and you have a square with extended corners. The centre area of the pastry should be 10 cm (4 inches) square, and the extended corners should be a further 10 cm (4 inches) from the centre section. Slice the extra butter into 2 mm (¹⁄₁₆ inch) thick slices and lay the slices evenly over the centre square. Fold the extended corners back over the butter to form a 10 cm (4 inch) square butter-enclosed parcel. Wrap the pastry in plastic wrap and return to the refrigerator to chill for 20 minutes.

Flour your work surface again and then gently roll out the pastry until it forms a rectangle, 30 cm (12 inches) long and 15 cm (6 inches) wide. Fold both ends of the rectangle into the middle to form a 10 x 15 cm (4 x 6 inch) rectangle of three layers. Turn this rectangle 90 degrees (a quarter turn) and roll the pastry out to form a 30 x 15 cm (12 x 6 inch) rectangle. Fold the pasty into the middle again as you did before, then wrap the pastry in plastic wrap and refrigerate for 20 minutes. Repeat the process exactly as above, wrap and refrigerate for 20 minutes and then repeat the process again. Wrap and refrigerate for 1 hour. Your puff pastry is now ready to use. It can be refrigerated for a couple of days or frozen for up to 1 month.

glossary

A lot of my recipes contain some hard-to-find vegetables, herbs and flowers. You can either get to know the growers at your local farmers' markets and find out if they produce what you need, or look at growing your own. Here are two of the best Australian websites to help get you started:
www.diggers.com.au
www.cornucopiaseeds.com.au

acquerello rice An aged organic carnaroli rice available from good Italian delicatessens or speciality food stores.

agar agar powder A setting agent derived from seaweed, available from health food stores.

amedei chuao This is considered by many to be the best chocolate in the world. Chuao is the name of the plantation and the Venezuelan peninsula where the beans have been selected into a natural 'cru'. For the first time these beans are processed in purity. The final result is a 70 per cent dark chocolate with great aromatic strength and the aroma of berries and exotic fruits.

banyuls vinegar An aged wine vinegar made from grapes grown in the French region of Banyuls-sur-Mer. Available from speciality food stores.

brik pastry A thin pastry from Tunisia, traditionally used for making pastilla. Available from speciality food stores.

combi oven Cooking at low temperatures overnight is a technique mainly used in commercial environments. Meat is usually cooked with a liquid, either a flavoured oil or stock, and this has replaced a lot of slow-braising that was done previously.

dried bamboo fungus Bamboo fungus is grown in bamboo forests and has a very interesting, sponge-like texture and a natural cavity that is ideal for stuffing. Bamboo fungus is available dried in most Asian supermarkets.

fresh wasabi Relatively new to Australia, fresh wasabi is grown in Tasmania by Shima Wasabi. Fresh wasabi has a much gentler heat and far more aromatics than the instant processed tube and powdered varieties.

garlic scapes These are the immature flower stalks of hardneck garlic.

green almonds These almonds are only available in October and November in Australia. When the almond kernels are not fully formed, they have a very soft paper-thin skin, which contains a jelly-like substance. Essentially they are immature almonds. When they are blanched, the rather tart jelly becomes sweet, almost resembling the flesh of a grape. They have to be removed from their fuzzy green outer shell. By December the almonds become more solid; they are crisp and tender and are also referred to as green almonds. By January and February the almonds are much firmer and they are then dried, with the outer shells removed — these are the almonds we are more familiar with.

ground black sesame seeds Available from Asian food stores.

hasuimo A rare Japanese vegetable — the stem from a green taro. You could substitute with celery heart.

homogenised Jersey milk A rich milk that contains around 4.5–5 per cent fat. Homogenisation makes the fat globules smaller so they sit evenly throughout the milk.

isomalt A hydrolised sugar made from sugar beet, which tastes naturally as sweet as cane sugar. Available from speciality food stores.

kamo eggplant An heirloom variety from Japan. The fruit is dark purple, with a sweet flavour and delicate texture. Available from farmers' markets and specialist grocers.

korean fine-cut dried chilli threads Available from specialist Asian supermarkets.

lecite A natural soy lecithin-based emulsifier. Available from speciality food stores.

palm heart The growing point of edible palms, consisting of the larger basal stem, growing shoot or heart and the new emerging leaves. Many palms produce an edible heart. In Australia they are very rare, with only a handful of restaurants being able to buy them from a supplier in North Queensland. The base portion can be used similarly to bamboo shoots without the need for pre-boiling. All portions are delicious raw, marinated, steamed or stir-fried. Each section has a different texture and appearance and can be used for different culinary sensations.

parsley root A root vegetable, native to the Mediterranean, that closely resembles a parsnip, but has a pale white colour rather than creamy yellow. It has a somewhat nutty flavour, with celery and carrot overtones. Look for it at farmers' markets or good greengrocers.

pearl oyster meat The flesh of the *Pinctada maxima* pearl oyster, which is almost as prized as the South Sea pearls it produces. Very small quantities are harvested annually and most goes directly to restaurants. Pearl meat is usually purchased snap frozen, as it is harvested a long way offshore. Available from specialist fishmongers.

pedro ximénez noble sour vinegar A sour–sweet vinegar made from Pedro Ximénez sherry. Available from speciality food stores.

preserved wild cherries Gathered in the Dolomite Alps, this cherry has a distinctive, aromatic flavour. From specialist Italian importer: www.lario.com.au.

preserved wild Italian mountain radicchio From specialist Italian importer: www.lario.com.au.

quenelle A French term describing an oval or mound of mixture. For creams, place a spoon in warm water before placing it in the mixture and, with a medium pressure, drag the spoon over the mixture so that it curls in the spoon to create a quenelle. For heavier mixtures such as mousse, ice cream or sorbets you may place the spoon in hot water. For larger quenelles, use two spoons, scoop the mixture into one spoon and then transfer the mixture between the spoons until a nice oval shape is produced and the quenelle is smooth.

salted jellyfish Salted jellyfish has virtually no flavour and is used more for its textural properties and for the fact that it absorbs the other flavours in the dish. It is available from Chinese grocers. Before use, rinse and soak in a couple of changes of water.

samphire A fleshy, smooth-branched herb with bright green tips that are crisp and salty. It grows on partially submerged rocks by the sea. Available occasionally from specialist seafood suppliers.

sous vide A cooking technique where food is vacuum-sealed in a plastic bag and cooked in a temperature-controlled water bath, usually for a long time. It is mostly used for meat, but good results can also be achieved with hard vegetables. Sous vide literally translates as 'under vacuum'. At home, a domestic food-saver vacuum-sealing machine is a good low-cost option. However, they are not as effective when there is liquid in the bag as they draw the air out and sometimes the liquid with it — cutting a bag longer than you require, or freezing the liquid first, can offset this.

temperature-controlled water baths These water baths are mostly used in commercial kitchens. At home you can heat water in a saucepan or deep roasting tin on the stovetop and use a digital thermometer to monitor the temperature, but you must pay close attention and adjust the heat to maintain a constant temperature.

titanium gelatine Weighs 5 g (⅛ oz) per sheet and is available from specialist food stores.

toma della rocca A soft Italian cheese made from cow's, goat's and sheep's milk. Available from cheese stores and good delicatessens.

vegetarian rennet Used for setting milk when making cheese. The usual source of rennet is the stomach of slaughtered newborn calves. Vegetarian cheeses are manufactured using rennet from either fungal or bacterial sources. Measure it out with a syringe. Available from health food stores.

virgin sesame oil Cold-pressed sesame oil with a different flavour to the toasted sesame oil, as it is produced directly from raw, rather than toasted, seeds. You can substitute 40 ml (1¼ fl oz) grapeseed oil mixed with just 10 ml (¼ fl oz) toasted sesame oil.

warrigal greens A native herb with arrow-shaped leaves, also known as New Zealand spinach. If using large quantities, blanch the greens for 3 minutes, discarding the water, as the leaves have a high oxalate concentration that can be harmful if consumed in large quantities.

white corn Available seasonally at farmers' markets.

wild hops purée This rare product contains the wild hops which is gathered as soon as it sprouts on the Dolomite Alps. Available from specialist Italian importer: www.lario.com.au.

xantana A brand of xanthum gum, produced by fermenting corn starch. It is extremely efficient as a thickener.

yuzu The Japanese name for a yellow citrus fruit (*Citrus junos*) with a distinctive sharp taste. Too acidic to be eaten raw, its zest is used to flavour dishes or to make condiments. Available from good Japanese food stores.

acknowledgements

First and foremost I have to thank my wonderful wife Kath. Without her support this book would not have been possible. Kath is my scribe and has worked on this book by my side.

My deepest gratitude goes to Leon Fink, the owner of Quay restaurant. Leon has been in the restaurant business for over 30 years and started Quay 22 years ago. I wouldn't be where I am today without his trust and support. John Fink joined the team at Quay as General Manager 3 years ago and has brought energy, passion and enthusiasm to the role. He has inspired and supported the Quay team to push the boundaries in fine dining in Australia. John has been a huge supporter of this book and was instrumental at the beginning of the process with Jane Lawson. The Finks have given their generous support to this project and have understood the time I have needed to devote to it.

From the very beginning, the team at Murdoch Books were passionate about this book. They have captured the essence of my cuisine, and through the pages and images have brought to life my passion for food and nature.

I would like to thank everyone at Murdoch who has worked on this project, starting with Jane Lawson, who immediately saw the potential for the book and steered the initial team behind it, and Reuben Crossman, the designer who set the tone and direction of the book. Reuben is an immensely talented professional who really understood the essence of my food and how to represent it beautifully on these pages. The photography by Anson Smart is simply stunning. The way he captured my food, its detail and the mood was so in tune with the feeling of the book that it is impossible to imagine this book without him. Thank you to David Morgan, who sourced all the plates and textural backgrounds for the images, and whose input was the third link in the creative partnership referred to by Jane Lawson as 'the dream team'. The finished result has far exceeded my expectations.

Thank you to the editorial team — managing editor Daniela Bertollo, food editor Sonia Greig and copy editor Kim Rowney — for their dedication and passion. Their eye for detail and all round professionalism impressed me greatly.

Working with the team at Murdoch has been like working with a finely tuned kitchen team in a top restaurant — creative, professional and dynamic.

The success of any restaurant is the sum of its parts. My kitchen team at Quay are a group of young dedicated professionals who work extremely hard to produce the very best food, day in day out. Their passion and drive is inspiring and gives me great hope for the future of Australian cuisine. I would like to thank my sous chefs, Analiese Gregory, Casper Christensen, Rob Cockerill and Richard Ousby, who all assisted me in producing this book. I rely on this team to maintain the standards at Quay and lead the kitchen team of 23 chefs and apprentices. Quay employs over 50 people and every single person has a vital part to play in creating the Quay experience. Kylie Ball, our Operations Manager, coordinates the team behind the scenes. Her professionalism and dedication to the job keeps Quay running smoothly. On the frontline is Ashley Scott, the Restaurant Manager, who leads the service team with great style and care for our customers.

Daniel Wegener is our Head Sommelier and is responsible for our wine team and extensive cellar. Daniel's passion for wine inspires both staff and customers and is a critical link in the dining experience at Quay.

To all the staff working at Quay, I would like to thank you for your support and the individual efforts that have made Quay what it is today. I would also like to thank all the people who have worked with me over the past nine years.

Peter Gilmore

index

Published in 2012 by Murdoch Books, an imprint of Allen & Unwin

Murdoch Books Australia
83 Alexander Street
Crows Nest NSW 2065
Phone: +61 (0) 2 8425 0100
Fax: +61 (0) 2 9906 2218
www.murdochbooks.com.au
info@murdochbooks.com.au

Murdoch Books UK
Ormond House
26–27 Boswell Street
London WC1N 3JZ
Phone: +44 (0) 20 8785 5995
www.murdochbooks.co.uk
info@murdochbooks.com.uk

Publishing director: Kay Scarlett
Publisher: Jane Lawson
Art direction, design and illustration: Reuben Crossman
Photographer: Anson Smart
Stylist: David Morgan
Project manager: Daniela Bertollo
Editor: Kim Rowney
Food editor: Sonia Greig
Production manager: Karen Small

National Library of Australia Cataloguing-in-Publication entry

Author: Gilmore, Peter.

Title: Quay: food inspired by nature / Peter Gilmore.

ISBN: 9781741964875 (hbk.)

Notes: Includes index.

Subjects: Cookery

Dewey Number: 641.3

A catalogue record for this book is available from the British Library.

Printed by 1010 Printing International Ltd in 2010. PRINTED IN CHINA.
Reprinted in 2010, 2011, 2012, 2013, 2014, 2017.

Colour separation by Splitting Image Colour Studio, Melbourne, Australia.

The Publisher and stylist would like to especially thank Dinosaur Designs
(www.dinosaur designs.com.au) for lending equipment for use and photography
as well as the following: Kris Coad (www.kriscoad.com), Shelley Panton
(www.shelleypanton.com), Samantha Robinson (www.samantharobinson.com.
au), Eco Outdoor (www.ecooutdoor.com.au), Paper2 (www.paper2.com.au),
Planet Furniture (planetfurniture.com.au).

IMPORTANT: Those who might be at risk from the effects of salmonella poisoning
(the elderly, pregnant women, young children and those suffering from immune
deficiency diseases) should consult their doctor with any concerns about eating
raw eggs.

OVEN GUIDE: You may find cooking times vary depending on the oven you
are using. We have used a fan-forced oven for these recipes. As a general rule,
increase the oven temperature by 20°C (35°F) if using a conventional oven.